A GRUESOME DISCOVERY

Andy Borisenko owned a red-painted cabin on the Bay of Quinte. One of his pastimes was fishing. A frugal man, he often walked the Quinte shoreline looking for lures. He was heading west around the bay when he spotted a green garbage bag by the water's edge.

Borisenko poked it with a stick. It appeared that the garbage bag was filled with soggy newspapers. The end was knotted. Borisenko bent down to see what was inside. Suddenly he jerked back.

The greyish lump was alive with maggots, their tiny white bodies clumped together. The smell of rotting flesh made him gag. But there was no mistaking the shape of a woman's breasts.

PRAISE FOR *CRIME STORY*:

"A fast-paced account of events. Enjoyable and exciting."
—Toronto Star

"This is an exceptional book. It has to rank among Canada's finest in its genre."
—London Free Press

"A slick, behind-the-headlines story."
—The Globe & Mail

"Lots of behind-the-scenes goodies from police officers."
—Times-Colonist

"Superior."
—Toronto Life Magazine

"[Donovan and Pron] bring us face to face with the egotistical killer, which makes the pages turn."
—Quill & Quire

CRIME STORY

The True Account of the Reporters, Cops, And
Lawyers On The Trail Of The Body-Parts Killer

Nick Pron and Kevin Donovan

SEAL BOOKS
McClelland-Bantam, Inc.
Toronto

CRIME STORY
Seal hardcover/November 1992
Seal paperback/September 1993

ISBN 0-7704-2566-6

CREDITS FOR PHOTO SECTION:

PICTURE OF INNOCENCE: Courtesy of the Ontario Provincial Police (OPP)
POSTCARD ROMANCE: Courtesy of the OPP
DINNER IN CHINATOWN: Nick Pron
TAKE DOWN: Photo by Jim Wilkes
THE PROSECUTORS: Photo by Jim Wilkes
THE DETECTIVES: Photo by Jim Wilkes
SOLE PROOF: (Two photos) Courtesy of the OPP
CULTURAL PARANOIA: (Three photos) Courtesy of the OPP
FACING THE MEDIA: Nick Pron
LONE MOURNER: Nick Pron
LAST MOVEMENT: Photo by Jim Wilkes
A GRISLY FIND: Photo by Jim Wilkes
MASK OF DEATH: (Two photos) Courtesy of the OPP

PRINTED IN CANADA

COVER PRINTED IN U.S.A.

UNI   0 9 8 7 6 5 4 3 2 1

For Lou Clancy, who wanted it done right.

TABLE OF CONTENTS

PROLOGUE

The woman with the raven hair stepped smartly from the streetcar, her violin case tucked under an arm. With her full lips and high, delicate cheekbones, she had a quiet beauty that caught the attention of several men that Saturday afternoon. She carried herself with poise, walking confidently along the busy street, stopping every now and then to window-shop. There was no need to hurry. She was early for the lesson. It was going to be a good weekend. There was a lot she had planned. She had certainly been right in telling friends that 1988 was going to be her lucky year.

It had not always been this good. In the five years she had been in the country since leaving her native China, her problems could be summed up in two words: men, money. There had never been a shortage of romance. Four suitors in five years. But each relationship had ended badly. It was always the same: she enjoyed the men's companionship but she didn't want their marriage proposals, even though settling down might solve her troubles.

She was in Canada on a student visa, one that was about to expire. She wasn't allowed to work, but that was exactly what she was doing, giving music lessons, always afraid immigration officials might catch her. How else was she supposed to support herself? Her parents didn't have any money. And she was too proud to ask her sister for help. If she married a Canadian, she could get landed immigrant status, the first step to becoming a citizen. Then she wouldn't have to worry about working secretly. But although there had been several offers, she didn't want to get tied down by marriage and a family. Her career, her dream of becoming a concert violinist, came first.

A letter was waiting for her at the house where she was giving the lesson. She frowned as soon as her student's mother handed it to her. She knew who it was from. She took off her coat and opened the violin case. Was this business never going to end? It would have to be dealt with. She couldn't ignore it any longer. She tore the letter open, read a few paragraphs, then threw the paper down in disgust.

Her student was waiting for her in the living room. She started the lesson, but it was no use. She couldn't concentrate. That damned letter! She apologized to the woman and the young boy. He stood with his violin, watching forlornly as she put on her coat and walked quickly out of the house, disappearing into the busy street. . . .

CHAPTER ONE

Dumping Grounds

The thing had been there since sunrise, lying across the yellow dividing line of the highway. A bus load of children on the way to a country school passed by it but didn't stop. A second school bus slowed, and innocent eyes gawked in confusion at the object on the road. Small faces pressed against the frosted windows, then the driver sped off along the deserted two-lane blacktop called the Thousand Islands Parkway. That morning in March, 1988, was bright and cheery, but the biting cold kept the thing from thawing, decaying.

Larry Mallory glanced at his watch as he finished scraping the frost from the windshield of his spanking-new Ford Blazer pickup. It was twenty minutes to eight; for once the thirty-two-year-old father of two was actually going to be on time for work. Not that being late mattered much this time of year. It was the off season in Rockport, a lonely hamlet in eastern Ontario on the banks of the St. Lawrence River, midway between Toronto and Montreal. Tourism was the only industry, and the season didn't start until school got out, nearly four months away. Mallory was a caretaker for an island lodge, one of many resorts in an area commonly referred to as the Thousand Islands. Like his father, he had been born and raised in the community, which was just large enough to support two bars.

Mallory got into the cab, turned the heat to high, and backed out the driveway onto a dirt road that went south to the Parkway. He had time for a quick breakfast at the Lighthouse. It was the town's only restaurant, and it seemed all people talked about there was ice hockey or the coming tourist season. Nothing much ever happened in Rockport during the winter.

Mallory was at the top of a hill overlooking the Parkway when he saw the school bus. He thought it strange the way it slowed, almost to a stop, then sped off. When he reached the highway, he signalled left. As he looked that way, to the east, he flicked down the visor to block out the brilliant sunshine. That's when he first noticed the crows.

There were two of them, big chunky birds, black as coal, the undisputed king scavengers of the road. They were perched on something, a long, slender object in the middle of the highway. Squawking, flapping their huge wings, they jockeyed for position, fighting for the best spot on whatever it was they were perched on. The larger of the two birds dug its beak into the thing, tore loose a chunk, threw its head back, and gulped it down. It cawed defiantly at Mallory as he drove past. For a moment Mallory took his eyes off the road and skidded onto the gravel shoulder. He braked hard, then turned back to stare at that strange tableau. There was something horribly, horribly wrong.

Leaving the motor running, Mallory got out of the cab and walked back. His thick-soled work boots made a crunching noise on the light cover of fresh snow that had fallen that night. The crows made angry noises as he got closer, as if they were trying to scare him off and protect their meal. Then they flew to a nearby tree, where they perched, watching and waiting. The thing on the road was shapely, smooth, like a limb from one of those mannequins in store windows, Mallory thought. But why were the big birds picking at it if it was made of plastic?

He knelt down and reached out to touch it, then yanked his hand back. His breathing quickened, and there was suddenly a funny, sick feeling in his stomach. He jerked upright, standing up so fast that he felt dizzy. He walked around the thing, moving in tight circles, oblivious to the fact he was in the middle of a highway. That wasn't a mannequin's leg. It was human.

At least, it was part of what had been a human being. The skin along the calf was dotted with little red gouges where the crows had been nibbling. The toenails were carefully manicured and painted a light pink, just like the shade his wife used. Mallory swallowed hard to keep down the bitter taste in his throat. The leg had been sliced off from the thigh just above the knee. The cut was even, neat. The top part of a bone was sticking out of the raw, red flesh. Mallory didn't notice the car that had pulled up behind him. The driver was leaning out the window.

"What the hell's that?" he asked.

Mallory turned with a start. The man was about his age, finely dressed in a camel-hair overcoat.

"I think it's human," Mallory replied. "Can you get help?"

The driver was silent for a moment as he looked at the leg. Then he shook his head.

"Uh-uh, not me, no way," he said, powering up his window and driving off.

Mallory watched him go. What in the world should he do now? he wondered. He just couldn't leave the leg lying there. Should he put it in the back of the truck? But that would mean he'd have to pick it up, and he wasn't about to do that. He looked down the highway. There wasn't another car in sight. He had to call the police, but the nearest phone he could think of was at his house. He ran to his truck and jumped in, squealing the tires as he spun it around.

His wife was washing dishes when Mallory burst into their house. He went straight to the telephone, ignoring her surprised look. She wiped her hands on a dishcloth and walked over.

"What's going on?"

Keep calm, Mallory kept telling himself as he started dialling, ignoring his wife's question. He had seen lots of road kill, but all animals, never anything human. What was wrong with the damned phone? He couldn't get the number he wanted. He hung up, then started again.

3

His wife gently took the receiver from his hand. "Let me do it," she said. "Who are you trying to reach?"

Mallory looked down at his hands and realized for the first time he was trembling. "Police."

"Are you all right?" his wife asked. "What happened?"

"Just . . . just dial the number. The police. Call the cops. Here." He pointed to the number that was written on a piece of paper tacked to the wall.

His wife dialled and a man answered.

"Ontario Provincial Police, Gananoque," he said.

She handed the phone to her husband, and he blurted out his story, repeating several times the description of the toenails. There was a silence at the other end, a long, disbelieving silence. Mallory repeated his story, his voice rising as he told it.

"I swear to God it's true!" he yelled into the receiver. "I saw it. It's lying in the middle of the road. It's got painted toenails, for Christ's sake!"

Out on the Parkway, two provincial highway workers were driving into Rockport when they spotted something on the road ahead. Roger Birtch and Jack Wallace, two long-time employees, had seen plenty of animals that had been hit by cars. But there was something different about this bit of carrion.

"That's no road kill," Birtch said to his partner as he pulled the truck to the side of the road. They got out, walked over.

"Hell," Wallace muttered. "What do we do with it?"

"Lot of school busses go by here," Birtch replied. "Better get it off the road. Kids shouldn't be seeing this."

While Birtch went for a shovel, Wallace got on the two-way radio in the cab. He called the Ministry of Transportation and Communications depot in Gananoque and told them what they had found. As he watched, his partner got a shovel and gingerly slid it under the frozen limb. Birtch carted it to the truck, holding it far away from his body. He put the shovel and the leg in the back of the truck.

Mallory was still trying to convince the OPP constable he was serious when a second caller, a provincial highway dispatcher, phoned in with the same story. Within moments, a cruiser was on the way.

Mallory drove back to the Parkway, but when he got there all he saw was a highway truck, and no leg. He parked and walked over to the truck.

"You guys see that thing on—" Mallory started to say to the two men sitting in the cab when one of them pointed to the back. Mallory went around to the rear and looked in. The leg was there, still resting on the scoop of the shovel. Mallory wasn't quite sure what to do next, so he just stood there, waiting for the police to arrive. He didn't have to wait long.

Ontario Provincial Police constable Peter Brian Kennedy, a soft-spoken father of two, had a lot on his mind when he started his shift on that Friday. His sister had cancer and he was worrying that she was not responding to chemotherapy. His thoughts were on her when a call came over the two-way radio directing him to the eastern end of Rockport, about thirty kilometres away. Something about a leg being found on the highway. Kennedy hit the roof lights and swung the cruiser around.

When he got there less than twenty minutes later, he found three men standing at the back of a highway truck. None of them looked very happy. While Kennedy took a look at the leg, one of the trio started apologizing for moving it off the highway, saying a lot of school busses went by and he didn't want children to see it. He hoped he hadn't made a mistake. Kennedy assured him it was okay, knowing it wasn't. Crime scenes are not supposed to be disturbed. He asked the three to wait while he called headquarters.

Within the hour, half a dozen black and white OPP cruisers were on the scene. It was the start of an investigation that would last more than two years and involve eight police forces from four countries. Kennedy, a devoted family man, didn't know it at the time, but he would be away from his home for most of those two years. It was ironic considering he had passed up promotions so he could be stationed near his family. On that cold morning in March, his only thought was containing the scene so that no other evidence would be disturbed. Until the homicide detectives arrived, he was in charge.

Kennedy got back on the two-way radio and ordered in a helicopter and a tracking dog. He got one of the other officers to take statements from the three men, then he organized a search along the banks of the St. Lawrence. There could be more body parts. All the commotion drew a crowd of curious onlookers who gathered around the cruisers and pestered the cops for information, while steam from the idling engines drifted slowly skyward. The officers told them little, mostly because they didn't know much themselves. Mallory knew as much as anybody at that point. He'd found a leg on the highway, probably a woman's, and that was about it. Somebody bought coffee for the police officers. That's the way things were done in a community not even big enough to be called a town.

The police officers fanned out in two groups from the place that Mallory had found the leg, one going east, the other west along the banks of the river. Kennedy was in the group that went east. He had combed through the bush about the length of a football field when he saw the green garbage bag. It was in a ditch, at the bottom of a steep slope by the Parkway. Just beside the bag was another leg, the left.

Kennedy got close enough to see that it, too, had been severed at the knee. Most of the flesh on the calf was missing, eaten away. One of the other officers said there had been a lot of foxes near the town that winter. There were tracks in the snow all around the leg — animal, not human. The paw prints went west. Most likely an animal, a fox or whatever, had found the legs in the bag, eaten one, and was dragging the other through the bushes across the highway to its lair when a passing car scared it off.

"If this keeps up, we'll have to call it the Thousand Islands Partsway," one of the officers with Kennedy said.

Mallory waited until noon, then, after checking first with one of the officers, got in his truck and went to the Lighthouse Restaurant for a coffee. He had long since lost his appetite and had forgotten about work. The roadside diner was packed. Mallory was the centre of attraction as soon as he walked in. A shy man, he felt uncomfortable with so many people staring at him, clamouring to get his attention. Everyone wanted to know what the hell was going on.

"How can you be so sure it was a woman's leg?" a man sipping a coffee at the counter asked.

"It was shapely," Mallory replied, "smooth — just as if it had been shaved." He told them about the manicured, painted toenails.

"You think it was anyone from around here?" was the next question.

Mallory shrugged.

Someone mentioned the name Doris Viola Taylor. The fifty-four-year-old woman from nearby Trenton, about a half hour's drive to the west, had left home four months ago and never returned. Could it have been her leg Mallory found? He didn't think so. The leg was slender, probably that of a much younger woman. Wayne Thompson, the owner of the restaurant, came out of the kitchen wiping his hands on his apron. He voiced the thought on a lot of minds that chilly morning.

There was a killer on the loose, he said. It might even be someone from town. Someone they knew. Maybe even somebody sitting in the restaurant that very moment. Several glanced around, trying to be as inconspicuous as possible. In a small community like Rockport, no one could believe — or wanted to believe — that a madman might be in their midst. Rockport was a safe place, not like big, bad Montreal to the east with its criminal gangs or Toronto to the west with its drug problems. It was the kind of town where you left your keys in your car and never worried that it would be stolen. Most people didn't even lock their front doors when they went to bed at night. No one wanted to believe the killer might be one of their own. There had to be some other explanation.

Perhaps the killer had just been passing by and decided to use their little community as a dumping ground for the body parts? That theory seemed more reasonable. Highway 401, the main road between Toronto and Montreal, was only a few kilometres to the north. The killer had detoured on the Parkway, taking it because in winter it was deserted. If that was true, then what really galled the customers at Thompson's restaurant that morning was the idea that some kook with a sharp knife had used their town as a garbage dump for human remains.

Mallory gulped down his coffee then got up to go. All this talk about a killer had worried him. In the excitement, he had forgotten about his family. His wife and two kids were at home, alone. The cruisers were still on the Parkway as he drove slowly by the spot where he had found the leg. A dark-blue, four-door Chevrolet had just pulled up to the scene. A heavy-set man in his forties with a hawk nose stepped out of the car. He walked like a drill sergeant, his back ramrod straight. From the way the uniformed officers gathered around him, Mallory figured the big man in the dark-blue trench coat was now in charge.

Lawrence Ivan Edgar had been about an hour's drive away when his pager went off that morning. He had heard only a few sketchy details over the phone before he headed south to Rockport, getting there around noon. Kennedy introduced himself, then told Edgar about the second leg. As they walked towards the spot where Kennedy had found it, Edgar fished around in the pockets of his trench coat for the package of Player's cigarettes. He was a two-pack-a-day man and he planned to quit, but not right now. He lit one and listened while Kennedy ran through what they had, which wasn't much.

The legs were probably female, maybe East Indian judging by the skin pigmentation. Both legs had been severed above the knee in neat cuts. An animal couldn't have done that. Some of the flesh from one of the legs had been eaten away, Kennedy explained. But other than that, both legs appeared quite fresh, not much deterioration of the flesh. Whoever had dumped the legs had done it recently. Edgar glanced across to the north side of the road, looking for homes. There were none, no one who might have seen a car or remembered a licence plate. Edgar scowled at the bushes lining the highway. The corners of his mouth curled down in a tight frown that made him look fierce.

It seemed that this was to be his second difficult investigation since his promotion to the rank of detective inspector with the OPP's Criminal Investigation Bureau. The first homicide case he had been handed, a double slaying in Lanark, a small town in eastern Ontario, had been frustrating the hell out of him. The case was already seven months old, and though he had plenty of suspicions, he lacked enough evidence to take to a jury. The victims, George Simpson, a building inspector, and his sister, Margaret, had been shot to death in their home late one night. There didn't seem to be any obvious motive for the double slaying. Both were well known and popular in the town. Neither had any enemies anybody knew of, at least not anyone who hated them enough to do them in. One theory was that there was a serial killer stalking the area.

Edgar was almost thankful when he was told he had another case. He needed something to get his mind off the Simpson slayings. But his mood had changed when he got to Rockport. As frustrating as the Simpson case had been, at least he knew the names of the dead people. "Jane Doe" murders were a pain. Edgar had been a cop for twenty-one years, and he had a gut feeling that this new case was going to give him more trouble than anything he had ever handled during his career.

A cruiser was parked at the spot where Kennedy had found the second leg. Edgar mashed his cigarette butt into the pavement with his heel as he glanced at the sky. A police helicopter was making slow passes along the banks of the St. Lawrence. Edgar told Kennedy he wanted the search carried out through the weekend. If there were any more body parts around, he wanted the police to find them first. What he didn't need was an animal eating up his evidence. He lit another cigarette, looked down the embankment where Richard McGarvey from the Identification Bureau was combing through the bushes around the leg, looking for anything that might be evidence. McGarvey picked up everything, from cigarette butts to tissue, and what later turned out to be a thorax of a bee. What if it wasn't a murder, Edgar wondered. Could this all be a sick prank? Maybe the work of some weirdo who grabbed a pair of legs from the morgue and dropped them on the highway for a few laughs. Or perhaps a satanic cultist had dug up a fresh grave and used the body for some ritual? It seemed unlikely. He stepped over the guardrail and made his way down the steep slope, almost slipping at one point. Wouldn't that have been great? he thought. The chief detective spread-eagled on top of his evidence.

McGarvey, a heavy-set man with slicked back hair, took pictures of the leg and the surrounding area. He repeated what Kennedy had said about the leg being neatly sliced above the knee.

"It was a very clean cut, just as though it had been dissected," McGarvey said.

Some blood-stained tissue was found underneath the leg, but it may have been there before, the leg falling on it, he said. McGarvey said he would run tests on everything, but he wasn't hopeful that the other physical evidence had anything to do with the case.

Edgar flicked his cigarette far from the scene and struggled up the slope. He watched from the road as the leg was bagged, carried up the embankment, and driven, with the other leg, to the detachment in Gananoque. He had been looking forward to a quiet weekend at home. But that's how it went when you were a detective with the force's élite unit. The twenty-four-man squad — and there were no women — was noted for putting in long hours with no overtime. They investigated about sixty murders a year in Canada's largest province, often travelling hundreds of kilometres along deserted highways in the middle of the night to reach a crime scene. But there were few complaints from the officers of the CIB. It was an achievement of honour to wear the gold signet ring engraved with the initials CIB, even though they themselves had to buy the ring, which cost about four hundred dollars. The only real perk they got was access to the wood-panelled officers' mess where entry was restricted by a numbered security code on the door. That and a car. The long hours didn't bother Edgar. He enjoyed the freedom given officers of the CIB to handle a case the way they chose. That was unusual for a police force. Working for the CIB was about as close to being your own boss as a policeman could be. You were left alone. Your hours were your own. You worked as hard or as easy as you wanted without much interference from your superiors. The way the force saw it, you had to know what you were doing to get there. Each officer set his own schedule and theoretically could pick anyone from within the ranks to help in a case. It was the team approach to solving a murder, and Edgar was the case manager, overseeing the investigation. Edgar liked Kennedy's thoroughness; he felt comfortable working with him. There were a few others he had in mind to help him — that is, if this case ever got rolling. Right now, without a name, there wasn't much they could do.

Satisfied there was nothing more he could learn at the scene, Edgar drove to the OPP's office in Gananoque. He called home as soon as he got there and told his two teenaged sons he wouldn't be home for the weekend. They had lived with him since he and his wife had separated. The other officers had gathered in one of the interview rooms down the hall. A police photographer was there, waiting for Edgar. The legs were lying on a table, still in the evidence bags. Edgar nodded at Kennedy, who put on a pair of latex gloves and carefully eased each leg out of its bag. He held the legs upright by the ankles, placing them side by side, while the photographer snapped several frames. For a few moments the only sound was the clicking of the camera's shutter. It was eerie — two severed legs standing upright on a table. Edgar lit up another smoke as he watched from a corner of the room. When that was done, McGarvey put the legs in the trunk of his cruiser and took them to the crime lab in Toronto for analysis.

Baby-sitting the police radio room in the Toronto *Star*'s newsroom was about the worst job a city reporter could draw. Dubbed the Cage, the Penalty Box, the Monkey House, and the Torture Chamber, the room was roughly the size of a prison cell. Reporters joked that the only difference was the radio room didn't have a lock on the door. It housed eight computerized radios that scanned police, ambulance, fire, and aircraft frequencies twenty-four hours a day, year round.

Every traffic accident, fire alarm, medical emergency, burglary, robbery, and other crime committed on the streets of the huge city were picked up by the scanners and blasted over small speakers that could be heard around the newsroom. The job of the person relegated to the Box was to make sense of the jargonized jumble of noises and pick out the few items that were newsworthy. In the confusion of sounds and police codes, the worst fear of any reporter sitting in the Box was that he or she might miss something big, like a murder or a fire at a nursing home. In the highly competitive newspaper wars in Toronto, where three dailies vied for readers, missing the big one could mean a stern lecture from the city editor, and perhaps a week of doing obituaries as punishment. One reporter feared the Box so much that she bribed a co-worker a week's pay to do her shift. As if the scanners weren't enough, there were two other pieces of equipment that reporters in the Box had to contend with: speakers linked with the headquarters of the Metro police and with the OPP. What normally came over the intercoms, besides a constant and irritating hum, was a steady diet of press releases and police blotter items, small stuff that most reporters ignored.

Nick Pron had gone through many low points in the fifteen years he had been with the paper, and he was well aware of the danger signs of an impending slump. His last major piece had been on a drug-smuggling ring based in Trinidad, but that had been nearly three months ago. The momentum and the praise he had enjoyed after those stories ran were dim memories. He had hoped his work on the series would earn him a regular beat doing special crime assignments, but to his dismay he had found himself right back in the radio room, a place where he had spent far too much time in his career. Doing filler items from the police blotter and phoning hospitals for condition checks on the victims of traffic accidents was a long way from the excitement of tracking a drug lord to his tropical island retreat. He desperately needed another big story to get him back on the front page. He was depressed, and when he got that way he ate too much. On that night in March it was a double hamburger and fries. At six feet seven inches, Pron was the tallest reporter in Toronto, but he kept his weight down by regular exercise and by working flat-out on stories. Lately, he wasn't doing much of either. And that made him even more miserable.

He was just starting his dinner when the grey speaker box beside the scanners emitted a sharp, piercing sound, the signal there was going to be a press release from OPP headquarters, a building just two blocks from the *Star*'s.

The bulletin didn't say much. Two legs had been found on a road in the Gananoque area. The police didn't know who they belonged to, but the person was probably a female. It was likely a homicide. If the public could help, et cetera, et cetera. Pron scribbled down the details while he took a bite of the hamburger. Then he went over and told a night editor about the find. He got no response. The eyes of most editors around the *Star* glazed over to almost any crime news that happened outside Metro Toronto. The paper's crime coverage was usually focussed inside the boundaries of Canada's largest city. The editor asked for a couple of paragraphs.

Pron went back to the Box and looked up Rockport on the map. Then he finished his hamburger. A few moments later another reporter wandered into the Box. Kevin Donovan had been standing nearby when the press release came over. Donovan's cheery good looks were a sharp contrast to his often abrasive personality. He and Pron had become friends after working — and being threatened — together on the drug-smuggling series, but Pron was not in the mood to be sociable.

"What's that I just heard about some legs being found?" Donovan asked, reaching over to grab a few fries.

Pron just shrugged.

Donovan persisted. "Was that the Gananoque area?"

"I guess so."

"Think there's anything to this one?"

"Who knows?"

Pron leaned back in his chair and slowly put his feet up on the desk. He reached for the *Sun*, the *Star*'s tabloid rival.

"Feeling sorry for yourself won't get you out of here," Donovan said, moving to the desk and picking up a copy of the OPP's internal phone book. He wrote a number on a piece of paper.

"What're you doing?" Pron asked.

"If you're not interested in working on a good murder," Donovan said, turning to go, "I'll call the OPP news bureau myself."

"Who said I wasn't interested? And don't bother calling the OPP. They'll just read you the press release, and I already got that."

Donovan threw up his hands. "Then tell me what they said."

"I was going to. I just don't like being rushed." Pron slowly reached for his notebook, carefully opened it, cleared his throat. "The cops found a nice pair of legs out east," he read, "or was it west? Whatever, there was no body to go with them." He put down the notebook and went back to his newspaper.

"That's it? That's all you got?" Donovan asked.

"If the cops know any more, they're not saying."

"Have you checked the library to see if there have been any stories about missing women?"

"Now how the hell am I supposed to do that? I'm stuck in here."

"I can do it for you."

"Yeah, and then steal the story—my story."

"I don't steal from the handicapped."

"One day you're gonna get charged with theft."

"You want me to look it up or not?"

"Why not? Gotta be someone out there looking for a woman—besides you."

The pretty, timid-looking woman was in her early twenties, and she had never been inside a police station before. She went with a male friend, and as they waited in the front lobby for an officer, she had thoughts of leaving. But she was too worried about her sister. She told the desk sergeant at 42 Division in Scarborough, a suburb of Metro Toronto, that her sister had been missing for two weeks. She was ushered into a side room where a detective took her statement and filled

14

out a missing person report. The young woman explained that her sister had not turned up for dinner at a restaurant two Sundays ago. "Have you checked her place?" the detective asked. The sister said she had and that's why she was so worried. All her sister's things were still there. The room was tidy, the bed made and her nightclothes neatly laid out on the pillow. What appeared to be her full wardrobe was hanging in the closet, along with two empty suitcases. In the top drawer of the bureau, she had found her sister's passport and bankbook. She had also found a four-page letter that her sister had written to her but never delivered. Did she have the letter, the detective asked. She took it from her purse and handed it to him.

The detective was kind and understanding, but there wasn't much the police could do, he explained. Each year, hundreds of people disappeared in the city of two and a half million. The police department didn't have time to hunt for each one. Besides, the officer said, most people who vanished didn't want to be found. If she was so worried about her sister, the officer wondered, why did she wait two weeks to notify the police? The young woman had no answer. Did the sister have a boyfriend? She gave the officer his name and address. He promised her a detective would be assigned to the case as soon as possible. Then he filed it away as missing person occurrence number 1635.

CHAPTER TWO

A Thirty-eight-point Match

Larry Edgar was restless. He had not slept very well that night, and on the drive in to work from Hamilton, his mind had wandered and he almost got into an accident on the expressway. He had been on the body parts case for what seemed like years, yet he was no closer to identifying his Jane Doe than he was that first day on the Parkway. He got up from behind his desk, walked over to the grey metal filing cabinets along the wall of his office, and rummaged through several drawers until he found the folder he was looking for. He glanced through it, then dropped it dejectedly on his desk, reached for a cigarette from the near empty package, and started pacing.

He was smoking too much and he knew it. His kids were starting to bug him about it. It was this case; it was driving him nuts. He was off running all over the province every time somebody thought they had found another body part. The "brain" had been found in Picton. It turned out to be the shell of a crab. A hiker stumbled over what was probably the skull in some bushes outside Toronto. It was a skull, all right. But it had belonged to a bear.

He finished his cigarette then lit another. He had almost finished his first pack of the day. He couldn't remember ever smoking that much. It was only after he made detective. He liked his new job but there was a lot more pressure. Things had been different when he worked on the biker squad. In those days he did all his talking with his fists. Real rough-house police work. He had been one of a group of cops, chosen for their size, who had cleaned up Wasaga Beach. Wasaga was a popular swimming spot on Georgian Bay, north of Toronto, but it had been taken over by biker gangs. Outfits such as the Satan's Choice, the Para-Dice, and the Vagabonds were treating Wasaga like their own little resort area. The OPP brass, getting heat from the politicians, who were hearing about it from the voters, wanted the bikers out or under control, and they weren't too fussy about how it was done. If the bikers got "stepped on" — well, too bad. Innocent civilians were getting hurt. At first, the bikers wouldn't listen to reason. But over time they found that squaring off against the cops led to lumps on their heads. Edgar had raided more than his share of clubhouses, shotgun in hand. But those days were over. The bikers had lost, and they faded from the scene. Occasionally they wore their colours and paraded through Wasaga on their Harley-Davidsons, but mostly they kept low profiles, doing their business in private, the business of crime. For Edgar, too, it had been time for something new, time to move on.

Nowadays he kept his gun in his briefcase instead of on his hip. The only time he drew it was on the firing range, where he went every so often for target practice. As a homicide detective, Edgar had little other use for the weapon. While his days on the biker squad had been dangerous, he hadn't found them stressful. Homicide investigations were different: long, drawn out, more exacting, psychological rather than physical. He was a case manager in charge of a team of detectives, a supervisor who co-ordinated the field investigations. It meant more responsibility and more stress. He wanted to quit smoking, even tried a few times, but it never worked. Now it would be harder. His third-floor office at OPP headquarters had become an informal smoke room for a few die-hards ever since smoking had been banned in the dull, grey brick building near Toronto's waterfront.

Edgar blew some smoke towards the ceiling and turned back to the desk, his glance playing over the stack of files. He had to be missing something. He was convinced there was a clue, some bit of information he had overlooked that would help him match one of those missing person reports to the body parts. Another piece of her body had been found a week ago, also on the Parkway. A motorist going to work almost drove over the left thigh farther east, about five kilometres, from the place that Mallory had first spotted the leg. But the latest discovery had not helped Edgar. He still needed that one break. There were times, mostly nights it seemed, when he wondered if he would ever get it.

Edgar glanced at the calendar on the wall. May 5. Two months and one day had passed since the legs had been found. Too long. The press kept bugging him for information. Calls came in daily from reports across Ontario, Quebec, and upstate New York, just across the river from Rockport. They all wanted to know the same thing. Who was the victim and were there any suspects? He had no answers for them. The brass had not been on his back about the slow progress in the case, but he knew that was only a matter of time. He lit another cigarette. As if he didn't have enough trouble, Edgar was also getting some heat from the residents of Rockport. They were afraid a maniac was on the loose. Were the police close to an arrest? they wanted to know. The thought that a killer was roaming free was making them uneasy. And with summer just around the corner, an unsolved murder was bad for the tourist business. Around the office, Edgar bore the brunt of a lot of sick jokes. The other detectives had dubbed the case the ''Snack Pack Mystery.'' Police officers he hardly knew greeted him in the hallway with comments like, ''Are you getting a leg up on that case?'' ''Stumped are we, Larry?'' or, ''Can I give you a hand, inspector? How about an arm?''

Edgar gazed out the window. Still raining. The day certainly matched his mood. His office overlooked the Gardiner Expressway, an ageing, elevated highway eaten away by salt and always under repair. Most days, the sound of jackhammers was as common as the squeal of tires. To the south, he used to be able to see the sparkling, although badly polluted, waters of Lake Ontario. But that view had recently been blocked by a row of drab high-rise condominium apartments. Not that he cared about the view. He spent most of his working time on the road. When he was in the office, he sat with his back to the window so he could see who was coming in the door. A cop's habit.

Edgar butted his cigarette, sat down, grabbed his briefcase, and put it on top of his desk. He thumbed the combination number, snapped open the locks, flipped up the lid, and reached inside for a folder, pushing the gun to one side. Clearing some space on his desk top, he laid the folder down. It was marked with the official stamp of the Ontario Coroner's Office. Inside were the details of the pathologist's examination of the two legs and the thigh. The pages were worn and creased. Edgar had gone over the report many times. Well, he was going to do it once more.

McGarvey, the identification bureau officer, had taken the legs to the forensic pathology building on Grenville Street in Toronto, where he made plaster casts of both feet with the same type of plaster dentists use to take a mould of the mouth for false teeth. Footprints, like hands, are unique, rich in detail. Although it was rarely done, a footprint could theoretically be used to make an identification. There was nothing unusual about the feet, except for a callus on the left foot, probably caused by a shoe that was too tight. Interesting, but not much help. Later, it would be.

The autopsy had been handled by Dr. Hans Sepp, one of the country's leading pathologists who had dissected nearly 5,600 bodies during his thirty-two-year career. Sepp confirmed what Edgar and the others had suspected, that the victim was a woman, possibly East Indian. The skin had a greyish colour due to the time it had been exposed to air, but just how long, Sepp didn't know. Each leg was fifty-six centimetres long from the heel to the top of the cut, which meant the woman had been about 162 centimetres (five feet, four inches) tall, average for a woman. The legs had been severed from the thighs about fifteen centimetres above the knee.

The cuts were precise, no rough edges where the legs had been sliced off from the thighs. There was no tearing of the skin or cartilage. The killer had most likely used a straight-edge rather than a serrated knife. The cuts had clearly not been made by an animal. The cuts on both legs were almost identical except for an angular chip on the bone of the right leg. Chunks of flesh had been bitten off both legs, probably by animals. There was a slash, several centimetres long, on the right leg. Sepp had no explanation for that.

It was the next part of the report that Edgar found the most perplexing. Sepp made special note of the total absence of blood. There was none in the veins, the main arteries, or in the tissue of the three limbs. Apart from a few reddish blotches on the skin, there was no lividity, the discoloration of skin that occurs when blood pools at the lowest point after death. Despite the lack of any quantifiable amount of blood, microscopic traces in the tissue enabled forensic technicians to do a partial blood typing. Tests revealed the blood was O type.

Edgar reached for another cigarette before starting to read the next report, dated March 30. It detailed Sepp's examination of a left thigh found by Shawn Patrick Edgell on March 29 on the Thousand Islands Parkway, about five kilometres east of where the legs were spotted. Edgell, a Rockport mechanic, had been on his way to work at about six that morning when he spotted a dark green garbage bag in the centre of the Parkway. Recalling the discovery of the legs three weeks earlier, he stopped the car and got out to have a look. Part of what looked like a large ham was sticking out one end of the bag, he later told police officers. The flesh was a pale pink. He poked at the bag with a snow scraper. It sank in, like a finger going into jelly.

Dr. Sepp confirmed that the left leg and the thigh came from the same person, although a connecting section of bone and tissue between the thigh and leg was missing. A section of the thigh bone, where it attached to the pelvis, was also missing, apparently bitten off by an animal, judging by the ragged ends of the bone. The cuts that severed the thigh were neat. As with the legs, Sepp found no blood in the thigh. Still hoping to get an exact blood type, Sepp removed a sample of marrow from the thigh bone and sent it to the lab for testing. Those results weren't ready. Edgar glanced at the photographs of the body parts before closing the folder in disgust.

Nothing.

He had seen nothing new, nothing he might have missed in the dozen other times he had read the reports. Edgar leaned back in his chair and wondered why he had ever left the biker squad. He was no closer to identifying his Jane Doe than he had been two months ago. How do you find a killer when you don't even know who was killed? Without a name, who do you question? Who were her friends? More importantly, who were her enemies? Did someone hate her enough to kill her? Or was her death a random attack by a lunatic, perhaps a serial killer, as some of the armchair detectives in Rockport seemed to think? Good questions, all of them. But he didn't have answers for any of them.

He was in charge of a team of investigators that was just itching to do some detective work: hunting down witnesses, interviewing friends of the victims, getting answers to all these questions. But all the detectives could do for now was pore over missing person reports, hoping to stumble on a match. Edgar had already ruled out the theory that the whole thing was a prank, the body parts stolen from a graveyard or funeral home. Pathologists had found no trace of formaldehyde or other embalming fluid in the legs or thigh. Edgar had never really bought that theory, but, as in all investigations, he had to eliminate every possibility, no matter how far-fetched.

The detective slipped his last cigarette from the pack and lit up, turning back to the window. Traffic leaving the city in the westbound lanes of the Gardiner Expressway was barely inching along, and Edgar was not looking forward to the long drive home. He decided to wait until it thinned out a little before leaving for the day. The traffic was stalled by some construction work in the inside lane, forcing motorists to manoeuvre around orange pylons into the other two lanes. Standing inside the pylons, oblivious to the blaring horns, a lone construction worker was leaning against the guardrail, smoking. Edgar couldn't make out the man's face but he was almost sure he was smiling, probably even laughing over the snarled traffic and the frustrated drivers, happy that his job was over for another day. Edgar envied the man. Leaving your work behind you at the end of the day — that was a luxury he didn't have.

He closed his eyes and tried to visualize what his Jane Doe looked like. She was average height, and she wore a size-eight shoe. A nice piece of information but it didn't bring him closer to identifying her. They hadn't found her shoes or any other item of clothing. At least if they had a shoe, they might be able to trace the make and lot number back to the store where she bought it. Maybe a clerk might remember her. Maybe. Right now that's what he had, a lot of maybes and no answers. Her blood type, O, was the universal donor. But the sub-group, Rh positive, made it rare. What were those statistics? Only one in five hundred thousand people had that kind of blood. Again, a potentially good clue, but it didn't fit any of the missing person reports. All it had done was rule out some people who had vanished. Dr. Sepp had theorized that the woman was East Indian, based on the colour of the skin. That information didn't match any of the reports, either.

Edgar wheeled around his desk for another cigarette. He was out. He searched in the side drawers for a fresh pack, but there was none. Maybe this was the time to quit. Everyone kept telling him that Player's were too strong. At least try a brand with less nicotine, they said. One of the secretaries came in for a smoke, and he borrowed one from her. When she asked him about the case, he shrugged in frustration. Although he didn't say anything to her, something else was bugging him.

Was the killer taunting him? How else could you explain the discovery of the left thigh on the same stretch of highway three weeks after the legs had been found? There hadn't been that much putrefaction of the limb, indicating that it had just been dumped. Had the killer come back and left another body part to tease the police? Daring them to catch him? Edgar wondered if he should have officers staking out the highway in case the killer came back a third time with more parts. It was a long stretch of highway. He'd need half the manpower in the south-east region to cover it. But even if he wanted to do it where would he hide the officers? In trees? If he was wrong, he would be the laughing-stock of the force.

What really bothered him was that they couldn't find the crime scene. The tracking dogs had sniffed around but they hadn't found a thing. Just where the hell was she killed? Nearby? Or hundreds of kilometres away? Edgar would have to accept the fact that he might never find the place she had been killed, cut up, and bagged, like meat in a grocery store.

And then there was the question of the blood, or lack of it. Every drop had been drained from the two legs and the thigh. What the hell was he dealing with here? A vampire? A human body contains about five litres of blood, and if there was none in the body parts, then where was it? Soaking into the soil somewhere? Or staining a basement floor? Not, he hoped, washed down a drain. Dr. Sepp had told him that it would be relatively easy to drain the large arteries, but the smaller veins were harder to empty. It could be done two ways. One was by pressure, with a suction machine like those used in funeral homes for embalming. Was his killer an undertaker? The other method of draining blood was by gravity. That opened up a realm of ghoulish possibilities.

Was she bled dry while she was still alive? Hung up like a side of beef while her killer cut open a vein in her throat, watching sadistically as the blood gushed out. This was a sick man, this faceless killer. But if she had been strung up, why were there no rope marks on the ankles? Maybe she had been held down in a bathtub? He just didn't have any answers. Dr. Sepp had pointed out that if the blood wasn't drained before death, it would have to be done shortly afterwards, within two hours after the heart stopped pumping, or else it would have thickened, causing lividity.

And just how was she killed? Was she shot? Or strangled? How could detectives find a murder weapon if they didn't know what they were looking for? Finding the torso and head might answer those questions. But what were the chances of finding the head? He would have to wait and hope for another lucky discovery. There had been enough co-operation from the public. Since the first find in March, it seemed as if everybody in eastern Ontario was on the look-out for body parts. All sorts of bones and tissue had been turned in to police stations. The crime labs had been working overtime.

But each and every find, including a kidney, were from cows, foxes, or other animals.

The intercom on Edgar's desk buzzed, interrupting his thoughts. There were two calls for him. A reporter from the Toronto *Star* was on line one.

"Put him on ignore," Edgar told his secretary. "Who's on two?"

It was Constable Garnet Rombough, one of the OPP detectives from the Picton detachment that he had seconded to his team. Rombough was calling with some fresh news. Right now, Edgar could use any kind of news.

One hundred kilometres west of Rockport an area of land roughly two thousand square kilometres was almost entirely separated from the rest of Ontario by a series of rivers and lakes, part of the Trent-Severn Waterway. All that kept it from being an island was a narrow bridge of land at its western end. In the days before Canada became a nation, fur traders often travelled the waterway to reach Lake Ontario. But when they got to the narrow, three-kilometre stretch of land they had to portage, carrying their canoes the short distance to the lake. That's how the area got its name, Carrying Place. Over the decades it grew from a collection of trading posts to a small hamlet known for its apple orchards and sweet cider.

Andy Borisenko owned a red-painted cabin on the Bay of Quinte across the bay from Carrying Place. In his early seventies, retired, Borisenko spent the winter months in his Toronto home in a suburb known as the Beaches, but preferred the solitude of the countryside for his summer retreat. On May 5 he had gone there to open his cabin, Happy Haven, for the coming season. After taking the shutters off the windows to air out the place, he made his way down the icy slope to the shore, using a fallen branch he had found for support. One of his pastimes was fishing, and Borisenko, a frugal man, often walked the Quinte shoreline looking for lures. Pickings were usually good at this time of year because the water flowing under the winter ice pushed debris inland. He was heading west around the bay when he spotted a green garbage bag by the water's edge.

Borisenko poked it with the stick. It appeared that the garbage bag was filled with soggy newspapers. The end was knotted. Borisenko kept nudging the bag until he tore the plastic. Inside was a greyish lump. After enlarging the hole with the stick, Borisenko bent down to see what was inside. Suddenly he jerked backwards, almost tripping over some driftwood. One end of the lump was moving.

Cautiously, he moved forward again, gingerly poking at the bag. The greyish lump was alive with maggots, their tiny white bodies clumped together, wriggling over the surface of what was obviously some kind of meat. The smell of rotting flesh made him gag. He pulled out a handkerchief and held it to his nose and mouth. There was no mistaking the swell of a woman's breasts. He didn't notice it at first, but when he looked closer he saw the maggots crawling into the exposed flesh where both nipples had been hacked off.

Two days after the phone call from Officer Rombough, the autopsy report on the torso was on Larry Edgar's desk. Dr. Sepp's examination of the skin concluded that the torso, two legs, and thigh all came from the same body. A series of X-rays of the lungs and pelvic area indicated the woman was young, probably in her early twenties. Sepp devoted several pages of the report to his analysis of six cuts that had been made on the torso by a sharp-edged object. Five of the cuts had severed both arms, both legs, and the head. A sixth cut, measuring twenty-five millimetres, had been made lengthwise on the torso near an arm, similar to the cut he had found on one of the legs. Sepp remarked on the smoothness of the cuts. So neat, in fact, that the limbs had been removed by carefully cutting around the ball-shaped joints that rotated in the torso sockets. While the maggots had damaged these areas somewhat, they had eaten much more flesh from the neck area. The head had been severed at the top of the fifth vertebra of the seven in the neck. Here, Sepp spent some time describing the intricacy of the cut. Instead of moving straight across, the sharp instrument had sliced carefully around the vertebra, first going horizontal, then vertical, without nicking the bone. The voice box, like the nipples, was missing. Cut out.

An internal examination revealed nothing unusual about the heart or other organs. Apart from the shallow cut near the arm, there were no other marks of violence, with the exception of the cuts to the breasts. Both the nipples and the areola, the area surrounding the nipple, had been sliced off. There was extensive putrefaction, or rotting, of the torso. This was due to the length of time it had been in the water.

Edgar read again Sepp's remarks on the intricacy of the neck cut. While the arm and leg cuts might conceivably be done by the average person, the precise cuts around the vertebra required a knowledge of anatomy. Sepp pointed out that a nurse or chiropractor could do the job, maybe even a hunter or a butcher, all of whom had experience cutting up meat. Then, of course, the killer could have been a doctor. Was that who Edgar was looking for, a deranged doctor? And what about the missing nipples and voice box? Did the killer keep them as souvenirs? As bullfighters did? As in the limbs, there was no blood in the torso, no lividity. While the torso had provided a few clues to his case, Edgar still didn't know how the woman was killed. He needed to find her head.

Five days later, late one Tuesday night, two friends set out to do some fishing on the Trent River, not far from the Bay of Quinte. That past weekend, Ken Yardley and Dean Stockwell had tried their luck in the annual Trenton Fishing Derby. They had enjoyed the contest but found the narrow river too crowded with other anglers. Many lines had been tangled and there'd even been a few spills into the chilly waters. The two men, who worked together at a factory in Belleville, were trolling near the McDonald Bridge in Yardley's twelve-foot aluminum boat when the small Evinrude motor stalled.

Yardley, sitting at the stern, was closest to the motor and tilted it back. Stockwell got out the flashlight. Neither was surprised to find fishing line tangled in the blades of the motor. More leftovers from the derby. Yardley started unravelling the line, while his fishing partner tugged on it to give him some slack.

''Feels like it's snagged on a boot or something,'' Stockwell told his friend.

He had to pull on the line several times before it came free. But what he pulled up wasn't a boot. It was a green garbage bag.

Holding the line with one hand, Stockwell reached over with a fishing net and hauled the garbage bag into the boat. The bag was slimy from river silt and felt cold as he tried to remove the hook. Then he froze.

"What's wrong?" Yardley asked, looking up from the propeller.

"It felt as though I just grabbed an elbow," Stockwell replied.

"You're joking."

"Grab your knife. Cut it open."

Yardley made a slit in the plastic with his penknife. Milky white water came pouring out, splashing onto his shoes. He gingerly picked up one corner of the bag and shone the flashlight inside.

"I think we've got another part to the puzzle," Yardley said.

He tugged at the bag, and an arm and hand fell out. The fingers were curled up, as if in a death grip.

The autopsy the next day revealed that the arm matched the torso. Like the other body parts, it contained no blood.

City editor Lou Clancy was in charge of more than 150 reporters and editors who worked for the Toronto *Star*. He decided what was going to be covered in Metro Toronto and who covered it. Clancy started in the business at the age of sixteen, as a copy boy. He'd done most jobs in the newsroom in the past twenty-five years, but what he liked was the hard-driving atmosphere of the city desk. The soft-spoken, one-time long-haired hippie seldom wore a suit or tie. He was more at home talking baseball with reporters in the newspaper's bar, the Print Room, than going out with the *Star*'s boardroom crowd to fancy restaurants. Clancy liked being in on a good news story, liked getting it fast, right, and exclusively. But in May, 1988, Clancy was more interested in a story in the rival *Globe and Mail*.

"Thought you boys were working on this," Clancy said, dropping the *Globe* in front of Donovan and looking at Pron, who was standing beside the desk.

Clancy was referring to a feature-length story on the discovery of the five body parts over the past nine weeks in eastern Ontario. With it was a map of the area, pinpointing the spots where the finds were made. Donovan scanned the story, then casually tossed the paper aside.

"There's nothing new here," he pronounced. "We've had all this. We ran stories on every find. All the *Globe* did was roll it all together."

Clancy glanced at the *Globe* and was silent for a moment, an indication he didn't like the answer. But he let it pass. "Just as long as we don't get beat," he said, and walked away.

"Nice bluff," Pron said to Donovan, when Clancy was out of earshot.

"Well, what can we do without a name?"

"The cops got almost a whole body," Pron said. "How long does it take to come up with a name? What's their problem?"

The body parts case was two months old when one of Edgar's investigators, Constable Angus McInnes ("Gus") Riddell, called him late one afternoon. Riddell said he had some information that could help him identify his Jane Doe in the body parts case. There was something he had to show him. Could they meet at the morgue? It was well after working hours by the time Edgar got to the building on Grenville Street. Riddell was waiting for him, along with Sepp. They went into the basement room where the bodies were kept in cold storage. Sepp opened the drawer that held the woman's remains.

"Just the legs," Riddell said to Sepp.

The pathologist put the two plastic bags holding the lower limbs on one of the dissecting tables. While they waited for the legs to thaw, Riddell explained what he had learned.

All along, the detectives had assumed the woman was East Indian because of the pigmentation of the skin. But what if she was an Asian? More specifically, said Riddell, what if she was Chinese? Riddell, who specialized in Asian crime, said he had been talking about the case with one of his underworld contacts. The man said it was common for Oriental women to have a double nail on each baby toe.

"It's got something to do with heredity, the way the women used to bind their feet to make them smaller," Riddell said. "I showed him the pictures of the legs. He couldn't tell for sure, but he thought there were double nails on each toe."

When the legs thawed, Sepp took them out of the bags. The two detectives and the pathologist leaned over to get a better look. After a moment, Riddell slapped his hands together in satisfaction.

"I knew it," he said excitedly. "I think I know who she is, Larry."

A woman had disappeared from a Scarborough town house about two weeks before the legs had been found in Rockport, said Riddell. The missing woman was twenty-eight years old. Sepp had speculated that the legs, arm, and thigh belonged to a woman in her mid-twenties. The height and weight of the woman who had vanished also roughly corresponded to the pathologist's estimates. The missing woman was a native of the People's Republic of China and had been in the country for seven years. Her sister had filed a missing person report with 42 Division of the Metro police.

Edgar asked the Metro force if they could send some officers to the woman's rented room to get something with blood on it. The detectives came back with a pair of the missing woman's panties stained with menstrual blood. The panties were taken to the Centre of Forensic Sciences. Tests were done almost immediately. The blood type on the panties was the same as the tissue sample from the body parts.

Good, but not conclusive.

Edgar wanted to be damn sure he had the right person before he went knocking on a relative's door to tell them their loved one was lying in pieces in the city morgue. He wanted another test done. He sent the detectives back to the missing woman's room for a pair of her shoes.

Feet, like hands, leave a unique impression. There was a test that specialists in the OPP's crime lab could do with a laser. It was exacting work, and could take days. The shoe would have to have a good imprint of the foot for the test to work, fingerprint specialist Brian Dalrymple told Edgar. Luckily, the impressions in the soles of the missing woman's shoes were sharp, probably because they were tight-fitting. That explained the callus. The shoes had only been worn a few times and apparently without socks.

Dalrymple had plaster castings made from the shoes. The laser measured the ridges along the foot and toes, then a computer reduced the information to a numerical readout. That information was compared to the measurements taken of the plaster moulds from each foot. Dalrymple usually considered ten points of comparison enough for a positive identification. After nearly two weeks, the tests were finally done.

Dalrymple was at his desk when Edgar walked into the lab. The tall, fair-haired scientist looked up at Edgar, took off his glasses, and rubbed his eyes. He had worked overtime to finish the tests because he knew how anxious Edgar was for the results.

"There are thirty-eight points of agreement," Dalrymple said, smiling. "I'd say we've got a match."

CHAPTER THREE

Two Days in the Rain

When the phone woke him at seven that Saturday morning, Donovan let the answering machine click in. It was his day off. He waited to hear who was on the line before deciding whether it was worthwhile getting out of bed. At the sound of Lou Clancy's gruff voice, he leaped up and flung the covers back. The woman beside him stirred in her sleep as he fumbled for the phone.

"Have you seen today's front page?" Clancy wanted to know. Donovan mumbled that he hadn't. "Call me back when you have," Clancy said, and abruptly hung up.

Donovan dressed quickly, grabbed a handful of change from the bureau, and rushed outside into the rain just as a police car, its roof lights flashing, raced by. His brownstone apartment building on Vaughan Road was in one of the city's highest crime areas, despite being just a two-minute drive from Toronto's wealthiest neighbourhood, Forest Hill. The bright blue Toronto *Star* box at the corner was splattered with mud. But the front-page headline behind the dirty glass was clear enough: SCATTERED BODY PARTS IDENTIFIED AS SCARBOROUGH WOMAN. The cops had a name, finally.

Donovan read the story as he walked back to his apartment. Selina Lian Shen had been twenty-eight years old when she was murdered. The story said she lived at a town house in Scarborough, played the piano, and gave music lessons. In a bit of a coincidence, her sister had reported her missing on

March 5, the day Mallory had found the leg. There were no suspects, or at least no mention of any in the story.

"You took your time," Clancy said when Donovan called him back.

Two city reporters had worked on the story the night before, after the press release came out. They hadn't found her family or friends, the key to advancing a murder story beyond the barest details of a police press release. Clancy wanted Donovan to give it a try.

"This was your day off, wasn't it?" Clancy asked. "You have anything planned?"

"A few things. I—"

"Good. Then you'll have something to do next weekend. I've already told city desk you'll be filing a story for tomorrow. Don't let me down."

Donovan changed clothes, trying not to disturb his sleeping bedmate. He put on a dark, pin-striped suit, one that made him look like a businessman. Going door to door for information was easier when you looked respectable. His battered grey Firebird was one of the few cars on the expressway as he drove to Shen's neighbourhood. He glanced down at the newspaper on the seat beside him. The story had just quoted the cops. Why hadn't the reporters talked to the relatives? They had her address. She lived at 250 Timberbank Boulevard. Was there something Clancy had not told him?

He couldn't miss the address. It was printed on a sign, a huge sign right by the curb. The number 250 was in big, block lettering. Number 250 Timberbank was not a single house. Number 250 Timberbank was a housing complex, a monster housing complex. Hundreds and hundreds of town houses. Dreary little half-houses that went forever, a maze of homes, walkways built in no particular pattern. All the units were the same size, like a child's building blocks. Some were painted white, some were brown, others a cream colour. Whatever, there were a zillion of them.

Those goddamn cops, Donovan thought, as he walked through the complex to a pay phone. They've only given out part of the address. No unit number. He called the OPP. Sorry, there wasn't a unit number on the press release, the woman in the communications room said. Just 250. Was there a problem? The detective in charge of the case, Larry Edgar, would clear it up, only he wasn't around. Perhaps if he tried back later? Had he looked in the phone book? Donovan did but there was no listing. He dialled information. Again, nothing. He called the rewrite desk at the *Star*, asked them to check the city directory. No Shens in the big book. No wonder Clancy had called him at home. It was a shit assignment that nobody else wanted. It would probably take all day, probably require knocking on hundreds of doors. Donovan stuck his head out of the phone booth, stared glumly at row after row of town houses. Little drops of rain were rolling down his nose. His feet were already cold, and he hadn't even started. His father was right. He should have been a lawyer.

A man with a beer belly wearing a Dallas Cowboys football jersey answered the door at the first house he tried. He made no move to invite Donovan in out of the rain. He didn't look happy to be bothered on a Saturday morning.

"Hi. I'm with the Toronto *Star*."

"There was someone here from the *Star* last night. If it's about that murder, I never heard of her. I told that to the other guy. Why do you guys keep coming around? Ain't you got nothing better to do? You sure you got the right address?"

"It's what the cops told us."

"And you believed them?" He laughed. "I think the cops are stringing you. That woman's not from around here."

A girl, about eight years old, came to the door at the next house. She was hugging a stuffed pink elephant, her eyes red from crying. She was Oriental. The sound of people arguing was coming from another room.

"Yes?" she asked, squeezing the elephant tighter.

"Is your mom or dad around?" Donovan asked. The girl nodded, but didn't move. "Could you get one of them?"

"They're fighting," she said.

"Oh."

"Can you stop them from fighting?"

"Oh, well, maybe. Could you get them for me?"

The girl turned and ran down the hall, taking the pink elephant with her. The shouting stopped. A man in his mid-thirties came to the door. He had on blue jeans and an under-shirt with food stains down the front.

"What do you want?" The tone was not friendly.

Donovan told him about the murder. He had trouble remembering Shen's full name and glanced at the palm of his hand where he had printed it.

"Why you come here?" the man scolded. "I don't know anything about this girl." He started to close the door.

"She was Chinese," Donovan said, leaning against the door. "I thought you might know."

"No, no. I Korean. Chinese lives over there." He made a vague gesture up the street before closing the door.

The next dozen houses were the same. It went like that for the rest of the morning. The only thing they knew about Shen was what they had read in the newspaper, or heard on tele-vision. Nobody recalled a young Chinese piano teacher. One man had a possible lead. A woman in unit 87 taught piano. Donovan went there, but the woman was out for the day. Neighbours said she was in her early sixties. Maybe Shen's mother? By noon Donovan wanted to quit. But what if a reporter from the opposition got the right door and beat him to the story? He decided instead to take a break.

He drove to a coffee shop and sat down at a corner table so no one could see him take off his right shoe. There was a hole in the sole and his sock was sopping wet. He stuffed in some newspaper over the hole. That's what he had been going to do that Saturday. Go out and buy a new pair of shoes. He checked his watch as he gulped down a coffee. Half a day gone and nothing to show.

Back at the complex he tried a different approach. Someone had given him the name of the woman who ran the residents' association. She was at home and she invited him in. He explained his problem. It was against policy to hand out a list of all the residents, but he did look cold. She left and came back a few moments later with several sheets of paper stapled together. Donovan scanned the names. Nobody named Shen was listed. He asked if he could borrow the list.

There were several dozen Chinese-sounding names. Don-ovan tried each house but came up with nothing. Maybe the man in the football shirt was right. Did he have the wrong address? He called the OPP back. Still no sign of Detective Edgar. Although it was an OPP case, Shen's sister had filed the missing person report to the Metro police. Maybe they could help him? He drove to 42 Division and explained his problem to a desk sergeant who was sympathetic but not very helpful.

"If the OPP didn't give out the number they must have had a reason," he said. "Love to help you, though, son. You tried the phone book?"

Donovan stopped at a shopping mall on the drive back to Timberbank Boulevard. Perhaps the dead woman had put up some flyers advertising her music lessons? The bulletin board was jammed with notices. But he was not looking for a trades-man to pave his sidewalk or a plumber to fix his toilet. It was nearly three. He couldn't put off calling the city desk much longer.

They would want to know what he had for tomorrow, which was zip. He tried a few more doors on Timberbank Boulevard then gave up. One thing was certain, he thought as he drove back to the office, when he got around to buying a home, it was not going to be a town house.

Assignment editor Robin Harvey had been looking for him all day. Why hadn't he called in? She wanted to know what he had for Sunday. There were a few leads he was working on. He went to the library computer and punched in Shen's name. The computer, called ALIS, for Advanced Library Infor-mation System, contained all the stories from the paper in the past three years. ALIS scanned its memory cells. In a few moments it had an answer.

"Zero documents satisfy your request."

He tried the words *Scarborough, piano,* and *teacher.* ALIS spit out seven stories naming a variety of music associations involved with piano teaching in Scarborough. Donovan spent the next hour calling officials from each association, but drew a blank. It was a rule at the *Star* that front-page stories had to be followed up for the next day's paper. He needed some-thing. Comments from the chief detective seemed like his best bet. But when he called the OPP, he was told Edgar was on the road and couldn't be reached.

Larry Edgar's pager had been beeping so much lately that he felt like throwing it in the toilet. He had left it on the front seat of the car as he drove home along Highway 33. Getting paged by his investigators on the Shen case was normal, but somehow several reporters had got his number and were calling him every few minutes. The most persistent was this guy named Kevin Donovan. The duty sergeant at OPP head-quarters complained to him when he checked in for his messages that this Donovan character was tying up their lines with nuisance calls. Tough luck, Edgar thought. We all have our crosses to bear. He had far too much on his mind, and no time for the *Star* or any reporters right now. Cops who talked to the press during a homicide case risked getting their ears pinned back by the boss if they said the wrong thing. So why talk to reporters at all? After all, the press was just there to be used. When he had put out a news release asking for anyone who knew Shen to come forward, it had suited his purposes. That was yesterday. Today, he didn't need their help.

Edgar had spent the day in Rockport, checking out what had seemed like a promising lead. An elderly woman thought she had seen Shen in a car driven by a man around the time the legs had been found. But the woman was having trouble remembering details. Her description of the car and the man driving it was vague. It had been a wasted day. But maybe not entirely. There was a hunch he wanted to check.

The parking lot of the hydroelectric plant was empty as Edgar pulled in. He got out of the car and headed for the walkway over the Trent River. His shoes sank into mud with each step. It had been raining all day. He stopped at a window of the red brick hydro plant and glanced inside. Two massive generators throbbed dully. There was a sign at a gate to the walkway over the river. It said: NO TRESPASSING. Edgar held the handrail as he made his way onto the metal grating that spanned the frothing waters of the short waterfall over the dam. He gazed downstream and lit a cigarette. Could the killer have stood on this very spot and hurled the green garbage bags into the raging waters just below his feet?

It was possible. The current was strong. It would take the bags downriver, to the place Yardley and Stockwell had fished out the arm. The river emptied into the Bay of Quinte, where Borisenko had found the torso. Maybe he should have divers check around the dam? What if a bag had snagged on the bottom and was still stuck there? He finished his cigarette and flicked the butt into the water. He made a mental note to have his investigators interview employees at the plant. Maybe they saw the same car the old lady had been talking about. It was a long shot but worth trying. Edgar got into his car and drove home. The phone was ringing when he opened the door.

"Inspector Edgar?" the caller asked.

"Yes?"

"My name's Kevin Donovan, and I'm with the *Star*. Can I ask you a few questions about the murder?"

Edgar grinned and shook his head. Now how the hell did that bastard get my home number? he wondered. He thought of the desk sergeant's complaints and wondered if it was him. Edgar had never dealt much with the Toronto media. He was used to small-town reporters who were not as persistent or aggressive as the ones he had encountered in Toronto.

"Oh, yeah, Kevin. I heard you were trying to reach me," he said. "I was just about to call you. I wanted to take off my wet clothes first."

"Yeah, lot of rain out there today. I'm pretty wet myself. Spent the day up at Timberbank Boulevard. Were you around there?"

"No. Out at Gananoque."

"Looking for more body parts?"

"Just poking around," Edgar said.

"Ah, I was wondering if you could help me, detective? I was up at Timberbank, but I couldn't find where Miss Shen lived."

"I can help you there, Kevin. It's a town house, number 250."

"Yeah, I know. But what unit number? It's a big complex."

"Gee, I'm not too sure, now that you mention it. All that stuff's at the office. Why don't you give me a call there Monday?"

"I appreciate that, detective. Thanks. But I work for a daily. Tomorrow's too late for me. See, I've got to write a story for tomorrow's paper. I need to find people who knew her. It would also be great if we had a picture. Can you give me one?"

" 'Fraid not there, Kevin. That stuff's all at the office."

"How about telling me a little bit about her — I mean, beyond that she was a piano teacher. She was a piano teacher, wasn't she?"

"Yeah, and apparently quite good. Actually, I don't know that much about her. We're just getting into the case."

"Do you have a suspect? Or a motive?"

"Kevin, I'm afraid that question's getting into evidence and I can't discuss that."

"There must be something you can tell me without hurting the case. I don't have to quote you directly. How about the body parts? Did finding the hand help you identify her?"

"That, too, is getting into evidence."

"Are you still looking for the head, and the other arm and thigh?"

"Oh, yes. We're hoping that the spring runoff might turn up something. Listen, I've got to get going. My pager has just gone off. Why don't you call Monday? Maybe I'll have something for you."

"How about her relatives or friends? Will you be interviewing them?"

"Oh, yes. I want to know everything about her. Who her friends were. Her enemies. Anything about her past that will help me find her killer."

"Who do you think did it?"

Edgar laughed. "Kevin, I have to go. It's been nice talking to you."

After he got off the phone, Donovan had twenty minutes to write his story. It ran across the top of page three the next day with a big, bold headline that read: DETECTIVES PROBE WOMAN'S HISTORY AFTER GRISLY DEATH. Donovan knew one thing after talking to Edgar. If he was going to learn anything more about Shen, it was not going to be from the chief detective.

He stayed at the office until midnight, calling his police contacts and people in the Chinese community. Nobody knew anything about Selina Lian Shen, except what they had read in the papers. Who was this mystery woman? Before he went home, he made one last call. There was still no answer at Pron's house. His friend had picked the wrong time to get away for the weekend.

It was still raining Sunday morning when Donovan pulled up to 250 Timberbank Boulevard. Puddles of water dotted the walkways. He had put some cardboard over the hole in his shoe, but the water was still seeping in. He cursed himself for not having a spare pair of shoes. But he was a victim of habit. Every spring he bought a single pair of black Florsheims, which he wore for the remainder of the year. That was it, just one pair every year. It was a habit Donovan had learned from his father, who died in his arms of a heart attack when Donovan was twenty. As he walked towards the first house, his foot cold from the wet sock, he decided it was time to get a new habit.

He started off with those units that he had marked "no answer" on his notepad the day before. He was not going to quit until he found out where Selina Shen lived. But what if the police had given out a phony address just to confuse the reporters? Why would they do that? Although Edgar hadn't told him anything, it seemed as if he was telling the truth about the address. He tried the house where the music teacher lived. A grey-haired woman answered his knock. She kept the outer door shut, talking to him through the screen. She said she wasn't related to the victim.

"I heard about the murder, but I can't think of any other piano teachers around here," she said.

Donovan started to leave when the woman remembered something.

"I got a flyer recently about music lessons," she said, "but it was for the violin. You sure she played the piano?"

Donovan said he wasn't sure of anything anymore, thanked her, and left.

"You look cold," the woman called to him as he walked away. "You should get out of the rain."

After several hours of going door to door, he was heading to his car to warm up when a woman in a housecoat with large purple flowers called out to him. She was in her doorway, waving him over.

"Aren't you the fellow who was here yesterday?" she asked, showing him into the hallway, shutting the door behind him.

Donovan nodded. He remembered speaking to her but she hadn't been helpful. The woman explained that her husband, Frank, who was downstairs, had been on a road trip and had returned late last night. She'd told Frank about the reporter and that apparently triggered something in the husband's mind. Did Donovan want to talk to him?

Frank had a bald head and a pleasant smile. He showed Donovan into the living room and pointed through the curtains at a house across the street. The number was 52.

"Have you checked that one?" Frank asked.

Donovan had, twice, but the people spoke only Chinese and weren't particularly helpful. Frank told Donovan to try again. Over the past two weeks, uniformed police officers had been there several times. Once the cops took away several bags. Frank couldn't be sure, but he thought it was clothing.

"I think your gal lived there," Frank said.

Donovan thanked him and walked over to the house. The woman who answered remembered him from the previous two visits.

"No, no, no, no," she said, trying to close the door. It stopped ten centimetres from the frame, at the point where it hit Donovan's shoe, the one with the hole the size of a quarter in the sole.

"Selina," Donovan said. "Selina. She live here?"

"No," the woman repeated. "No."

Just behind her a man and a woman watched. Donovan eased the door open with his shoulder, just enough to squeeze his body inside.

"Selina Shen," he repeated. "She live here?"

It was the man who spoke this time. He had only a few teeth left in his mouth, and those were discoloured. "No Selina. No here."

"Look, I'm not with the police," Donovan persisted, pushing his way farther into the hallway. "And I'm not with immigration. I work for a newspaper. I have come to see about Selina Lian Shen." And then, angrily, added: "I'm not moving until you start telling the truth."

The trio chattered to each other for a few moments. Donovan had manoeuvred himself fully into the hallway. He stood rigid, his arms folded across his chest. It was the man with the bad teeth who spoke again.

"Selina gone," he said. "She rent up there." He pointed to a room at the top of the stairs. "She stay here two week, she move out."

Donovan moved towards the stairs. "I want to see her room," he said. The man tried to block his way.

"No see, nothing, just bare room."

Donovan went around him and up the stairs, ignoring their shouts to stop. The elderly trio followed close behind, yelling at him in Chinese. The door to the room was open. What if the police were still checking it for fingerprints? He paused for a moment, looked for something that said keep out, found nothing, and went inside.

The room was tiny, not much larger than a bathroom. It was completely bare, except for the curtains on the window. The closet had also been cleaned out.

"Go, you must go." It was the man speaking.

Donovan ignored him. It had taken him two days to get here, and he wanted to savour the moment.

"How much did Selina pay?" he asked.

"I tell you, then go," the man said. But when he kept answering questions, Donovan kept asking.

Selina had moved in around the first week of February after seeing their ad in the paper. The rent was cheap, just two hundred dollars a month. Though the family told her she was welcome to share their food, Selina ate out for most of the two weeks she lived there. Occasionally, when she did eat with them, it was a light salad or soup that she brought home with her. She was a good tenant, and they were surprised when she disappeared without any notice. The rent was paid and all her clothes were in the room. The police had taken her belongings away.

"Where's her piano?" Donovan wanted to know. The man was confused. Donovan repeated the question.

"Not piano, violin," he answered. "Very beautiful girl, very beautiful music. Violin she play. Violin."

Donovan groaned. No wonder nobody knew about a slain piano player. It was the wrong instrument. Was that another deliberate lie from the cops? Donovan, never particularly fond of cops, was starting to hate them even more.

"When the police came, did they tell you anything?" he asked.

"Police tell nothing."

"Did they ask you who might have killed her?"

The man with the rotting teeth seemed confused. He glanced at the two women, said something to them in Chinese.

"Who do you think killed her?" Donovan asked, turning to the two women. "The killer, who do you think is killer?"

One of the women suddenly burst into tears and ran into another room. The man with the bad teeth watched her go. Then he turned to Donovan. His voice was angry.

"You go," he ordered.

Donovan ignored him.

"I need to know about Selina's family. I must know family," he said.

The woman who had disappeared into another room came back holding a calendar in one hand, wiping her eyes with the other. The calendar was from a bank and had a picture of a wild animal with each month. She turned the calendar over and thrust it towards Donovan.

"Sister," she said. "Sister."

On one corner of the calendar was a telephone number. Donovan wrote it down in his notepad. He thanked them and left.

He stopped at a pay phone and called the number. There was no answer. He asked rewrite to cross-check the number for an address. The sister's number was unlisted.

When he got to the office, he tried the sister's number again. He set up his tape recorder. It was always difficult talking to the next-of-kin of someone who had just been killed. You could never predict how they would react. He recalled one *Star* reporter who was knocked unconscious when he was punched in the face by a dead man's brother. Pron had told him about the time a cop threatened to shoot him because he wanted to write an obituary on the man's father. How forceful should he be with Shen's sister? Her sister had been butchered, cut up like some cow.

After two rings, a woman answered. Her voice was soft, unsteady.

"I'm really sorry to bother you. Are you Selina Shen's sister?" he asked.

"Who is calling?" the woman wanted to know.

Donovan identified himself.

"I'm Sophie. Her sister."

"Can I talk to you for a second?"

"I can't talk. I'm not to talk to anyone."

"Can you at least clear up something? Did your sister play the piano or the violin?"

"I'm the pianist, she . . . Selina plays . . . played the violin."

"Everyone says she was a good player."

"She was a beautiful violinist. We came from a musical family," the woman said. "Both our parents are musical."

If he could write a good story about Selina, it might help the police catch the killer, Donovan said, using an old reporter's tired but proven line. Could the sister help with some details? She said she would like to but was frightened. She did not want to be killed for talking. She would tell him a few things if he promised not to say in the story that it came from her. Donovan readily agreed. At this point he wasn't fussy about conditions for an interview.

Selina Shen had studied music at a conservatory in Hong Kong after leaving China while in her teens, the sister said. She majored in violin, but also took courses in the piano. Sophie and Selina had come to Canada five years ago as visa students. They enrolled in the Scarborough Christian School to study English. To support herself, Selina taught music at a Chinese school called Wei Du, and also gave private lessons in violin. Working could have got her deported, but Donovan didn't bring that up.

What about a boyfriend? he asked. There was a pause at the other end of the line. Finally Sophie answered. The boyfriend was a businessman. Selina had lived with him for nearly three years, leaving him and moving into the town house on Timberbank Boulevard shortly before she disappeared. Sophie said she got worried after Selina failed to show up for a dinner date. Sophie could not believe Selina was dead. She admitted that her parents in Hong Kong still didn't know. She didn't have the courage to call them.

Donovan pressed for more information on the boyfriend. A name would be nice.

"He has many names," the sister replied.

"What are they?"

The sister refused to say. "I've told you too much, I don't want to say any more."

Donovan asked for a picture of her sister. "Sometimes it brings people forward with information," he said.

"I don't know. I'll see," she said, and hung up.

Donovan played the tape. Sophie Shen sounded as if she was holding back something more than Selina's boyfriend's name but he didn't know what. At least he now had the correct musical instrument, no thanks to the cops. He sat down at the computer to write the next day's story. He was working on the lead when his phone rang. It was Pron. He was finally home. He had read Donovan's story on the murder and was anxious to know what was going on. But first he had some good news. A contact had called with a tip about the murder. His source told him that Selina had been neatly cut up, almost with a surgeon's precision. There was something else, something weird. Not a drop of blood had been found in the body parts. Was there still time to get that in tomorrow's story?

CHAPTER FOUR

The Man with Many Names

Sometimes the information that reporters leave out of stories is more important than what they put in. Like the name of a person's high school. Sophie Shen had told Donovan that she and her sister had gone to the Scarborough Christian School but Donovan had left the school's name out of his stories on purpose.

Since the murder was getting extensive coverage by the media, reporters from other papers and television stations were scrambling around trying to find out what they could about the dead woman. And what better place to start than at her school, where there was a wealth of information waiting to be tapped? Was she a good student? Who were her friends? More importantly, who were her enemies? Schools also had yearbooks, and Donovan needed a picture. The trick was getting into the school and convincing the principal that giving up all that information was in the public's interest, a view most principals didn't share. The last thing Donovan wanted was a dozen nosy reporters following his trail. He had slogged through the rain for two days to get this far. Why should he tip the opposition to his next move? So he had just referred to it as a school in Scarborough. It would be his first stop Monday morning. Pron went with him.

The school was in the north-eastern part of the city, a wasteland of bland town houses and dreary shopping malls. It was an old brown brick building, with crumbling front steps. Portable classrooms were scattered on a muddy playing field at the back. The lobby was crowded with students, mostly Orientals. The woman sitting at a desk in the office looked as though she had missed her morning coffee. She glanced up when Pron cleared his throat but went back to her work.

"We're looking for Mr. Davies," Pron said. The name was on a directory in the lobby.

"He's busy."

"It's important."

She shuffled a few papers before looking up again. "Do you have an appointment?"

"No."

"He's in a meeting."

"It has to do with a police matter," Donovan said solemnly.

The woman immediately stopped what she was doing and looked intently at the two men in dark trench coats standing before her.

"Oh." Her tone was apologetic. "You should have said so right away." Pron and Donovan stared back stony-faced. "I guess I better get him."

She got up and left the office, returning a minute later. "Mr. Davies will be right with you. Why don't you two gentlemen wait in his office."

She showed them into a tiny, cluttered room then left, closing the door softly behind her.

"One day we'll get charged for this ruse," said Pron.

"For what?" asked Donovan. "We never said we were cops. And it's no crime to look like one."

Donovan went to the door and watched. "Somebody's coming," he warned.

A man with an armload of books and a flustered look on his face hurried into the cramped office and dumped the books on the desk. One fell on the floor. Donovan reached down and picked it up.

"Oh, oh, thanks. I've got to clean this desk up some day. Sorry to keep you officers waiting."

Donovan stuck out his hand and told Davies who they were.

The principal looked from one reporter to the other, confused. "My secretary said you were police officers."

"No, just reporters," Pron clarified.

"I wonder why she thought you were police officers?" Davies said.

Pron smirked. "Must be the trench coats. All cops wear trench coats."

Davies thought about that for a moment, then sat down and beckoned the two reporters to sit in the chairs in front of his desk.

"Is there something I can do for you?" he asked. "My secretary said something about a police matter?"

"We're doing a story on one of your students," Pron said. "Selina Lian Shen."

It took a moment for Davies to recall the name. "Yes, yes," he said enthusiastically, "wonderful girl. Such a pleasant person. A musician, right? Yes, uh, the violin. She played the violin if I'm not mistaken. And quite good, really an excellent musician. Brilliant, as a matter of fact. We had great expectations for her. Quite devoted to her music. We were sure she was going to go on to better things. I think I recall something about her wanting to try out for the Toronto Symphony Orchestra." He smiled, folded his hands on top of his desk, and leaned forward. "So now what is it you want? Are you doing a story on Selina?"

Both reporters nodded.

"A feature? You don't look like entertainment writers."

"We're not," Donovan replied.

"But there was something about a police matter?"

Donovan took a newspaper clipping from the inside pocket of his trench coat and handed it to Davies. The headline read: SCARBOROUGH MUSICIAN'S BODY DRAINED OF BLOOD.

Davies glanced at the story but shook his head as if he still didn't understand.

"I gather you haven't heard?" Donovan asked.

"Heard what?"

"About Selina. She's dead. Murdered. Whoever did it cut up her body. Remember reading stories about all those body parts found in eastern Ontario the past few months? Leg on the highway . . . arm in the river . . . torso washed ashore."

Davies's upper lip curled.

"Right. Selina. Someone murdered her. We are trying to find out a few things about her."

Davies slumped back in his chair. "My God!" He looked down at the article and read through it more carefully. "My God," he repeated several times as he read. "I just can't believe it."

"When was the last time you saw her?" Donovan asked.

It was either in 1985 or 1986, Davies wasn't exactly sure. He called his secretary on the intercom and told her to pull Selina Shen's file. The records showed she had studied at the school from 1983, the year she had arrived in Canada, to her graduation in December, 1985. Davies started to put the file away when Pron reached over and grabbed it.

"Can I see that?" he asked, thumbing through the records and making notes while Donovan engaged Davies in small talk about the school.

Selina had a degree in music from the Canton Musical Institute in Guangzhou, in the People's Republic of China. Her marks at Davies's school weren't that great. She got a fifty-seven in economics, sixties in English, math, and geography. Her best mark was in music, a seventy-five. Tuition was three thousand dollars a year. Selina had paid in full when she left.

"This school just for foreign students?" Pron asked, handing the file to Donovan, pointing at the thumbnail-sized, black and white picture of the murdered woman.

Davies said about half the students were from overseas. Many, like Selina, couldn't speak a word of English when they arrived and had to take extra language courses. Maybe she was weak in English but she sure didn't need any help with her music, Davies said. Every time he saw her in the hallways, she was carrying her violin, stopping to practise whenever she had the chance. Often she played for her fellow students at impromptu gatherings in empty classrooms. The

49

last time he saw her was on graduation night, when she had a solo performance.

"She wanted to become a concert violinist," he recalled, smiling sadly. "It was entrancing when she played—just like angels singing."

"What's this?" Donovan asked, holding up Selina's academic record. "How come she wasn't at school between January and September in 1985?"

Davies tugged at the lapels of his sports jacket. He looked away. "Well, it's sort of delicate. Personal."

"That's what a murder is. Very personal," said Pron.

"I don't think she wanted people to know."

"No offence here, Mr. Davies," Donovan said, "but I don't think that matters much anymore."

Davies was silent for a moment. "Actually, I'm surprised you haven't heard."

What was that? they wanted to know.

"That's when she had her baby," he replied. The two reporters glanced at each other. It was the first time they had heard Selina was a mother.

"What baby?" they both said.

She got pregnant during her second year, Davies explained. Not many people at the school knew she was expecting. She quit just about the time her stomach started to swell. As far as he knew she had the baby, then gave it up for adoption. People being people, there were plenty of rumours floating around when she resumed her studies, he said. But he didn't like to repeat hallway gossip.

"Don't worry," said Pron. "We always double-check our facts before we do a story. Can you tell us anything that would give us a lead on this baby? Who do you think the father is?"

Davies shifted uncomfortably in his chair. Well, there was a lot of talk about the father being from South America, he said. He had heard several names but he wasn't about to repeat them. But there was one thing he knew for sure.

"Oh, yeah, what was that?" Pron enquired.

"The father, he wasn't anybody from this school," Davies answered. He had heard that the man was black. When Selina returned to school in the fall of 1985 she never talked about the child to anyone. He didn't know what became of the baby or the father. He assumed Selina gave the child up for adoption, but he couldn't be sure.

"Who were her friends . . . enemies?" Donovan asked.

Selina didn't have any enemies, Davies answered.

"You're wrong there," Donovan corrected. "She had at least one."

Davies picked up a class list and read off some names of the people who knew Selina. Pron scribbled down each one in his notebook. One was a man named Victor. They were close, but Davies didn't think there was anything romantic between the two. Another was a former officer in the Taiwanese army, Chin. Davies remembered the two often argued over who were the real rulers of China, the Communists or the exiled government in Taiwan. She had lived with a group of students while she was at school. He gave them the address. There was one thing more the reporters wanted.

"This picture," Pron said, picking up the file again and opening it to the page where the snapshot was glued to the top left-hand corner. It was a picture of a woman with a sweet, wide, innocent smile. Perfect teeth. She was wearing a sweater with a ruffled collar. Her shoulder-length black hair was cut in bangs. "Could we have it?"

Davies tore it from the folder. He gazed at it for a moment before handing it to Pron. It had been taken when Selina was twenty-three. Davies said she looked older, more mature, and more beautiful when she graduated.

Pron stuck the picture on the dashboard between them as they drove to one of the addresses Davies had given them. He flicked on the police scanner. Two men had held up a branch of Canada Trust in Don Mills. One of the men had a black handgun. The other talked with a lisp. The North York fire department was putting out a second alarm at a blaze in a tire factory on Finch Avenue. Someone had started a bush fire in a ravine along Highway 401. The fire was spreading rapidly, an anxious fire captain told the dispatcher. It was still spring but already the ground was dry from the unseasonably warm weather.

"Looks just like a kid," Pron said, glancing at the snapshot. "Real picture of innocence."

"I think you're getting ready to hit me with some of your sappy lines," Donovan challenged.

"Nothing wrong with being sappy," Pron shot back. "She looks like a real nice kid. Why would anybody want to kill her?"

"Anybody ever warn you about getting too emotionally wrapped up in your stories?" Donovan said.

"Yeah, you. About a thousand times."

"Well, this is one thousand and one."

"So what's wrong with showing some feeling?"

"It's a waste of energy. The only thing that really matters is getting the story. I'd like to find the killer before the cops do. I hate those stories that go on and on about how sad everybody is that somebody got killed. About how they're such nice, quiet people and all their friends are so shocked. That doesn't tell me anything. I want to do more with this story. It's bizarre, the way she was cut up." Donovan snatched the picture from the dashboard. "I want to know some dirt. Sure, she looks innocent, but is she really that innocent? I doubt it. We just found out she had a kid. What else was she doing that she shouldn't have been doing? There's gotta be more we can dig up."

The voice of an excited cop came over the scanner. A motorist had got into an accident with a bus and, not surprisingly, he was the big loser in that one. The cop said the driver was wearing the steering wheel for a necklace. He told the dispatcher to call for more cruisers to block off traffic.

"Wanna know something?" Pron said, turning down the scanner. "You can be really callous. Anybody ever tell you that?"

"Yeah, you. About a thousand times."

"This is one thousand and one."

The building they were looking for was at the end of a small side street, lined on both sides with other high-rise apartments. The landlady was a short, plump woman in a bright red, floral print dress. She remembered the students well, a look of disgust coming over her face as she thought about it.

"Fifteen of them, that's what there was. Fifteen!" She shook her head in disbelief. "You believe people could live like that? That's the Chinese for you. Sure as hell didn't know they had fifteen in there. Never would've let them get off with only paying $460 a month. Sleeping together on the floor, in the hallways. Taking turns with each other, too, I'll bet. God knows what was going on in there. And them pretending to be such religious people, I mean, going to that Christian school up on Finch there. Learning how to be good Catholics. I never seen a place left in such a mess. And you wanna know who had to clean it up? You wanna know!? Eh? You're looking at her. Me. The place was a pigsty. It stunk! You should've seen the mess when they left. Garbage everywhere. We had to kick them out. Fifteen people in a two-bedroom, can you imagine? There were a dozen mattresses on the floor. The way they lived. Had to fumigate twice to get rid of the cockroaches. Must've thought they were back home. I got nothing good to say about any of them."

Donovan showed her the picture of Selina. The woman thought for a moment.

"Oh, yeah, I remember that one. Only one who didn't seem to fit in. Like she had more class or something. Seemed cleaner than the others. What was that name again?"

"Selina Shen," he said.

"Yeah, Selina. That was it. Nice girl. Like I said, she wasn't like the others. What you interested in her for? Who are you guys, anyways? You cops?"

"No, ma'am, we're reporters. We're doing a story on her."

"What kinda story?"

"She's dead. Murdered. Whoever killed her cut her body into pieces."

The woman stepped back from the door. "You say she's dead? I don't want my name in the paper. I got enough trouble."

"We're just trying to find out more about her. We won't use your name."

"The cops, they got anybody?"

"No," Pron said. "Can you tell us anything about her? What about the other tenants? Do you know where they moved to?" He read out the names they had got from Davies.

"Christ, it was a long time ago. Over two years."

"Could you check?"

The woman sighed deeply but said she would. She shut the door, opening it again a few minutes later. She handed Pron a piece of paper with a name and address scribbled on it.

"This guy," she said, pointing to the paper. "Victor. He was okay. He collected rent from the others and always paid on time. This address may not be any good, but it's the best I can do. You want anything more—pay me. I don't read the *Star* anyways." She slammed the door shut.

Their next stop was Chinavision, the local Oriental television station. The head office was in North York. They went there on a hunch. Since Selina was an artist, chances were she had appeared on one of their shows. Maybe somebody at the station would remember her. The hunch paid off. The Shen sisters had been interviewed the year before. One of the station hands played the tape and translated for Pron and Donovan.

It was a brief interview. Selina did most of the talking. "I was surrounded by music since I was young," she told the interviewer. "My parents taught me how to play. They sent me to Canada to further my career."

"Hope they didn't buy her a return ticket," Donovan said to the technician as he rewound the tape.

They went back to the office and started working the phones, hunting for Selina's old friends. The newsroom was being renovated, and that day there was a full crew demolishing a wall. The men in overalls seemed to have an uncanny knack for turning on a whirring power saw at the crucial point of a telephone interview. Donovan was sure the workers got a bonus for every reporter who went insane.

The *Star* switchboard found Victor, one of Selina's roommates. An operator tracked him down in Sarnia, a city in southern Ontario near the American border. He worked as a computer analyst for a real-estate firm there. Victor had heard about the murder and was anxious to talk.

He recalled how plain-looking Selina had been when they first met at the high school. But her appearance changed dramatically during that first semester. She let her hair grow, used make-up, wore fashionable clothes. Far away from home for the first time in her life, free from the restrictions of Chinese society, Selina blossomed. It was no secret around the school, Victor said, that the fine jewellery and additions to her wardrobe came from her many male admirers. Selina liked to flirt, playing on her looks. But despite her beauty and charm, Victor remembered she could be very arrogant at times.

"She always thought of herself as quite smart and clever. You could see it in the way she dealt with the guys who liked her. She treated them very badly."

There were several suitors. One was a former officer in the Taiwanese army. They had dated briefly during school and often debated who should rule China—the same thing Davies had mentioned. Another man who wanted to marry her was a car mechanic whose family had sponsored the Shen sisters when they came to Canada.

"He really liked her. He bought her shoes and clothing; he took her out. He wanted to marry her, but she always told him no. He felt cheated. But she told him it was one thing to take his gifts, quite another to get married."

"Think he killed her?" Pron asked.

Victor didn't know. He went on to say that the most important thing in Selina's life was staying in Canada.

"It was all she talked about. There was no way she was going home."

He always believed she would do anything to stay here. Anything. With her student visa about to expire, he was surprised she never accepted any of the marriage proposals. And there were enough. Marrying a Canadian would have given her the landed immigrant status she desperately wanted.

"She could always leave the guy later," Victor said. "It's done." But, he said, she was probably too proud to stoop to a marriage of convenience.

Pron asked him about the baby.

Victor said Selina had always been very secretive about her personal life. She never talked about the baby with anybody. Not even him, and they were good friends. Although she tried to keep the baby a secret, almost everybody in the school knew she had one. He had heard the same rumours about the South American. And there was more.

"Selina got raped," he said. "I don't know why she had the baby. Maybe because she was religious."

He had heard she gave the baby up for adoption as soon as it was born. As far as Victor knew, the South American had never seen his child. Could this man from out of her past have been angry enough to kill her because she gave up the child? Victor didn't think so. He wondered if the police had questioned the South American.

Pron said the detective on the case wasn't exactly giving him hourly progress reports. The only way they were getting any information was through her friends.

Donovan was still on the phone when Pron went over to his desk. He scribbled something on a piece of paper, which he handed to Pron. On it were the words: *Li Ling, boyfriend, argument. Argument* was underlined.

When Donovan got off the phone, they went down to the cafeteria to escape the racket in the newsroom. A cloud of fine dust hung in the air from the demolished wall. At a nearby desk, one of the night copy editors was coughing and swearing as the dust swirled around him. Donovan had located a man in Vancouver named Paul who was a close friend of the Shen sisters. He had some interesting things to say.

Back in early February, shortly after Selina disappeared, a distraught Sophie had called Paul, asking for help. He immediately flew to Toronto. They started searching for Selina, first going door to door in the neighbourhood to which she had moved, then combing through the three Chinatowns. They had even taken out ads in the Chinese newspapers. But no one had seen Selina since the day of the lesson. Finally they went to the police. Sophie was afraid to go, afraid the police would ask too many embarrassing questions about Selina's immigration status. Selina had been working even though that was forbidden under the rules of a student visa. They even went to a local politician, hoping he would pressure the police to step up the hunt for the missing woman. There was one more thing they did, he said.

They asked Selina's former boyfriend to help. He was a businessman and a writer who had several pen names. One of the names was Li Ling. He was in his mid-thirties and involved in the import-export trade. He was also the editor of a magazine called *China Voice*, which supported the fledgling democracy movement in the Communist country. Li Ling had once lived in Montreal, where he had published a similar magazine, *China Spring*, with a Dr. Wang at McGill University.

Paul said Li Ling was an ambitious man. Li Ling professed to be a prolific author and reader and an expert on world affairs, Paul said.

"But for all his worldly wisdom, his talk about democracy, he could be quite narrow-minded," Paul had told Donovan. "At the same time as he was preaching about people's rights, he was treating Selina like a servant."

They had met shortly after Selina had finished school. Selina moved into Li Ling's house on Puma Drive in Scarborough. Paul didn't understand how Selina had stayed with him for three years. He was too domineering for her, Paul said. She was becoming more independent every day, less willing to follow the cultural tradition of her homeland, where the woman's job was to serve the man. Selina had left Li Ling twice, moving in with her sister each time, he said. But she went back to him both times. He promised her things would get better. And for a while they did.

But then Li Ling's older brother, Jia-Wen, left China and moved in with them. Right from the start, Selina and Jia-Wen hadn't got along, Paul said. They quarrelled incessantly, usually about the housework. Selina didn't think it was her job to do all the cooking and cleaning. But Li Ling always sided with his brother. Finally Selina had had enough. After three years she moved out for the third and last time. She rented a room at the town house on Timberbank Boulevard. She was happier, he said, saying that 1988 was going to be her lucky year. Two weeks later, Selina vanished.

Paul said Li Ling had a grocery store in Chinatown, but he wasn't sure of the name or the address. All he remembered was that it was on Gerrard Street.

"He probably meant Chinatown East," Donovan said. "Shouldn't be a problem. It's not as big as the main Chinatown. I mean, how many grocery stores can there be?"

They went back to the newsroom and wrote their story. When they finished, they put in their usual call to Detective Edgar. It was Pron's turn to call. Donovan was sick of getting the run-around. An OPP secretary told Pron that Edgar was in but tied up in a meeting. She said all calls were being referred to the news bureau. Would Mr. Pron like that number? Pron said he already had it.

"So what's next?" Pron asked, leaning back in his chair and putting his feet up on the desk. "How about we quit for the day and have a nice, fresh start in the morning?"

Donovan scrunched up his face.

"Uh-oh. I know that look," Pron said. He took off his glasses and rubbed his eyes. "It means you want to keep going. Right?"

"There's just too much to do. What if the *Sun* is on to Li Ling? Or the South American? What if they find them before we do? We have to keep going."

Pron sighed heavily. He turned slowly in his chair and slid his long legs off the desk, letting them drop heavily to the floor. They landed with a thud. He sighed again, looked away from Donovan and, with great effort, picked himself out of the chair. Shuffling his feet, he followed Donovan out of the newsroom. They walked to the car in silence.

"You're really pissed off, aren't you?" Donovan said as they drove out of the parking lot. He was going through his notebook.

"Look, it's been a long day and I'm tired. I mean really tired. What else can we possibly do tonight that we couldn't do tomorrow morning?"

"Why don't we just cruise through Chinatown and eyeball the grocery stores on Gerrard?"

"Donovan, I'm a lot older than you. I want to go home and relax. I want to see my wife. I told you the last time we worked together I wasn't going to go day and night on a story."

Donovan closed his notebook, put it into his pocket. "Okay, let's quit."

On the scanner a policeman said he was going to arrest a man who was stealing clothes from a Salvation Army drop box. Someone else said over the air he needed a pair of pants, preferably grey.

For the next few moments the only sounds in the car were the voices of police officers putting in orders for clothes, then laughing.

"Okay," Pron said finally, "where to?"

"Chinatown."

There were about six hundred thousand people of Chinese descent in Canada, and more than half of them lived in Metro Toronto. Their community was concentrated in three areas, the largest and oldest in the city's downtown core, which stretched for about fifteen city blocks along Dundas Street, branching off into a maze of side streets. To the north-east, in Scarborough, was the newest Chinatown, in Agincourt, dubbed "Asiancourt." In between, both geographically and in age, was Chinatown East, the area in which Li Ling supposedly had his store.

Most of the grocery stores were closed for the day by the time Pron and Donovan got there. The streets were lined with garbage. As they drove slowly along Gerrard, Pron was counting out loud.

"Twenty-seven . . . twenty-eight . . . twenty-nine. You're right, Donovan. This should be a breeze," Pron said, his voice heavy with sarcasm. "There can't be any more than 178 grocery stores."

About a dozen officers from the two forces, Metro and the Ontario Provincial Police, gathered that afternoon. They met in the boardroom of a building that from the outside looked like another of the many office complexes on the side street in North York, one of the five cities and one borough that made up Metropolitan Toronto. The one-storey building housed the offices of the super-secretive Intelligence Unit of the Metro police, a squad that was set up in 1982 by the chief at that time, Jack Ackroyd, to gather information on organized crime gangs. Investigators from different police forces often gathered there on joint cases.

On that day, Detective Inspector Larry Edgar chaired the meeting. Its purpose was to plan how the two forces would handle the joint investigation into the murder of Selina Lian Shen. Although the investigation had started out as a Metro case with the disappearance of a Scarborough woman, the OPP had taken over because Shen's remains had been found in their jurisdiction. Missing person occurrence 1635 was now a homicide case.

"We need a name for this operation," said one of the officers seated around the table.

The room was starting to fill with cigarette smoke. Kent Bradbury, a vocal non-smoker with the Metro force, coughed loudly and waved his hands before his face, but the smokers in the room ignored his protests.

"How about Project Mandarin?" suggested another officer. The investigators would be dealing mostly with Orientals, many of whom spoke Mandarin. It seemed a logical choice.

"I have no trouble with that name," said Edgar.

One of the problems with joint investigations was communication. Each force had its own way of conducting interviews and writing up reports. Because the Shen investigation had taken so long to get going, Edgar wanted to set some ground rules to avoid snags that sometimes befell, and delayed, other joint forces operations.

He told the investigators to keep daily logs, and to funnel all reports back to him. There was going to be a mountain of paper work, and Edgar assigned Garnet Rombough the thankless task of keeping track of all the reports. Officers from Metro had already talked to a number of people who knew Shen. These people would have to be reinterviewed now that the case was a murder. Metro reports would have to be rewritten and put on OPP forms, another time-consuming but necessary job.

Although the victim's sister, Sophie, had been helpful, Edgar felt she was holding back information that might be vital. Before Selina moved in with him, Sophie had lived with Selina's boyfriend, Rui-Wen Pan, who also went by the name Li Ling. Sophie said she had asked Pan to help find Selina, and the two had gone out looking for her. It was clear, though, that Sophie didn't like Pan, didn't trust him, and suspected he was the killer.

While she was pointing her finger at the boyfriend, he was making his own allegations, accusing a language instructor at the University of Toronto of having something to do with Selina's disappearance. This accusation was reported by Sergeant Michael Norton, who had interviewed Pan. Pan told him that Selina was romantically involved with Robert Fisher, whom Pan described as a "professor who wasn't a professor." He said Fisher became interested in Selina after the two met at a dinner Pan had held at his house. It was soon after Selina met Fisher that she left Pan for the third and final time. Pan got angry whenever he mentioned Fisher's name during the interview, Norton said. Pan said the last time he saw his former girlfriend alive was in early February, about two weeks before she vanished.

Edgar told the officers he was no closer to finding the crime scene. He didn't even know if Selina had been murdered and butchered in the same place. Although he didn't know where she was killed, he was fairly certain he knew when the murder had taken place. The mother of one of Selina's pupils, Virginia Lawrence, had called police after reading about the murder in the paper. She said Selina was supposed to give her son a music lesson on Sunday, February 21, but never showed up, even though Selina had called two nights before to confirm the appointment. Selina had been giving Virginia Lawrence's son lessons every Sunday for nearly a year and was always very punctual, calling ahead if she couldn't make it.

There was a second witness who knew where Selina was on Saturday, the day she disappeared, said Edgar. She had gone to a house on Gerrard Street to give a violin lesson to another of her pupils. This other witness, a seamstress named Eng Siew Chan, had told investigators Selina had cut short the lesson after reading a letter that Pan had left there for her.

"Do we have the letter?" asked one of the investigators. "Do we know what was in it?"

Edgar shook his head. Mrs. Chan hadn't read it, and Selina took it with her when she left. Pan had previously left other letters for Selina at Mrs. Chan's house, and he had dropped off another one for her on Tuesday, three days after Selina was last seen alive. Since Selina didn't show up for the music lesson on Sunday or a dinner date she was supposed to have that same evening with her sister, it was likely that she had been killed between the time she left Mrs. Chan's house on Saturday and Sunday evening, Edgar said.

Edgar broke the officers into teams to handle further interviews. Two investigators from Metro who had been investigating Shen's disappearance, Constables Bradbury and Jim McClelland, would stay together as a unit. Edgar wanted them to keep talking to Mrs. Chan, who appeared to be very nervous about being a witness in a murder case. The two constables were known as the Scotch Tape Gang for a prank they once played on another officer who kept complaining that they always took his tape and never returned it. When the officer came to work one day, he found his desk completely covered in tape, wound around it in strips so that the desk looked as if it was inside a cocoon.

Gus Riddell and Brian Kennedy, with the OPP, were another team. Riddell, with his dimpled cheeks and easy-going manner, was the "good cop," while Kennedy, a dark-haired, feisty Irishman, could easily be the counterpart "bad cop" in interviews. Edgar wanted them to talk to Pan. The last two weeks had been difficult for Kennedy, whose sister had lost her battle with cancer and died the first week of March. Before the investigation was over, tragedy would strike twice more.

Ken Yates, with Metro, a specialist in Asian crime, was assigned to reinterview Fisher and his ex-wife, Anna Leung. Fisher's background and alibi would have to be checked. Stuart McDonald, a soft-spoken OPP officer with a walrus moustache, was assigned the task of getting judicial permission for the inevitable wiretaps and search warrants.

The meeting went well, lasting less than an hour. As he gathered together his papers, Edgar could only hope the investigation would go as smoothly.

CHAPTER FIVE

China Spring

"No Li Ling here!"

The dumpy man standing at the cash register brought the palms of his gnarled hands down on the counter with a loud smack, shaking it. A package of bean sprouts teetered at the edge, then fell to the floor. The storekeeper glared at the two men in front of him. "How many time I tell you! No Li Ling here."

Donovan bent and picked up the package of vegetables. "Look," he said, tossing the cellophane bag from one hand to the other, "we were told somebody named Ling works here. I'm betting that's you. What are you trying to hide? You know we're not leaving until we talk to him." He put the bean sprouts on the counter and glanced at Pron, who stood beside him, arms folded across his chest.

Behind them in the tiny store a line of customers laden with groceries had formed. Some were yelling at the owner in Chinese. One woman, her grey hair tucked under a straw hat, tried to push her way around Pron, who didn't move, didn't even seem to notice she was there.

"You got a licence to run this place?" Pron asked.

"Sure I got," the owner replied, pointing to a piece of tattered, yellow paper taped to the wall. Pron walked around the counter, squeezed past the dumpy man, and looked at it.

"Says here the owner of this store is a guy named Ling."

"Yes, Ling. But I John Ling. Not Li Ling. John, John Ling."

"Maybe Li is your middle name," Donovan said. "I still think you're trying to hide something."

"I not hide anything. My name John, John Ling. You go away, I have customers."

The storekeeper beckoned to the lady in the straw hat to put her groceries on the counter. She shoved her way around Pron, who smiled at her, then started making his way to the back of the store.

"Mr. Ling," Donovan began, glancing at Pron, "just help us out and we'll go away. Last night we went up and down this street looking for a guy named Li Ling. Finally somebody tells us, 'Come to this store. That's where Li Ling works.' So we came here but you were closed. That's why we're here this morning, hoping that you could help out. Now the licence says your name is Ling. Maybe we've got the wrong first name, I don't know. The man we're looking for was the boyfriend of Selina Shen. She's the woman who was murdered." The storekeeper looked up from the cash register. "That's right, murdered. And cut up. Cut up into many little pieces." Donovan made chopping motions against his arms and neck. "Like that, sliced apart. Maybe even killed with a knife like you'd use to cut vegetables."

"Killed? Who killed? Li Ling killed?"

"No, Selina Shen, she's the one killed."

"Nobody killed. Nobody chopped up. Now go away."

Donovan took a black and white picture from his pocket and handed it to the shopkeeper. "Selina," Donovan said. "Dead."

The shopkeeper studied the picture for a moment. "Not know girl," he said, dropping it on the counter. He looked to the back just as Pron pushed aside a curtain and walked into the storeroom. "No go there! No go back there!" he shouted at Pron.

Arms waving, he scurried after Pron, shoving past the line of impatient customers and running into the storeroom. One man near the front of the line glared at Donovan, put down his groceries, and walked out of the store. A woman who had been on the street putting some apples into a display box came in and waited on the remaining customers. Within moments, Pron emerged from the storeroom, the shopkeeper right behind him, still waving his arms and shouting at him in Chinese.

Pron turned to him, smiled, and shrugged to indicate that he didn't understand. Then he ambled up the narrow aisle piled high on both sides with tins of food, stopping every now and then to pick items off the shelves, not being too particular where he put them back. The shopkeeper was right behind him, retrieving each item and returning it to its proper place. At a display of kitchen utensils, Pron grabbed a cheese grater and turned to the shopkeeper.

"How much?"

The shopkeeper's round face softened. He craned his neck to look up at Pron. "Two dollar ninety-five."

"Good deal." Pron walked over to the counter, the shopkeeper right behind. "Spot me a few bucks, Donovan."

"What the hell for? You're not buying that, are you?"

"Just pay the man, Donovan. Humour me on this."

Donovan pulled out his wallet and handed five dollars to the storekeeper, who eyed it suspiciously, then tugged it from his hand.

"You got a really nice shop here," Pron said, looking around the store as the shopkeeper went behind the counter and rang up the purchase. Bits of produce littered the floor. A plump tomato had been flattened by someone wearing a waffle-soled shoe. Cabbage leaves and pieces of cardboard from packing cases made a soggy carpet in front of the vegetable stand. The front window was coated in grease and smudged with fingerprints. "Yeah, real nice place."

The owner closed the till but said nothing. He shuffled around the bean sprout packages, moving them to one side of the counter. Then he looked at Pron. "Let me see picture."

Donovan handed it to him.

"This girl," the shopkeeper said, "maybe I remember. Others talk about her yesterday. Say she used to go to butcher store."

"Which butcher store?"

The shopkeeper walked to the window. "Down there," he said, pointing up the street. "Butcher store, down there.

Everyone say that girl, she went there to buy meat. Talk to Eric. Eric know her. The man with beard.''

Pron thanked him. As they walked out the door, he suddenly shoved Donovan to one side.

"What the hell did you do that for?" Donovan yelled, shoving him back.

Pron pointed at the air-conditioner sagging from its plywood perch over the doorway. A steady trickle of water was dripping from one corner of the sputtering unit, forming a puddle on the concrete.

"Didn't you read about those dead Legionnaires in Atlanta?" Pron said. "They got that disease from air-conditioners. Bacteria grows in the water. You've got to be careful around them things."

Donovan looked up at the air-conditioner and shook his head disbelievingly. Pron smiled back, then pitched the cheese grater he had just bought into the gutter.

"What the hell you doing that for?" Donovan shouted as he hurried to pick it up.

"I don't need it," replied Pron.

"Then why the hell buy it?"

"To help us get information. Donovan, you should spend more time trying to be nice to people. You might get further with finesse."

"Just don't forget who spent two days finessing his way through the rain to get us where we are," replied Donovan. "Besides, you shouldn't litter. You're forever littering."

"Your name can go first on the next story," Pron said, as he turned in the direction of the butcher shop.

It was hot and muggy, unseasonably warm for May. The weather forecasters were predicting a record-breaking heat wave that summer. Steam rose from the pavement of Gerrard, the main street in Chinatown East, slick from an early morning rain shower. The sidewalks were teeming with shoppers. In front of nearly every store were makeshift wooden stands, piled high with goods that spilled onto the sidewalks. Shoppers were picking through mounds of fresh produce, piles of tangled clothing, stacks of second-hand books, magazines, comics, and cassette tapes. In the shade of some store awnings, old men sat in rickety chairs around card tables, smoking pipes and playing Chinese checkers on colourful wooden boards.

Gerrard Street was jammed with traffic, cut back to one lane in places by delivery trucks double-parked in front of grocery stores. Horns blared constantly as angry motorists manoeuvred slalom-style down the street. The butcher shop was beside a laundromat on the other side of the street. An ambulance, roof lights flashing, weaved slowly through the traffic, heading for an accident farther up the street. A car had rammed into a pole, and the driver was standing beside the wreck, holding his head while a crowd gathered around him.

The customers in the butcher shop crowded around the window, looking at the accident. There were five butchers behind the meat counter. Three of them had beards, and none was named Eric. But when shown the picture of Selina, one of the butchers remembered her. She had come into the shop, maybe once a week, always to buy the same thing. Chicken. Did she ever say where she lived? No, but she often joked about where she worked. In what way? She said she wouldn't have far to go if she died. That's because she worked across the street from a funeral home.

Ten blocks east on Gerrard Street they found the funeral home. Nearby were two variety stores. They went into one and Donovan bought a package of gum, then struck up a conversation with the man behind the counter, asking him if he was Li Ling. He wasn't. Did they try the store across the street?

There was a sign taped to the inside of the glass door of the other shop. On it someone had written in blue crayon the words, CLOSED. BACK SOON. The front of the store was one big window, parts of it covered with homemade posters advertising sales. The bright sunshine made it hard to see anything inside the darkened shop. Pron cupped his hands and leaned against the glass, peering in. There were two aisles crammed with merchandise. Tins of food, pots and pans, toys, radios and cassette players, erotic prints of scantily clad women, school supplies. Behind the counter, cardboard boxes were stacked to the ceiling. Several at the bottom had split open, the contents falling out onto the tiled floor.

"Pron," Donovan said, tapping him on the shoulder and pointing to a display in the window.

It was a flat box propped up on a plywood stand, about waist high. The lid was off. Inside, arranged in a semicircle, were six butcher knives and a meat cleaver. The handles were black, the blades gleaming. In block lettering underneath the knives were the words: OLYMPIA SWORDS. STAINLESS STEEL. PROFESSIONAL.

"I think we just hit the jackpot," Donovan said.

"What are you saying, Donovan? Every shopkeeper who has a knife display in their window has killed their girlfriend?"

"No," Donovan said, pointing to a second display. "Only the ones that also sell handcuffs."

There were several sets. Some were play ones, made of plastic, but one set was real, advertising itself as the kind used by the police.

"Okay, great. We got a guy selling knives and handcuffs. But how do we know this is Li Ling's store?"

"Like this," Donovan replied.

He walked over to the mailbox at the corner of the store and started playing with the lock on the lid.

"Great," said Pron. "Two days into the story and you're committing a federal offence."

"I'm not going to open the letters. Just look at the name and address on the outside."

"I understand—but will a jury?"

"Got any better ideas?"

Pron thought for a moment, looked around the street. "Uh, why don't you try fishing out the letters with the arm of your sunglasses?"

Donovan took off the glasses and poked the curved end of the arm inside the mailbox slit. He played it back and forth for a few minutes, then finally pulled out a letter. Pron hovered over him as they read the outside of the letter. It was addressed to Rui-Wen Pan, Bouji Daily Supplies.

"Who is this Pan guy?" asked Pron.

Donovan stuck the end of his sunglasses into the mail slot and pulled out a second letter, this one addressed to Li Ling. The address on the envelope was the same, Bouji Daily Supplies on Gerrard Street. Were Li Ling and Rui-Wen Pan the same man? After all, Donovan and Pron had been told he was a man with many names. Li Ling wasn't listed in the phone book, but maybe Pan was.

Pron went across the street to check at a phone booth. Bouji Daily Supplies and Pan were listed to the same address on Gerrard. Pron dialled directory assistance and asked for a home number for Rui-Wen Pan. It was unlisted. However, there was a second listing for a Bouji Daily Supplies, this one at 320 Broadview Avenue, in the heart of Chinatown East. Pron joined Donovan at the side of the store. A sign was leaning against the wall. Donovan tipped it back. On it was printed BOUJI DAILY SUPPLIES. Parts of the sign were missing, smashed out, as if it had been lying there a long time. Three cars were parked in a row close to the side of the store. A fourth car was up on blocks in front of a small mechanics shop at the back of the building. They walked into the shop and over to a man in greasy overalls working under the hood of a blue Pontiac Strato Chief.

"I used to have a car like that," Donovan said, leaning over the engine. "That a 350 in there?"

Glancing up, the mechanic said, "Three-fifties are for boys. That's a 452 you're looking at. You want something?"

"We're looking for a guy named Li Ling."

"Never heard of him."

"How about Rui-Wen Pan?"

"Yeah, he owns the store around front."

Donovan took out the picture of Selina, showed it to him. "Ever seen her around?"

The mechanic reached out an oil-stained hand and grabbed the picture, studied it for a moment, then handed it back to Donovan. "Kinda young lookin', but I'm pretty sure that's Pan's girlfriend, the one who was killed."

About a week ago he'd seen Pan carting boxes from his car into the store late at night. Two Oriental men who worked in the store were helping him. He didn't know their names.

Had the shop been open today? Not for about a week, the mechanic said. Did he know where Pan lived? He didn't. The landlord, Peter, might know, but he was away for a few days. Could the mechanic tell them anything about Selina? Not much. She worked the cash register. Friendly girl, but she never seemed happy.

"Funny thing about that shop," the mechanic said, leaning over the engine.

What was that?

"I don't know how he made his money. Always bringing stuff in, but he was only open for a couple of hours a day." He shrugged. "Nice fellow, though. Just a little odd. You tried that music store down the street? You might get something there."

The music store owner didn't know Selina until Pron and Donovan assured him they were reporters not immigration officers. Then he became quite talkative. Selina had worked part-time as a music teacher, giving violin lessons out of this store and another he owned up in Agincourt. It was no secret she had overstayed her student visa and was working in Canada illegally. He said he felt sorry for her because it seemed she always needed money, especially after she left her boyfriend and moved out on her own. She had talked about enrolling in the music program at the University of Toronto and needed money for tuition. Although she worked for her boyfriend, he paid her little, if anything. So the music store owner paid her, cash, for each lesson. The last one had been in early February. Sure, he was taking a little risk but he needed help, and she was an excellent violinist and a good teacher.

Pan's Broadview store was in the basement of a new building. The shop was closed, the entrance blocked by black burglar bars. Although they had passed the store during their search, they had never bothered to check it out, since it wasn't on Gerrard Street. The inside of the store was about the same as the one they had just visited, maybe a little cleaner. The store appeared to have been closed for some time. Newspapers and garbage bags were piled against the bars. Pron fished through the mailbox, found a few bills addressed to Pan.

They went into the store next to Pan's, a shop that sold wedding dresses. The Oriental woman at the counter spoke only a few words of English. She recognized the picture of Selina and smiled at the mention of Pan's name. But though she chattered away, half in English, half in Chinese, Pron and Donovan didn't understand much of what she said. Finally she wrote a name on a piece of paper, then took them out to the street and pointed at a nearby Chinese restaurant.

"You go there. She know. She help you," the woman said.

It was early evening. Editors expected reporters working on a breaking story to keep them informed with regular calls throughout the day. But Pron and Donovan hadn't called in once. And now they were afraid that if they did call in, Clancy would want to know why they hadn't interviewed the boyfriend. They had nothing to show for their work except the addresses of two stores, both of them closed. So they didn't call in. Instead, they walked up the street to the restaurant.

Stores were closing. The evening crowd was slowly taking over Chinatown. Gone were the shoppers. In their places, teenagers in black leather jackets lounged against the empty food stalls, talking and smoking. Young women in short, tight skirts, with heavily made-up faces, were taking up their nightly positions near street corners. Police cruisers prowled past them, slowing but not stopping. The restaurant that the store clerk had pointed out looked more like a butcher shop. They walked up a flight of stairs and went inside, passing through a short corridor to get to the dining area. To one side, a row of slaughtered pigs, bellies cut wide open, hung upside down from steel hooks. Their throats were slit. Blood dripped to the sawdust-covered floor.

"Maybe that's what the killer did to Selina," Donovan said. "Strung her up by the heels, slit her throat and let all the blood drain out before he hacked her up."

The restaurant was long and narrow. There were tables and chairs along one wall and a row of black stoves against the other. Several cooks, all wearing T-shirts, stood over the stoves. Pron and Donovan stopped near one of the gas grills.

They were the only Caucasians in the place. The other patrons stared at them for a few moments before turning back to their meals. Finally a stooped old man walked slowly over. Pron showed him the name the seamstress had written on a piece of paper. The old man pointed towards the back of the restaurant where a woman was leaning against a wall, smoking.

She was tall and slender, probably in her mid-forties. Her hair was pulled straight back and done up in a bun. She had on a tight red dress with a slit up one leg. She was talking to one of the cooks, who looked over and saw the old man pointing. The cook nudged the woman's arm. She turned, looked right at Pron and Donovan, then butted out her cigarette and walked over.

"Can I help you?" she asked, her face solemn.

Donovan showed her the picture. "This was Selina Shen. Her boyfriend was Rui-Wen Pan. Do you know either of them?"

The woman hardly glanced at the picture before shaking her head. She turned abruptly, walked to the cash register, and sat on a stool.

"Did you see the look on her face?" Donovan said. "She's lying."

"Let's stay here, get something to eat. She'll talk."

They sat down at a table right next to the cash register. The woman in the red dress eyed them warily. Pron picked up a menu, wet from spilled food.

The old man with the stooped shoulders came over to the table. They ordered wonton soup, since they didn't understand anything on the menu. The woman in the red dress was watching.

"That woman, Donovan, she's got worried eyes. She knows something. Now's the time for some of that phony charm of yours. Pretend you're her long-lost son."

"If you talked to her," Donovan said as he turned around, "you could pretend you were her father."

Donovan turned, smiled at her. "We hear Selina spoke very highly of you," he said. "We hear she really loved this place. Sorry if we upset you. We're writers, with the Toronto *Star*, and we're trying to do a nice story on Selina. Can you help us?"

"You knew her?" the woman asked, getting up from behind the cash register. She walked towards their table.

"Well, not exactly. But we've talked to so many of her friends we feel like we know her. Please," Donovan said, pointing to a chair.

She sat down at their table, the slit on her skirt going up well past her knee. She lit a cigarette and blew some smoke to the ceiling, where a fan kicked around the stale air.

"I guess you two were close," Donovan continued. "Did you know she was having a rough time of it in the last few months?"

"You are reporters? Why do you care about her? She just one person, not even your kind. A nobody. If the police don't care about her, why should a big paper like Toronto *Star*?"

"Somebody has to," Pron said.

"I don't want to get in trouble. Why should I get involved?"

"A friend, a real friend, would want to find out who killed her," Pron said.

The woman looked silently at both reporters for several moments. She took another puff on her cigarette. "You promise my name won't be used, if I tell you something?"

They nodded.

The woman took several more puffs. The old man brought the soup. She said something to him and he came back with two platefuls of steaming rice and chicken, which he placed before the reporters. The woman motioned that they should try it. She watched them eat. Finally she spoke.

Two years ago the woman had gone to a dinner party in Scarborough hosted by Jay Payne, a teacher who was giving her English lessons. Payne had also invited Rui-Wen Pan, his partner in an importing business. She had never met Pan but she'd heard about him, a shrewd businessman who was making a name for himself in the Chinese community. When she went into the kitchen to freshen her drink, Pan followed her in and started talking to her. The subject was music. He professed to be an accomplished violinist. He tried to flatter her, saying he had listened to her sing at one of the local festivals, telling her what a wonderful voice she had. But despite the compliments she didn't like him.

He was a nice-looking man who dressed well, but he was ill at ease. She made an excuse to leave but it didn't register. He kept talking. Bragging. About what a wonderful businessman he was. And how he was such a great writer and editor with a magazine that had a world-wide circulation of four million. He also boasted about being a doctor who had trained as a surgeon in China and had taken further medical courses in Canada. He asked her out for a date, and grew quite persistent even though she said no. When she tried to leave, he grabbed her and kissed her, right on the lips. She would have slapped his face but she didn't want to make a scene. Later in the evening, she was shocked to find out that Pan was not at the party alone. He had brought a date, the woman he lived with, Selina Shen.

In the months that followed, she and Shen became good friends, often meeting for lunch or going out after concerts at which they performed together. The woman admired Selina's devotion to her music, her dedication to it as her life's career. But she felt sorry for Selina, who put in long hours at Pan's stores, time that would have been better spent practising the violin. She thought Pan was taking advantage of Selina, making her do menial labour when she should have been practising her music. Selina had said that discussing that subject with Pan was a waste of time. It only led to arguments. Although Selina was hesitant to talk much about her personal life, she admitted there were plenty of arguments between the two. She'd even left him twice, but returned when Pan promised things would improve. Hearing all this, the woman was tempted many times to tell Selina of Pan's advances at the party, hoping that it would convince Selina to leave him. But the woman never did. It would have hurt Selina too much. "Selina really loved him."

The last time she had seen Selina was a few days before she vanished. Selina had come to the restaurant. It was only a brief visit. There had been something different about her that day; she was not the Selina the woman knew. She seemed agitated, scared. Selina was convinced she was being followed. That someone from out of the past was after her, trying to kill her.

"Who was after her? Pan?" Donovan asked.

The woman had asked the same question, but Selina had refused to answer. She just kept saying it was somebody from her past. The woman said she thought it had something to do with an immigration scam, where Chinese students were brought to Canada illegally. Perhaps Selina had threatened to expose the people running the scam. As far as the woman knew, it was all over between Selina and Pan. The two hadn't seen each other since Selina moved out from Pan's home on Puma Drive some weeks before. Before leaving the restaurant that day, Selina gave the woman her new address and telephone number but begged her not to tell anyone where she lived.

The woman stopped talking. She turned away, looking absently at the stoves while she finished her cigarette. One of the cooks called to her but she dismissed him with a wave of her hand. She turned back to the reporters.

"I read that Selina was cut up. I think I know why that was done. In ancient Chinese custom, person who really hates somebody cuts up the body to keep the spirit from finding eternal rest."

"Who hated her that much?" Donovan asked. "Pan?"

"No, not him. He loved her."

"But the police have told us her body was . . . uh . . . cut up neatly — with surgical precision," added Pron. "If he really was a doctor, maybe he did kill her?"

"I know I didn't like him, but I don't think he killed her. Maybe he knows who did it, but Pan kill . . . no."

They wanted to talk to Pan. Could she help? She'd heard that Pan had sold the house on Puma Drive and moved to another one in the west end of Toronto shortly after Selina disappeared. She didn't know where. The best she could do was show them what Pan looked like. She had a videotape of Selina's last performance. At one point Pan joined her on stage. Maybe seeing Pan would help them find him. The tape was at home, but she didn't want the reporters following her there. Could she drop it off somewhere tomorrow? No, they needed it that night. Reluctantly, she agreed to meet them in a bus shelter down the street when she got off work, at eleven that night.

Pron and Donovan left the restaurant and went to the *Star*. It was almost nine o'clock, just a half hour before deadline. The night editor was not pleased that neither reporter had bothered to call in. He reminded them they worked for a daily paper, not a monthly. He cheered up a little when they told him they had a story, plus a chance of getting a fresh picture of Selina in a few hours. Pron started writing the story while Donovan had the switchboard put in a call to New York. He was looking for Dr. Bingzwang Wang, co-founder with Pan of a magazine that promoted democracy in China, called *China Spring*. The tip had come from Paul, his contact in Vancouver, who had told him to call McGill University in Montreal. A friendly clerk in the university's records section had dug up a home telephone number for Dr. Wang, who had moved to New York after completing his doctorate. The phone was answered by Dr. Wang's wife, Amy. He was out of the country on business, but she knew Pan well and wanted to talk.

Wang and Li Ling, whom they now knew as Pan, had met in early 1982, discovered they had similar political leanings, and formed a partnership to publish *China Spring*. Pan had emigrated to Canada on a student visa in July, 1981. He chose Montreal because his uncle and sponsor, a man named Jony Mark, owned a Chinese restaurant there. Amy Wang said Pan spoke little English when he arrived, but learned it quickly after taking courses at Concordia University. Pan, who had studied at a university in China, also took some biochemistry courses at Concordia. She said he bragged about being a doctor, but neither she nor her husband had ever seen a certificate. For about a year, Pan and Dr. Wang had worked closely on the magazine. But then there was trouble.

Pan thought Dr. Wang, the senior editor, was getting credit for work he had done himself. Dr. Wang, on the other hand, felt Pan was too uncooperative to be a good partner. Pan left Dr. Wang and the magazine in early 1983. A month or two later, in March, the Wangs got a call from Pan. He was in jail in St. John, Quebec, a Canadian border town. Pan had been caught using another person's U.S. immigration card, commonly known as a green card, to cross the border. Pan's student visa had expired, and he was in Canada illegally. Despite the ill feelings between them, the Wangs arranged for a lawyer and bail for Pan. To avoid being deported, Pan made a claim for refugee status on the grounds that, if he returned to China, he would be jailed or executed because of his anti-government stance. Pan was granted refugee status three months later.

The Wangs had heard about the murder, but all they knew was what they read in the *Chinese World Journal*. Amy Wang suggested they get a copy of the magazine Pan was now publishing, the *China Voice*. She also gave him the name of another of Pan's girlfriends, a Montreal real-estate agent named Vcrinza Tong. There was more she could tell them but she had to check with her husband.

On their way to the bus shelter, Donovan read over a printout of the story Pron had written. They had decided to leave out the part about the boyfriend being a doctor until they spoke with him. They worried about a libel suit. Saying he was a doctor was pretty incriminating, given the neat way she had been cut up. Their frequent references to the bitter argument Selina had had with Pan three weeks before she disappeared was damaging enough. It made it seem as though the boyfriend was the killer. Normally, newspapers focused on the victim. Reporters never went out to solve a crime. That wasn't their job. But already Pron and Donovan were crossing the line into police work. By mentioning the argument they had shown a possible motive. If they went another step and called Pan a surgeon, they gave him the means to commit the crime. If they were going to brand him a suspect by calling him a doctor, they wanted to be pretty damn sure of their facts. Although they had never identified Pan by name, all he had to do was prove he was the boyfriend to make his case that the newspaper had libelled him. After all, Pan had not been charged with anything. If it turned out the murderer was a cleaning lady from Winnipeg, Pan would win the libel suit. And the Toronto *Star* could start writing cheques to Pan, and stop writing them to Pron and Donovan. The more Pron started thinking about the direction the story was taking them, the worse his stomach felt. He had just bought a house and signed a big mortgage. Donovan, single and a renter, told him to relax.

Pron pulled the car over to the side of the road, stopping in front of a store. He went inside, came out a moment later, a package of Winston cigarettes in his hand. He lit one in the car, inhaled deeply. It was his first cigarette in ten years.

"Donovan, if I die of cancer I'm going to hold you personally responsible. My family will, that is."

When they arrived at the bus shelter, there was no one there except a vagrant passed out on the bench. They went in and stood there, watching him.

"See that guy, Donovan? He used to be a young, hot-shot reporter at the *Star*, just like you."

A passing police cruiser stopped in front of the shelter, and the two officers stared briefly at the trio in the shelter before driving off.

"Think she chickened out?" Pron asked. "I can't believe we didn't follow her home. We always follow people home."

He looked up the street towards an imposing Gothic structure, Toronto's Don Jail, the oldest in the province. It overlooked the muddy, pollution-clogged Don River, which has been described as an open sewer flowing into Lake Ontario.

"That's where they had the last two hangings in Canada. A cop killer and a hit man, Ron Turpin and Arthur Lucas. They strung 'em up back to back. I think they twisted for about fifteen minutes or so until their hearts stopped. That was back in '62."

Donovan looked at his watch, started pacing in the booth. "Maybe she isn't going to show. Gimme one of those." He pointed to the cigarette package.

Pron started to say something, but let it pass. He handed him the smokes.

"I can't believe I'm smoking," said Donovan, lighting one up. "I don't smoke. I don't even know how to smoke. How do you smoke?" Donovan asked, trying to inhale. He blew out some smoke, coughed, then threw the cigarette away. He was still coughing, his face flushed, when the woman in the red dress walked into the bus shelter. Under her arm was a brown paper bag. Pron offered her a cigarette. He lit it for her. Donovan was still coughing.

"I give you this," she said, "but you must promise not to tell anyone who gave it to you."

She handed Pron the bag. They thanked her and started to leave. Suddenly she reached out and grabbed Pron by the arm.

"I think I know why you two are here," she said, squeezing his arm for several moments before letting go. "I think maybe you were sent by God." Then she turned and walked quickly away.

"Either God or his earthly representative, Lou Clancy," remarked Donovan, snatching the bag from Pron and taking out the tape. "This is the first time I ever got a video pick-up of a dead person. I can't wait to see what's on it."

"Look at the time. Surely you don't mean right now?" pleaded Pron.

"Of course I mean right now," replied Donovan as he hurried off towards the car.

Three scruffily dressed men walked quickly towards the row house with the screened-in front porch. The man in the blue-jean jacket took out a pick and inserted it in the door lock, played with the tumblers for a few moments until he heard the click, then opened the door.

"We're in," the taller of the two men behind him said into the small two-way radio.

The man in the blue-jean jacket stood by the door while the other two surveyed the small, messy house, moving quietly around. The only sound was the throbbing of the pump on the fish tank in the kitchen. One of the two men had a black bag. He put it on the floor and opened it, taking out the small listening device known as a probe.

Across the way, a man with a thick moustache parked his car in a back lane so that it was facing the house. Although his face was calm, his eyes darted nervously up and down the street. Resting between his legs was a two-way radio. It was warm out that night but the windows of his car were rolled up tight. A woman with spiked heels and a skirt that barely covered her rear walked in front of the car. She noticed the man with the moustache and smiled, striking a seductive pose with a hand on one hip. He ignored her, turning his head to look the other way. The woman watched him for a moment, then turned and walked towards Queen Street where a red streetcar was rumbling by. Several minutes passed. In the stuffy car the man with the moustache was starting to sweat. Suddenly he sat bolt upright. He grabbed the two-way radio and swore into it.

"Shit," he said. "We've got trouble."

A thin Oriental man carrying a white shopping bag had just turned off Queen Street and was walking towards the row house with the screened-in front porch. The man with the moustache reached for the door handle, at the same time pressing the repeater of the two-way radio.

"We got company," he said to the three men in the house. "You guys gotta hurry. I'll see if I can stall him."

The man with the moustache leaped out of the car and ran towards the small Oriental man, who had reached the front driveway of the row house. When he got to him, he grabbed the Oriental man by the shoulder and forcefully swung him around.

" 'Scuse me,' he slurred, rocking back and forth on his feet. "I think I'm lost. I'm looking for Ossington. This Ossington Street?"

The Oriental man shook his head, waving his hand in front of his face.

"No understand," he said, trying to break free. "No understand."

The man with the moustache teetered and almost fell on his rump. He grabbed the Oriental for support and started walking him towards Queen Street.

"Well, which way is it?" he said, shoving his face so close to the other man that he jerked backwards in an attempt to get away. But the man with the moustache had him firmly by the shoulder.

"No English. No English," the Oriental said, still trying to push the other man away, but not having much luck.

"Show me," said the man with the moustache, pushing the other man towards Queen. "I'm lost."

Inside the house, the two men were on the second floor. They turned into the front bedroom just as a blue four-door Chrysler drove by and turned into the lane. The man behind the wheel eased the two-way into his lap and hit the receiver.

"How you guys doing in there? I don't know how much longer we can stall out here."

"Need a few more minutes, at least," was the reply.

The man with the moustache had the Oriental on Queen Street and was forcing him to walk west. The Oriental was squirming as he tried to break free from the bigger man's grip. Several passing cars were slowing to take a look.

"Izzit that way?" the man with the moustache asked. "Ozzington?"

"No understand. You go."

The man with the moustache suddenly wheeled around, swinging the Oriental with him.

"Or maybe dat way?"

The man driving the Chrysler was on the two-way radio again.

"You guys better hurry."

The radio was silent for several moments. Then an excited voice came over.

"We're done."

The man in the Chrysler watched as the three men walked out of the house and disappeared quickly along the street. Then he got out of his car and walked towards the man with the moustache who had lost his grip on the Oriental.

"John," he shouted at the man with the moustache. "Where the hell you been? I been looking all over for you. You get lost again?"

The man with the bushy moustache smiled, staring at the Oriental who was walking quickly away.

"Let him go," the other man told him. "They're out. They got them planted."

CHAPTER SIX

Freeze Frame

Jim Wilkes slowly opened the door, shaking his head as he squinted at the two visitors in the hallway, not liking what he saw.

"Don't you guys know what time it is?" he said, running a hand through his tousled hair, tightening the belt on his blue bathrobe.

Donovan slapped Wilkes cheerfully on the shoulder as he brushed past him, striding through the foyer and into the living room of the condominium. Wilkes was a two-way man at the *Star*, someone who wrote stories and took pictures. He also had a better assortment of video equipment than anyone else at the paper, a collection Donovan now stood in front of. He took the video cassette from the bag, then started fiddling with the myriad knobs and buttons on the high-tech gadgets.

"Sorry, Jim," Pron said, shaking his head, his feet dragging as he walked slowly past Wilkes and into the apartment.

"How do you turn this thing on?" Donovan shouted from the living room. "Where's the on switch?"

"It's on remote," Wilkes said. "Like your head."

"How 'bout a couple beers, Jim? Got anything to eat? Pron, check the fridge. See if Jimbo's got any of them, uh, them . . . mini pizzas. Yeah, hey, Jimbo. You got any of them pizzas? God, I'm starved. This investigating stuff sure builds up a fierce appetite."

"Why don't you guys make yourselves comfortable?"
Wilkes said. He walked over to an old sea chest on which
was a neat row of remote-control devices. He picked one up
and handed it to Donovan.

Donovan stared at it blankly. "Uh, why don't you do it,
Jim?" He handed back the device. "Can I get you anything?
Hey, Pron, grab a beer for Jim."

"How about just telling me what's going on?"

"We need a favour. We didn't wake you up, did we?"

"Who, me? Why would I sleep? I thought I'd stay up all
night. Considering I have to be at work in five hours."

Pron came in with the beers. "We were sort of wondering
if you could take a picture for us off a video," he said.

Wilkes walked to the closet. "I don't know why I do this,"
he said, taking out his camera bag. "Is this about that Shen
case?" he asked, putting his bag down in front of the television. "Give me that." He grabbed the video cassette from
Donovan's hand, put it into the machine, then hit the play
button.

"So where's that food?" Donovan asked.

"I've got some cold chicken wings in the fridge. Is that
good enough?"

"It'll do," Donovan said, taking his beer and sitting down
in front of the television.

The video opened with a picture of an empty auditorium
stage. For a few moments, the camera jerked amateurishly
from side to side, out of focus. When the camera steadied, a
woman was standing at centre stage, alone, shrouded in
darkness, a violin by her side. A spotlight came to rest on
her.

"That's her," Donovan said.

Selina had on a floor-length, white gown, drawn in tightly
at the waist. Around her neck was a thin gold chain, fully
exposed by the low-cut gown. Her only other jewellery was
a pair of small, silver-coloured earrings. The camera zoomed
in on her face. Her lips were coloured a deep red, her cheeks
tinged rose. Her eyebrows were pencil thin. She tossed her
head back, throwing her long black hair off her shoulders.

Selina brought the violin to her chin and started playing. Her face impassive, she drew the bow slowly across the strings. Her gaze stayed on the violin. The spotlight cast her shadow on the red curtain behind her.

Wilkes brought a tray of food into the living room and set it down on the sea chest. They listened in silence to the delicate, wavering melody Selina coaxed from her instrument. She played for about four minutes, then acknowledged the applause from an unseen audience with a polite curtsy, but no smile. Wilkes picked up the remote control and froze Selina's image on the screen.

"She's really beautiful," Pron said, leaning forward on the couch. "How could anybody kill that?"

"Kind of fragile," Wilkes added, "like a China doll."

"Hey, these are great wings," Donovan said, reaching for a napkin to wipe the grease from his hands.

Wilkes set up a tripod in front of the television screen, took a Canon AE-1 camera from his bag, and clipped it to the stand. He photographed the screen but did not look pleased.

"Not enough light for a good shot," he said, hitting the play button on the remote control.

A singer followed Selina on stage, then an oboist. Selina returned to play a duet with another woman. The lone camera focused on her, occasionally turning to the other performer. Behind the duo, scenes of China were flashed on a giant screen. Most were of lakes and waterfalls. When they finished, the duo bowed and Selina smiled for the first time before following the other woman off stage.

"The lighting's not very good," Wilkes repeated, fast forwarding through a segment where a man was playing the xylophone. "Anything I take off the screen will come out too dark for the paper."

"In other words," said Pron, "we're wasting your time."

"You're the ones who are wasting your time."

Selina returned to the stage for what was to be her final public performance. She played alone, for about twenty-five minutes. Wilkes snapped off several frames but he was still shaking his head, annoyed because a microphone was in front of Selina, blocking his shot. He slumped down on the chesterfield and picked up some food, but didn't eat. His eyes were fixed on the screen. Suddenly Wilkes jumped up and grabbed the remote control.

"There!" he yelled excitedly, rewinding the tape, playing it again past a close-up of Selina's face. "Did you see that?"

"See what?" Pron asked, yawning.

"All I see is that we're out of chicken wings," said Donovan.

Wilkes rewound the tape, then went through it in super slow motion before stopping it. "There," he said. "There. That's the one I was looking for."

A close-up shot of Selina's face was frozen on the screen. The violin was tight against her chin. To one side her shadow loomed ominously. Wilkes was fussing with his camera.

"Someone in the audience took a picture of her with a flash," he said, double-checking the setting on his camera. He pointed to the television screen. "Right at that moment. It's all the light I need. That's the picture that will make the paper."

When he was finished, Wilkes hit the play button. Later in the tape, Selina was having trouble with the microphone. The curtain parted behind her. A man stepped out from the shadows. His shoulders were rounded, his body slightly stooped. He had on a narrow black tie and a short-sleeved white shirt. He took quick, birdlike steps towards Selina. She turned to him and smiled. Very briefly. He had a soft face with no wrinkles. Beard stubble showed under his nose and around his chin. Selina watched him closely. He kept his eyes down, fumbling with the stand, finally lowering the microphone a notch. He glanced at Selina, adjusting his eyeglasses. Then he smiled. Wilkes took the picture. Selina Shen with Rui-Wen Pan.

Wilkes rewound then removed the film from his camera. "Who gets the bill for this?" he asked, tossing it to Donovan.

"You know the old saying, Jim," said Donovan, "friendship means more than money."

"Just get out of here so I can get some sleep."

"Just one more favour, Jim. Can I use the phone?"

Donovan called the office for messages. A drowsy copy boy answered.

"Some guy keeps calling for you and Pron," he said to Donovan.

"He leave a name?"

"No. Wouldn't say. Sounds Chinese."

"He what!" Donovan slammed down the phone. "Pron, we have to go into the office," he said, brushing past Wilkes and striding out the door. "Pan is calling us." He ran down the hall towards the elevators.

"Thanks, Wilkesey," Pron said, slowly following his partner out the door. He turned back to Wilkes. "I'm working with a guy who's a mental case. I guess that makes me one, too."

The morning edition was rolling off the presses when they got to the *Star*. The murder story was on page one. The headline read: BUTCHERED VIOLINIST AWARE OF STALKER WEEKS BEFORE DEATH.

There was a handful of people in the vast newsroom. The cleaner was vacuuming the carpet in the business section. After dropping off the film in the darkroom, Donovan went down for coffee, telling Pron to put his feet up, relax, and watch the phones. Instead, Pron went looking for the copy boy. He found him sleeping in the wire room, oblivious to the chatter of the teletype keys punching out news from around the world. Since the advent of computers, the wire machines had been relegated to a back-up role, moved from their place of prominence in the centre of the newsroom and dumped into a squalid little room often used as a place for a smoke or a nap.

"Hey, Robbie," Pron said, rousing the copy boy from his slumber, "that guy Pan call again?"

"Who?"

"That Chinese guy, Pan. You told Donovan he'd been calling for us."

The copy boy sat up and lit a cigarette. "No," he said.

"Terrific," Pron said. "Go back to sleep, Robbie."

Pron walked to his desk and waited for Donovan to come back with the coffees. When Donovan got back, they sat in silence reading the paper and drinking coffee for half an hour.

Then Pron got up and walked towards the elevator, not even looking back. He was hitting the button when Donovan called to him. He had the phone cradled in the crook of his neck and he was waving his arms frantically in the air. Pron sighed, walked back. Donovan put his hand over the mouthpiece.

"It's Pan. He says he wants to meet with us."

CHAPTER SEVEN

No Tears to Cry

Rui-Wen Pan strode confidently into the lobby of the Harbour Castle hotel, stopping in the foyer to scan the crowd, absently pushing a lock of oily, jet-black hair off his forehead. He was flanked by two Oriental men, who, like him, were wearing three-piece business suits. His gaze settled on the two men walking towards him.

Donovan thrust out his hand and introduced himself. Pan shook it reluctantly. His grip was soft, his skin smooth, cold.

"You're a very tall man," Pan said, looking up at Pron as he shook hands.

Pan introduced the two men with him as his business associates, Peter Wang and Andrew Fang. He said something to them in Chinese. All three laughed.

"I'm very sorry I'm late," Pan said, as they walked towards a lounge, empty except for a bald-headed man with a pot belly at the bar. Pan directed the group to a corner table. "We sit here," he said.

Pron and Donovan sat on one side of the table, Pan and his two associates on the other. For several moments no one spoke. Then Pan pulled out a cassette recorder, placed it in front of the two reporters, and turned it on.

"For my own protection," he explained.

Donovan reached into the breast pocket of his suit jacket and pulled out a mini cassette tape recorder, set it down on the table in front of Pan, and turned it on.

"For our protection," he said.

"Before we start interview, have to go over rules. First, no name is to be used," Pan stated. "You agree?"

"Which name don't you want us to use?" Donovan asked. "Rui-Wen Pan or Li Ling? If there are others, you'd better tell us now."

Pan stared at Donovan for several seconds but didn't answer. A waitress came over to take the order, breaking the silence. Pan was unsure what to drink and asked the waitress for advice. She shrugged. Pan settled on an orange juice for Wang and Fang, a piña colada for himself.

"It was Selina's favourite drink," he explained.

"Why do you have two names?" Donovan asked.

"Before I answer question, do you agree, no name?"

"No, I don't agree. Why do you have two names?" Donovan persisted.

Pan took several moments to answer. "Like you I am writer," he said finally. "I publish magazine on democracy under the pen name of Li Ling. I have family in China. I have to protect them. My writings have made me most famous. My articles appear around the world. Millions read my magazine. I am freedom fighter for democracy. I have many enemies. Many people want to see me hurt."

"That sounds reasonable," said Pron. "Is Pan your pen name or is Li?"

"Pan is my name. Li is pen name."

"Look, Mr. Pan," Donovan said, after the waitress brought over the drinks, "we'll agree not to use any of your names for this interview, Li or Pan or whatever, but we've got to identify you as Selina's boyfriend or it won't be much of a story. Right?"

"Yes, that is okay. But no name." Pan picked the tiny pink umbrella out of his piña colada and set it on the table.

"Fine, we won't use your name. But you've got to prove to us who you are. For all we know, you could be someone playing a joke on the real Mr. Pan."

Pan reached into his breast pocket and pulled out a wallet, took out his driver's licence, and put it on the table. The name on it was Pan and his home address was listed as the store on Gerrard Street. Donovan handed the licence back to Pan.

"We've been to this store of yours several times," Donovan said. "You're never home very much."

"I don't live there. That is just my store."

"Where do you live?"

"That is my business. I do not wish anyone to know where I live. I am in mourning. For my beloved Selina."

"We realize this is a difficult time for you," Pron said. "I guess we're wondering why you called us."

"I call because there are many mistakes in what you write. Many error. Eighty percent not truth and fact."

"What mistakes?" Donovan challenged, leaning forward in his chair.

"First, you write there was argument between me and Selina. There was no argument."

"That's not what we heard," said Donovan.

"What you write — all wrong."

"Many of the people we talked to say you two fought all the time."

"Who are these people."

"We can't say. Like you, Mr. Pan, they don't want to be identified."

"How can all these people make rumour about me? I haven't done anything to them."

"Forget about what people are saying. Why don't you tell us your story."

"There are so many rumours going on about her death. Most are unfair to me. This is Canada. A democratic country. Why are these things allowed to continue?"

"People want to know about this murder. They're interested in it. They're fascinated by it. They want to know how something like this could happen."

"Everything said about me is wrong. You say there was bitter argument, there was no bitter argument. Eighty percent of what you write all wrong, not truth and fact. You say she wanted to be a student at the University of Toronto. That all wrong."

"We just wrote what we were told."

"Who told you? Did Selina's sister tell you?"

"No. Others did."

"You should get your information from police."

"We've tried, Mr. Pan," said Pron. "But they don't tell us very much."

Pan smiled over that, turned to his two associates, and said something to them in Chinese. Wang and Fang listened attentively, hands folded in their laps. Neither touched his drink. Neither spoke. Both stared straight ahead. Like two mannequins.

"I am working with police to help them solve case," said Pan. "I have talked many times with Larry Edgar. He is top of guy at OPP. I give OPP reference material to help them catch the killer. I give them picture of Selina."

"What reference material?" asked Donovan.

"Some are photocopies of letters. I can't answer all these questions directly. You should check with police."

"Can we ask your two friends here any questions? Did they know Selina?" Pron glanced at Wang and Fang. "By the way, do these two gentlemen talk?"

"I talk for them. They do not speak English."

"You said they were your business associates. Do they work in your stores?"

"Yes."

"What about your businesses? How long are they going to be closed?"

"They have been closed for two weeks. I lose so much money every day."

"But why are they closed?"

"How can I open them when there are so many rumours and lies about me? After I learned about her death, I couldn't eat or sleep. I just lay down on the bed. I lost fifteen pounds. Nobody knows how much I suffer." Pan paused to take a sip of his drink. "Rumours can kill a person. There is Chinese proverb says if rumour repeated one thousand times it become the truth."

"I don't get it, Mr. Pan," Donovan cut in. "Here we've got your girlfriend, a woman you lived with for three years, a beautiful woman, horribly killed and chopped up. But all you talk about is how it has bothered you. Where's your sorrow for Selina?''

''I have sorrow. Much sorrow. How can you say such a thing, Mr. Kevin Donovan. I loved her. I cried so much I have no more tears to cry. It was just like the end of the world when she left.''

''If you loved her so much, how could you let her work in your stores and face deportation?''

''But she make no salary. As a visitor on student visa, she wasn't allowed to make salary.''

''We heard that Selina and your brother argued a lot.''

''No, no argument. There were a few troubles between them. They do not like each other, but I was dealing with the problem.''

''What do you mean, 'dealing with'?''

''I cannot answer this right now.''

''Mr. Pan, you say you loved Selina. But we were told that you went to Hong Kong with a girlfriend from Montreal since Selina disappeared. That doesn't sound like you were too broken up.''

''That is not true, I never went to Hong Kong with a girl. Who told you this lie?''

Donovan checked his notepad, flipping back a few pages. He ignored the question. ''What about this, Mr. Pan. Were you in trouble before, ever in jail?''

''No, this is also lie. I was never in jail. Where do you get all this?''

''How about March, 1983, crossing the U.S. border. Do you remember that?''

''I canot talk about this now. You must be bad man, Mr. Kevin Donovan, to ask me questions like this. Maybe you are police.''

''Some people say you are a surgeon. Is that true?''

''More rumours. I was not a surgeon. I took biochemistry in Montreal, but I am not a surgeon.''

''Look,'' Donovan said, slapping his fingertips against the edge of the table. ''We're not getting anywhere here.'' He finished off his drink, pushed the empty glass to one side. ''If you want to tell your story, you're got to answer our

93

questions." He leaned forward across the table. "And quit beating around the bush. Now, answer me this. Did you kill her?"

"I beg your pardon?"

"You heard me, Pan. Did you kill Selina?"

"Kevin," Pron interrupted. "Could you lower your voice a bit? The waitress is looking."

"Did you kill your girlfriend?" Donovan persisted.

Pan's hands tightened on the arms of the chair. But he remained silent.

"Did you kill her and cut her up into little pieces?"

Pan slumped in his chair, crossed and uncrossed his legs, then said something in Chinese to his two associates. His face flushed. His eyes widened. He stared at Donovan. For several seconds he looked at him without speaking. Finally he answered the question.

"Of course not. I loved her. I didn't kill her. How could you ask such a question?"

Pan turned to Fang and said something in Chinese. They talked for several moments, ignoring everyone else. Pan pushed aside his drink, picked up the pink umbrella and put it into his pocket. He reached for his tape recorder and looked for the waitress, as if he wanted to pay the bill. Then he stood up.

"You're not leaving, are you, Mr. Pan?" Pron asked, getting up with him. "You understand we have to ask these questions. It is our job. We don't mean to offend you. Right, Donovan?"

Donovan looked out the window and said nothing.

"Look, why don't you just tell us about your relationship with her? We'll order another round and maybe you could tell us about that." Pron searched out the waitress, waved his forefinger in a tight circle over his head. The waitress nodded. "You must miss her deeply. She was a very beautiful woman."

Pan paused, said something to his associates, then sat down. He put the tape recorder on the table, flipped over the cassette and turned the machine on.

"What I did for her I don't think anybody in the world would do," he said. "What I did was generous."

"You must have loved her very much," Pron said.

"I asked her to marry me several times. Once last spring I asked her in front of her mother and sister. But she always refuse. My dream was to have kids and a family. All that is finished now."

"That must have hurt you."

"She did a lot of things to hurt me but I always forgave her."

"Why did you stay with her?"

"She was a very special lady. She's the type of lady that really needs love and protection."

"When did you last see her?"

"The truth of the fact is on Saturday, February 6, at around eight o'clock, she left. She took everything, all her personal belongings, and she left. Even when you check out of hotel you have to give notice. But she . . . she tell me nothing. Is very cruel."

"Do you know why she left?"

"No, there was no problem. No argument. If there a financial problem, people might argue. But there was no problem like that."

"There had to be a reason."

"Maybe reason but she not tell me. I come home and she is gone. No explanation. She gave me nothing. Before, she left two or three times but she always came back. There was somebody she was afraid of."

"Who?"

"I cannot tell you. She called me five days after she left. She called for help. I can't tell you what she said. That's part of the investigation. She was in a hurry to go, but I tried to keep her talking. She was terrified, someone was after her. I gave two letters to friends to give to her, to tell her that I forgave her. But I never see her again."

"You say someone was after Selina," said Donovan, getting back into the conversation. "Who was it?"

"A man who has troubles with his mind."

"What's his name?" .

"I know the wife of this man. She told me her husband is sick. The wife told me her husband fooled around with a married woman and a university student."

"His name, Mr. Pan. Tell me his name."

"Right now I cannot answer this question because I want the police to arrest the suspect as soon as possible."

"Him or somebody else? What kind of answer is that, Mr. Pan? Do you know his name or don't you?"

"I think maybe she was target of blackmailers who prey on immigrants working illegally. These blackmailers bring Chinese and others from Hong Kong, Thailand, and mainland China. Selina knew these people."

"Did she threaten to turn in the blackmailers?"

"I cannot answer that. I am working closely with police. It would hurt investigation if I talk."

"Who were these blackmailers?"

"There were several. They were calling her all the time. I have them on tape."

"Can we hear the tapes?"

"These conversations are in Mandarin. You would not understand."

"We'll get them translated," Donovan responded.

"No. I cannot answer any more questions on this. Don't ask me any more."

"Okay then," Donovan said. "Answer me this. We hear that Selina had a baby a few years ago. Something about a black man being the father, maybe even that he raped her. Could the father have anything to do with her death?"

"How you know of such a thing?"

"We found out, okay? That's not the point. What I want to know is, could the father be a suspect?"

"If you write such a thing it would greatly hurt her reputation."

"But is he a suspect?"

"Right now, I cannot answer that." Pan looked at the table, moving his half-finished drink around in tiny circles. "Maybe, if I were to tell you the truth, that would help my reputation but hurt hers."

Donovan banged his glass down on the table, then stood up. "This is going nowhere," he declared. "Mr. Pan, you're not telling us anything we don't already know. Every time we ask a question, you make up some reason not to answer it. We're really wasting our time. And what about these two guys?" He pointed to Wang and Fang. "Can they talk for themselves? What about it, fellas? Do you know who killed Selina? Huh? Do you?"

"Don't ask them questions," Pan interrupted. "They are not here to answer questions."

"They're grown men, Pan. Let them speak for themselves."

Wang started to say something but Pan raised a hand, cutting him off. The three spoke in Chinese then got up to go.

"We really appreciate you coming to talk to us, Mr. Pan," Pron said, holding out his hand. Pan shook it reluctantly.

"I have talked a lot today," Pan replied, packing away his tape recorder.

"Can we talk again?"

"Maybe I will tell you more but right now I don't want to hurt the investigation."

"What if I called you? Can I do that?" Pron asked. "Can you give me your number? I can come to your house and talk if that would be better."

"That is private. But I will give you my number," Pan said. He wrote it on a napkin and handed it to Pron before walking away.

Donovan reached for his wallet, then threw a few bills on the table for the drinks. He caught up to Wang and Fang as they walked to the door and started peppering them with questions. They just looked at him, smiled, and said nothing. Pan grabbed Pron by the arm, motioned him aside.

"Please, be fair to me, Mr. Nick Pron," Pan said, shaking hands again. "There have already been too many rumours and slanders against me in the media. This trial by publicity can kill a person."

"Of course, Mr. Pan, we'll be very careful."

"Your friend," Pan said, nodding at Donovan, who was standing a few feet away, still trying to cajole Wang and Fang

97

into talking. "He lacks maturity. He speaks without thinking. He has the traits of a lower-class person."

"He's young, Mr. Pan. He'll learn," Pron said. "This man you think is the killer, I'd like to find out more about him."

"Yes, you should find out."

"If you know a lot, maybe you should tell me, or the police. Aren't you worried that the police might make you the main suspect?"

"No, I am not worried. The difference between a democratic country and a dictatorship is that in a dictatorship they can charge you without any reason. But here, if you haven't done anything wrong and somebody knocks at your door at midnight, you are never scared. That is a Chinese proverb."

Pan glanced at Wang and Fang and said a few words in Chinese. They walked over and the three went out the revolving doors without looking back.

"I'm young? I'll learn?" Donovan said, firing a glance at Pan and his two associates as they walked away.

"Donovan, I had to say something. Don't you think you were overacting your role? I had to smooth things over."

"Who was acting? It's obvious he did it."

"And what do you base that on?"

"Why were you being so nice to him? The man's a killer."

"I thought we agreed that's the way we'd play it."

"That's before I realized how guilty he was."

"And my answer to that is, how can you be so sure?"

An elderly couple, loaded down with luggage, turned and stared as they walked by.

"What are you looking at?" Donovan challenged. The couple turned and walked quickly away.

"You're wrong about this one, Donovan. There's no way that guy killed anyone. He just doesn't have it in him. He doesn't look the type."

"What is the type? I knew he killed her as soon as I shook his hand. No warmth. No feeling. No compassion. That's the type."

"Oh, I get it, Donovan. From now on, whenever a judge wants to know if someone is guilty we'll just have them shake hands with you."

"He was just too evasive. Why would an innocent man beat around like that? The way he lied about his immigration. And the baby."

"Maybe he didn't know about the baby. What if Selina never told him?"

"And I guess he didn't know he was in jail, either."

"What about this guy with the troubled mind?"

"More bullshit. He just made that up. That story is probably the only thing keeping him out of jail. The cops are still checking it. Yeah, sure."

"Donovan, if Pan was a suspect, the cops would be watching him. But I didn't see anyone in that bar who looked remotely like a cop."

"How do you know they weren't there? Maybe the waitress was a cop. She was hanging around our table a lot."

"We should've followed him," Pron said, as they walked back to the *Star* building. "We always follow people around. How come we didn't tail Pan?"

"We'll do it next time."

They filed a story quoting but not naming Pan. The headline read: SLAIN VIOLINIST CALLED A TARGET OF BLACKMAIL.

Sophie Shen remembered the telephone conversation quite well. She had called Pan the day after her sister had failed to keep their Sunday dinner date to ask him if he had seen Selina.

"Even before I identified myself, he knew it was me on the phone," Sophie told Larry Edgar and Gus Riddell. The two investigators were interviewing her in the kitchen of her home. "He said, 'It's all your fault.' He was very angry."

"Your fault about what?" asked Edgar. "That she had moved out, or that she had been killed?"

"He just said, 'It's all your fault.' I asked him to help me find my sister."

"And what was his response to that?"

"He said she had moved out. He said she was with some Canadian guy."

"You mean Robert Fisher?"

"He never told me his name," Sophie Shen replied. "He said it was a Western guy who had mental problems. He said he knew where she went. After I got off the telephone, I went to his house to see him."

"This was his place on Puma, right?" asked Edgar. "The one he sold?"

"Yes, that's where I went. I wanted him to help me find her."

"And did he?" asked Edgar.

"He told me to come back later. He said he had some business to do first. He said to come back at ten that night."

"And you went back?"

"I went back, but with a friend."

"Why was that?"

"I was nervous. I didn't want to go alone."

"This friend, what's her name?"

Sophie told him and Edgar wrote it down in his notebook. "And then what happened?"

"They were having dinner," Sophie said.

"Who?"

"Pan and his brother."

"Jia-Wen?"

"Yes."

"Did you and your friend go into the house?"

"No. She was watching from her car. I told her to wait there for me."

"While you went inside?"

"Yes."

"And then what happened, Miss Shen?"

"Pan said again that Selina had met this Western guy and she must be at his place. He said he knew the man's ex-wife. I asked him for the address, but he wouldn't give it to me. He said we had to go there together."

"Did he tell you her name?"

"He said her name was Anna Leung. I didn't know who she was."

"So you went to see her, with Pan?"

"We drove in my car."

"And what about your friend?"

"I told her to go home. But I told her if I didn't call her by midnight she should call the police."

"You were being very cautious," remarked Riddell.

"I was scared."

"But still you went in the car with Pan?" asked Edgar.

"Yes."

"That was very brave."

Sophie didn't answer. She smiled weakly. Her eyes were starting to redden. Edgar gave her a moment to compose herself. She looked a lot like her sister, he thought. Although the two had not been that close, it was clear that Sophie loved her elder sister. Their parents were separated, she had told Edgar. The two girls had grown up in different cities, Selina in Hobai, and she in Shanghai. Both had come to Canada in 1983 on student visas. But while a brief marriage in 1984 had given Sophie a Canadian citizenship, Selina was still trying to get landed immigrant status. Sophie had met Pan first, and had lived with him for three months before she left and her sister moved in. If she didn't like Pan, why did she introduce her sister to him? Edgar wondered.

"So you drove Pan to Anna Leung's house?" asked Edgar. "And what happened then?"

"We knocked on the door but nobody answered. But there was somebody in the house."

"Why would you say that?"

"I saw a somebody, a man, at a window when we knocked. Pan wanted to go to a pay phone and call."

"Did you?"

"Yes."

"And did anyone answer?"

"Yes."

"Who?"

"A man answered. He said Anna Leung was on holiday."

"Then what happened?"

"I made an appointment to go out with Pan the next day. He said we should go to the Ontario College of Art because that's where this woman worked. We went there but she wasn't there. He said that we should go to the Toronto Western Hospital."

"Why was that?"

"He said this woman worked there."

"And did you go there as well?"

"Yes. But she wasn't there."

"Then what happened?"

"We made another appointment to go look for Selina, on Thursday. But I cancelled it."

"Why?"

"I went to Selina's house instead."

"On Timberbank Boulevard?"

"Yes."

"And what did you find?"

"Everything was there. Her dresses were in the closet, her sleeping gown was on the bed. All her toiletries were in the bathroom."

"Did you talk to Pan again?"

"Every day, on the phone."

"Why did you wait so long before you reported her missing?"

"Pan said we should go, but not right away. He said if we went and Selina came back the next day, we would look foolish."

"But you kept looking for Selina, on your own?"

"I called all around, all her friends. I even phoned her old boyfriend in Australia."

"Do you have his name."

She told Edgar and he wrote it down in his notebook. "I gather no one had seen her?" asked Edgar.

Sophie shook her head. Her eyes started to redden again. Riddell gave her a tissue from a box on the kitchen counter.

Edgar put away his notebook and got up. "You've been very helpful," he said. "We have a few things to check out but we'd like to talk to you again."

Sophie nodded.

"There's just one more thing," Edgar said, putting on his coat. "After your sister moved out, you said she seemed very happy?"

"Yes. She said this was going to be her lucky year."

"We know from talking to her landlord that she left early every morning and came home late at night. Her landlord said this was because she had a job."

"Yes, she was working."

"You see, this is where we're having trouble. We're unclear what exactly happened during that two-week period after she moved out. We know she had a job, but we don't know where. Do you know where she worked? This would be a big help in our investigation."

Sophie looked away. She folded her hands across her lap. "No," she said.

"Well, thank you, Miss Shen," Edgar said as he and Riddell walked to the door. "We'd like to talk to you again. We'll have more questions."

"When will you arrest him?" she asked.

"Who?"

"Pan."

"We have a lot more investigating to do," Edgar said. "We'll be in touch."

Edgar waited until he was in the car before he lit up a Player's.

"Keep talking to her, Gus," he said. "I don't know why, but she's not telling us everything she knows about where Selina worked after she left Pan."

CHAPTER EIGHT

Dangerous Driving

Rui-Wen Pan was having tea at the kitchen table with Peter Wang and Andrew Fang when he saw the article on the murder of Selina Shen in the Chinese newspaper. After he finished reading it, he threw down the paper in disgust.

"They are trying to crucify me," he said, pointing at the story.

Fang picked up the paper and started reading the article, while Wang, the taller of the two, looked over his shoulder. The two men had become friends in Vancouver, where both had settled after coming to Canada on student visas. While on holiday in Montreal, they were introduced to a man named Li Ling who shared their distrust of communism. Ling said he was the editor of a magazine that was promoting democracy for China. Neither Wang nor Fang liked the Communist system, and they were impressed by Ling's desire to rid their homeland of totalitarian rule. Like Ling, they had left China in search of a better life. Wang and Fang wanted to stay in Canada and were trying to get landed immigrant status, the first step to becoming Canadian citizens. They wanted to move to Toronto, but told Ling they didn't have any place to stay. He offered them jobs at his stores, and said they could live at his house. It was only after they arrived in Toronto that they found out his real name was Rui-Wen Pan and that he was being vilified in the Chinese press because his former

girlfriend, Selina Shen, had been murdered, and her body
cut into pieces.

The article said that Selina Shen's boyfriend was mentally
deranged. It went on to say they had split up after a bitter
argument. But the article never identified the boyfriend.

"Everyone knows that I am boyfriend of Selina Shen," Pan
said to Wang and Fang. "I wrote that letter, but I said nothing
to frighten her. I wrote her three letters. I wanted her to come
back to me. Why do they say such a thing in the paper?"

"Maybe they are mistaken," said Wang. "You should ask
them where they got this information."

"Yes, that is what I will do," Pan replied. Then I will have
legal proof that the newspaper is wrong. I want you to come
with me." Pan nodded at Wang. "You will be my witness.
Later, I want both of you to come with me to meet the reporter
from the Toronto *Star*. I need a witness for that interview."

Larry Edgar was starting to get a better picture of the last two
months in Selina Shen's life. The year had started off well
for her. Until her death, there were promising signs that 1988
was indeed going to be her lucky year, as she had told her
sister. Early in January, Selina had gone to an immigration
consultant who told her she had a good chance of getting the
landed immigrant status she so desperately wanted, despite
the fact she had been working illegally. She wanted to
improve her English and had signed up for language courses.
On February 6, she moved out of Pan's house and found a
room in Scarborough. Unlike the previous two times she had
left Pan, on this occasion there were no signs of a reconcilia-
tion. She had a telephone installed in her room, the number
unlisted. Investigators had seized her bankbook from her
apartment and, after checking the records, had learned that
she had transferred her account from a branch of the Royal
Bank near one of Pan's stores to a branch of Canada Trust
close to her new home on Timberbank Boulevard. That had
been done the day before she disappeared. Her sister supported Selina's move from Pan's house, and in those last two

months, it appeared the two women were forming closer bonds.

Then there was Robert Fisher, the lecturer at the University of Toronto. Fisher had also been very supportive of the move. The two had met at a dinner party at Pan's house on January 16. Fisher freely admitted in his interview with Yates that he liked Selina, had spent a lot of time that night talking to her, and wanted to know her better. Fisher told Selina that when she moved out from Pan's house, she could stay with him if she couldn't find a place of her own. Fisher told Yates he had called Selina several times after the dinner party. Once, Pan got on the line and warned him not to get involved with Selina because she was having mental problems. Although Pan told investigators that Fisher had something to do with Selina's disappearance, Fisher said he had seen Selina only one other time after the dinner party, at the School of Continuing Studies in downtown Toronto, where Selina was signing up for a course in English. Yates had been impressed with Fisher's openness. He had an alibi for the weekend Selina disappeared, one that was being checked by Edgar's investigators.

Although the investigation was going well, there was a two-week gap in those final two months of Selina's life that bothered Edgar. This was between February 6, when she moved out from Pan's house, and February 20, when she vanished after the music lesson at Mrs. Chan's house. He knew where she lived during that time but didn't know what she did. He assumed she had a job, but he didn't know where.

Edgar's investigators had talked to several of Selina's friends, but none of them knew what she was doing. One suggested that because Selina was very proud she wouldn't have told them where she worked if she had been ashamed of her job. That wasn't much help. Edgar had to find out what she did all day during those two weeks. What if she met her killer during that time? A co-worker perhaps? It was a longshot but it had to be thoroughly checked. That's what a murder investigation was, eliminating all possible suspects while hunting for the killer.

Donovan winced. He couldn't believe his eyes. Across the street, his friend and partner was heartily shaking the hand and cheerfully patting the back of a man Donovan was convinced was a killer. Donovan shook his head as he slumped even farther behind the steering wheel of his Firebird to avoid being seen. The plan had been to lure Rui-Wen Pan to the Sutton Place Hotel in downtown Toronto, have Pron do a quick interview in the bar, then tail Pan home, talk to his neighbours and check to see if his house was being watched by police. But that was three hours ago, the interview was just wrapping up, and it was dark. Pan and his two associates, Wang and Fang, were headed towards their car, an early-model Chevette, while Pron walked the other way up the street to his. A minute later, the two-way radio on the seat beside him crackled.

"Donovan, you on channel two?" the voice asked. It was Pron.

"Yeah, I'm here. What the hell took so long? He confess?"

"Nice try. He just rambled."

"Heads up," Donovan said. "They're moving. Looks like it'll be west on Wellesley, then probably south on Bay. That's what I'm guessing."

"He saw me get into my car . . . knows what I'm driving. I'll have to hang back so I won't spook him," Pron said.

Donovan dumped his half-finished coffee out the window, shifted the Firebird into gear, and slowly eased away from the curb, just far enough into the next lane to get a good jump. Other motorists, forced to manoeuvre around him, honked angrily. Donovan ignored them. His eyes were on Pan's battered Chevette, with its missing front grill and cracked windshield, coming up to the intersection at Bay Street, just ahead of him.

Pan turned left and headed south. Donovan pulled out to follow but had to slam on the brakes as a Ford Tempo appeared out of nowhere and stopped just in front of him. Donovan, penned in, leaned on the horn. The driver of the Tempo stared straight ahead, as if he didn't hear.

"Move, fuckhead!" Donovan screamed.

He honked again, seething as Pan's Chevette went through a green light and disappeared in traffic. Donovan swung around in his seat. There was room, about a car length. He banged the stick shift into reverse, the car tires screeching as he backed up, hitting the front fender of a parked car. Donovan turned sharply to the left, shifted into first gear. He accelerated out of the parking spot and wheeled around the Tempo, sneering at the driver as he sped by him. The light at the intersection just ahead turned red. He went through it.

"Just ran a red," he shouted at the two-way to Pron. "Some jerk cut me off. I'm a half block away from him, going south."

Pron was stuck in the turning lane on Wellesley behind a line of cars. He pulled out of the line and cut off several cars as he turned south on Bay. About a block ahead, he saw Donovan's distinctive taillights, a bulb on the left burnt out. Pron gunned the engine, racing to catch the light at the next intersection. A Ford Taurus in front of him slowed to a stop, even though the light was still green. Pron tried to back up, but another car had pulled up tight to his rear bumper. He rolled down the window, stuck his head out.

"Move your fuckin' car, asshole," he screamed.

The driver of the Taurus glanced back and gave him a shrug of the shoulders. Pron reached for his two-way radio.

"I'm stuck at the lights at Elm, behind some idiot. How far ahead are you?" Pron asked.

There was no answer from Donovan. He had just passed the twin curved towers of City Hall. Pan was several car lengths ahead, turning west from Bay onto Queen Street. As Donovan reached Queen, the car ahead stopped at a yield sign, even though there was no oncoming traffic. When the car didn't move, Donovan downshifted and sped around him. He went up the curb and over the traffic island, bouncing the front fender heavily on the pavement of Queen Street. He grabbed the two-way.

"Somebody cut me off again! I'm going west on Queen. I can see Pan."

A white Mustang came up quickly on Donovan's left and veered in front, cutting him off, forcing him against the curb. Donovan drove up on the curb, hubcaps grinding against the concrete. He raced ahead, around the Mustang, passenger wheels straddling the sidewalk, then down onto the road. The car rocked on its springs, Donovan's head banging against the side window. He gave the Mustang driver the finger. Pron's voice came over the radio.

"Donovan, I'm almost at Queen. Which way?"

"Stay off Queen. Something funny's going on. Go west on the next street."

Pan was still going west on Queen. He had just crossed University Avenue, eight broad lanes with a boulevard in the middle. When Donovan got to University, the light had just turned red. He took a quick glance in either direction, then jammed the gas pedal to the floor, racing through the intersection. The chase had taken him into the fashionable restaurant district of Queen Street West. Two cars separated him from Pan's Chevette. His radio crackled.

"I'm west on Richmond," said Pron. "Just coming up to University. Where are you?"

The car in front of Donovan, a blue Ford Topaz, slowed to a crawl, then stopped. To Donovan's right were parked cars. He tried to go left, but an oncoming streetcar had just stopped and was letting out passengers. Ahead of the Topaz, Pan's car was getting away. There were no cars in front of the Topaz, yet it wasn't moving. Donovan leaned on the horn.

The driver of the Topaz, a tall, burly man with shoulder-length blond hair, got out. He turned to look at Donovan, then walked around to the front of the car. He fumbled with the latch for a few minutes, then lifted the hood. He stood there looking at the motor for a few moments, his hands thrust deep into the pockets of a red windbreaker. Then he slammed the hood shut, but took his time getting into the car. Finally he drove off, but very slowly. Pan was nowhere to be seen.

"Donovan, where are you?" Pron repeated.

"I've been cut off," Donovan replied, his voice agitated. "I've lost Pan. I'm going to follow the guy who boxed me in. I'm sure he's a cop."

Pron took a side street onto Queen and kept going west. Pan's car was nowhere in sight. He called Donovan.

"I've lost him, too. Where are you?"

"This guy's just leading me in circles. Let's meet. Queen at Spadina, northeast corner."

Pron got there first. He was leaning against the side of his car when Donovan pulled up.

"What the hell happened?" Pron asked.

Donovan described his ride from the hotel to where he lost Pan. "I had all these guys trying to knock me off the road," he said. "Then this other guy waits for a streetcar and picks that time to find out if he's still got an engine. It had to be cops. It was too organized to be a coincidence."

"I knew there was something going on," Pron said. "There was this guy back at the hotel who kept hanging around our table, staring at the prints on the wall. He didn't look like an art collector."

"Did you notice the cars? All new Fords. Like they were rented from the same place," Donovan said. "At least we got one of our questions answered tonight."

"What's that?"

"The cops are keeping a pretty close eye on our friend Mr. Pan. There must have been at least five cars blocking us off. Pan must be a suspect."

"Where to now?" asked Pron.

"Let's stake out his store," replied Donovan. "He might go there."

It was dark inside Pan's shop on Gerrard Street. The tinny sound of a bad radio came from one of the old cars parked at the side. Pron tapped on the car roof.

"Hello?" he called through the car's open rear window.

A dirty hand poked up from behind the front seat and grabbed the headrest. An Oriental man pulled himself to a sitting position.

"Yes? Who is there?" He had on a tattered plaid jacket and a small woollen cap. "Something wrong?"

"We're looking for Mr. Pan," Pron said. "You're not his brother, are you?"

The man's eyes widened. He laughed. "Me? I'm Korean. Pan is Chinese. Big difference." He laughed again.

"Do you know him?" Donovan asked, walking around to the open passenger window and crouching to look in. A few cans of beer had rolled out of a plastic bag on the floor. An open can sat on the seat beside the man.

"Mr. Pan is my tenant." He squinted at the reporters. "Why are you here? I already talk to police."

Pron told them who they were.

"Reporters? You going to write story about Mr. Pan?"

"We already have," said Donovan.

The man pointed to the back door. "You want to sit in here? Have beer?"

They got in. The man, who said his name was Peter, passed back two beers. "Maybe you guys could write a story and help me collect my rent from him. He owes two months!"

Pron took out his cigarettes, handed one to Peter. "What kind of a guy is he?"

"Mr. Pan or his brother?" Peter reached over and turned the car radio down. "You know, this radio only thing on car that work." He laughed again. "Work more than Pan."

"Mr. Pan doesn't work, is that what you're saying?"

"I can't figure him out. He opens store two hours a day. Not many customers come in. Then he leaves. Strange guy."

Pron took a swig of beer. "What about his brother?"

"He yelled at me once. Got real mad because I ask him about rent. Just shouted and shouted at Peter."

Donovan put down his empty beer can. Peter handed back two more, saying he had lots in his house next door.

"What are the brothers like together?" Donovan wanted to know.

"Sometimes mean. Like they are more important than I am. I have good job in Oshawa at the food terminal and I own this building. But they act like they are better. Smarter. My only dumb thing was buying this building last year and not checking who were tenants."

"And Selina? His girlfriend?"

"Very pretty. Nice. That store not a good place for girl like that to work. Could you write a story to get my rent?"

"How much a month?"

"Eleven hundred and fifty dollars."

Pron cracked open his second beer. "How come you're sitting out here?"

"It's quiet. I like to come here, have beer, cigarette, relax." He straightened in his seat. "And watch."

"Watch?" said Donovan. "Watch what?"

"All sorts of things. Things different than Korea. Funny things happen."

Pron stubbed out his cigarette in the door ashtray. "What kind of things?"

Peter asked Pron for another cigarette. "Late at night, Pan and his friends come here. Sometimes take boxes in, sometimes take boxes out. Funny guys."

Donovan leaned back. "What about Selina getting killed?"

"I read about," Peter said. He squeezed his beer can, hard enough to crush the sides. "Really sad." He gave a short laugh. "Funny things around here. After she go away, I see Pan. I notice hand." Peter held up his right hand. "Injured. Wrapped with bandage. I ask him what happen? He say he fall down, hurt himself. Very strange."

Just then, two men in windbreakers walked past the car, stopped to glance in at Pan's store, and then kept going.

"Have to be cops," Pron said.

He and Donovan got out of the car and walked along Gerrard Street, past the two men in windbreakers who were standing in front of a shop near Pan's store. A diminutive Oriental woman opened the door. One of the men took something out of his pocket, flipped it open, and held it in front of the woman's face. They went inside.

Pron and Donovan went to the corner, turned around, and walked back, stopping in front of the shop. The curtain across the front window was partially open. The two men in windbreakers dwarfed the woman, who was standing beside a sewing machine. There was a second sewing machine in the store and a pile of dresses nearby. The woman was wringing her hands nervously. She was crying.

Jim McClelland turned around and saw the two faces in the window staring at them. He nodded to Kent Bradbury, who walked over and closed the curtains. Bradbury had heard about the two *Star* reporters who were making a nuisance of themselves in the murder investigation, and he wondered if the two men at the window were them.

CHAPTER NINE

A Midnight Stroll

Rui-Wen Pan turned the Chevette onto Hammersmith Avenue, a side street in an area of Toronto known as the Beaches. He parked near the end of the road, not far from the waterfront. It was late, nearly midnight, and the street was deserted.

"There is some business I must do," Pan said to Peter Wang and Andrew Fang. They had just come from a restaurant and were heading home when Pan made the unexpected stop.

A car turned on Hammersmith and came slowly down the street towards them. Pan watched it with suspicion, squinting in the darkness to get a better look at the driver, but the car went by too fast for him to see who was behind the wheel.

"What is it?" Wang asked, glancing around to look at the car.

Pan watched the car until it turned the corner at the end of the street.

"I must be so careful," he said, a line that Wang and Fang had heard many times before. "But tonight I have taken precautions. There is something important I must do. I have some *China Voice* magazines I must destroy. The policemen should not see these magazines."

Pan got out of the car, went around to the back, opened the hatchback, shifted around some cartons, and reached deep into the well. He took out a white carton and a plastic shopping bag with something inside.

114

"I want you to wait in the car," Pan said to Wang and Fang, reaching up to close the hatchback. "I will not be long."

He walked south on Hammersmith towards the lake, the plastic shopping bag in one hand, the white carton tucked snugly under his armpit. Everything was going as planned. There were no police around. If there had been, he would have noticed them by now. He had been watching for them. Still, he had to be cautious, on his guard. Was somebody in that parked car over there? He stopped at the corner to get a better look. No. Just a shadow.

He turned on Hubbard Boulevard, a street that ran parallel to the lake, and headed east. It was a calm evening, with a clear sky and a full moon — a pleasant night for a midnight stroll. He took his time. He was in no particular hurry. There were a few other people about, but they were strolling on the boardwalk. He had not gone far on Hubbard when he noticed someone walking towards him.

He was a big fellow and was also walking at a slow pace. Someone out for a walk? Or was it those damned police? He would have to find out, just to be safe. He stopped, knelt down, and carefully laid his packages on the sidewalk, shuffling them around and stalling for time as the big man got closer. He put the white carton into the bag, then took it out again. The big man was only a few feet away. Who was he?

The big man, who had a bushy moustache, stopped beside a newspaper box and started fishing through his pockets. He took out some change, dropped the money into the slot, got his paper, then turned and continued walking north, without even a glance at Pan. When he was almost out of sight, Pan picked up his bag and his box and cut across the park to the boardwalk. He soon came to a concrete pier that stretched into the lake. He looked around to make sure he was alone, then turned onto the pier.

The water was calm that night, as still as glass. Tiny waves broke gently on the shore, a sound as soft as two bedsheets coming together. Moonlight sparkled on the lake and lit up part of the pier, but the far end was dark. Pan walked towards the end, disappearing into the night.

A few minutes later, when he was finished, he hurried off the pier, barely glancing at a vagrant sleeping on a park bench. He walked into the park and over to a garbage can, where he ripped up the empty white box and dropped the pieces into the trash. He threw the bag into a second garbage can, then headed back to his car. Wang and Fang were dozing when Pan got behind the wheel and started the engine.

As the Chevette drove away, a man stepped out from the shadows behind a tree, tucking in his shirt-tails and straightening out his jacket. Once the car had disappeared around the corner, he ran back to the garbage cans, lifted out the bags, and carried them to his car. He was a big man, well over six feet tall, with a bushy moustache. He got into his car, reached under the seat for the two-way radio, turned it on, and pressed the transmitter switch, checking first to make sure there was no one around.

"He's thrown something into the lake," Andrius Kaknevicius said softly into the mike. There was an edge to his voice.

Kaknevicius was on one of the surveillance teams that had been watching Pan for weeks. It seemed like years. He and four others had been following Pan since early afternoon that day, taking over from another team at one of Pan's variety stores on Gerrard Street. They worked in twelve-hour shifts, literally waking him up in the morning and putting him to bed at night. Following him was boring, and that made it more tiring. Pan never did anything unusual. Every day was like every other day. From his home to work, then back home again. He made the odd trip to Brampton, a small city near Toronto, where he rented a warehouse for his merchandise, but otherwise he stuck to his routine.

Pan, along with his two sidekicks and a woman, had gone to a restaurant that night after work. Later, after dropping her off, Pan and his two companions appeared to be heading for home. Everyone on the surveillance was thankful for that. They were looking forward to quitting on time for a change. But then, unexpectedly, Pan started "spinning."

Instead of going west, he turned south, towards Lake Ontario. Normally a slow, cautious driver, he began to drive oddly: speeding up, then slowing down, making sudden U-turns in the middle of the road, pulling off to the side and studying the cars that passed, obviously checking to make sure he wasn't being followed. But his tactics were amateurish, almost laughable for the team of four men and one woman, surveillance professionals whose sole job was watching people and recording what they did, without their knowing about it. With five sets of eyes watching Pan, there was little chance he would elude them.

After about a half hour of evasive manoeuvres, Pan turned on a side street near the waterfront, apparently satisfied he wasn't followed. Kaknevicius drove by Pan's car, parked around the corner, and waited. When Pan got out and walked towards the lake, Kaknevicius got out too, glad for the chance to stretch his long legs, which had been cramped behind the steering wheel of his car for nearly eight hours. Kaknevicius had watched Pan walk out on the pier, then had lain down on a park bench, pretending to be a vagrant. Although he was close, it was too dark for him to see what Pan was doing. He heard sounds coming from the end of the dock. A splashing noise. Was Pan throwing something into the water?

An hour later, there were a dozen police officers by the pier. A police truck with huge floodlights was parked at the end of the pier, the beams trained on the water. Two police motor boats were anchored not far off shore, one on the east side of the pier, the other on the west. Metro police diver Martin James Hunt was in one of the boats, a twenty-two-foot Boston Whaler. At 1:50 that morning, the balding, fifteen-year veteran of the force slid backwards over the edge of the boat into the darkened waters.

He began a pendulum search of the sandy bottom, starting at one side of the pier on the water's edge, swinging out around it in a semi-circle until he got to the other side. The first sweep was close to the pier. Kaknevicius had heard splashing but couldn't tell where it came from. A yellow nylon rope tied around Hunt's wrist acted as a guide, keeping him within the search radius. Sergeant Ed Riekstins from Metro police stood at the end of the dock and held the rope taut. Hunt had to go slow; he could only see a few feet, even with the powerful lights shining on the water. At the end of the first sweep, all he found was a pop bottle. Riekstins let the rope out one and a half metres, marked it with a string, and Hunt went back into the water.

A passerby noticed all the activity on the dock and walked over. One of the police officers went out to meet him.

"What's going on, officer?" asked the man, craning to get a look around the policeman, who was blocking his view.

"Could be nothing, sir," the officer replied. "Someone heard some screams near the dock. We're just checking it out."

"You mean someone drowned?"

"We don't know at this point. Apparently there were some screams, maybe for help. As I said, we're just checking."

"So you haven't found anything, yet?"

"Not yet, sir."

"There're some nasty undertows around here," the man said, as he started walking away. And then, as an afterthought, he added, "Well, good night."

"Good night, sir," the officer replied, nodding.

Hunt had about an hour's supply of oxygen in his tanks when he started his second sweep, this one about three metres from the dock. He didn't know exactly what he was looking for. One of the OPP officers had told him it could be more of Shen's body parts, or maybe even a murder weapon. He hoped it was hardware. Almost all his dives were for bodies, people who drowned in the frigid waters of Lake Ontario. Most of those bodies had been in the water for a long time when he found them. They were never intact. When the soggy corpses were pulled to the surface, the skin colour changed rapidly from blue to black to brown once they hit the air. It was revolting work, but whatever was in the water, he would find it. He was confident of that. The water might be murky, but the bottom was clean of debris, with a light layer of silt over the sand.

Hunt was coming to the end of the second sweep, on the opposite side of the pier. His knees hit bottom and he stood up. He looked over to the dock and shook his head. Half a dozen faces lined up on the edge of the pier looked back, and there was disappointment on each one. Hunt turned around, nodded to Riekstins, who let out another one and a half metres of rope, then he went back into the water and continued the search.

Many of the officers involved in the case had made their way down to the dock after hearing that Pan had thrown something into the water. Brian Kennedy, Gus Riddell, and Garnet Rombough were there from Larry Edgar's homicide team. Kent Bradbury and Jim McClelland, two officers from the Metro police Asian crime squad who had investigated Shen's disappearance when it was still a missing person case, joined them. Kaknevicius and the other members of the surveillance team, leader Nigel Tilley, John Moffatt, and Patti Rumley had stayed on, even though their shift was over. The fifth member of the team was staked outside Pan's house, watching just in case he decided to return to the pier. Even though it was late, the lights in Pan's house were still on. He was having a long conversation with Wang and Fang. Although they were speaking in Mandarin, wiretap specialist Stuart McDonald, who was listening in from OPP headquarters, said that Pan was doing most of the talking.

"What the hell about, I wonder?" Riddell asked Kennedy, who just shrugged back.

The one person who wanted to be there the most, but couldn't make it, was the man in charge of the case, Detective Larry Edgar. He had organized a family reunion for that day, and although he wanted to leave and join his investigators at the dock, they persuaded him to stay home and enjoy his night off.

Hunt was in the middle of the eighth sweep, and was about twelve metres from the dock, diving in about three metres of water, when the yellow rope in Riekstins' hand stopped moving.

"I think he's found something," Riekstins announced to the others on the dock.

They crowded around him, peering into the darkness, their eyes following the yellow cord that disappeared into the water. The line went slack.

"He's coming up," said Riekstins.

The searchlights were aimed at the spot where the yellow cord snaked into the water. There was a flurry of bubbles on the surface. For a long moment no one spoke. The only sound was the gentle lapping of the waves on the shore. Everyone was at the end of the pier, jammed close together, trying to get a better look at the illuminated spot on the lake where the water looked like it was boiling over from the diver's oxygen bubbles. And then something broke the surface.

CHAPTER TEN

Trial by Media

"Let me get this straight," the television reporter said to Donovan. "The cops haven't accused this guy of killing her, right? So why is he holding a press conference to say he's innocent?"

Donovan shrugged. He was staring at a corner table in the Chinatown restaurant where Rui-Wen Pan was sitting, surrounded by reporters jostling for position and television camera operators setting up their equipment. The floor around the table was thick with black cables, and a knot of microphones was on the table in front of Pan. Pan squinted every time a television light was flicked on in a test, but otherwise he stared impassively ahead, occasionally turning to whisper something to his constant companions, Wang and Fang. Behind them, a waiter set up several bamboo screens to give the lunchtime diners in the second-floor restaurant some privacy.

"So tell me, what's this all about?" the television reporter asked again. "Why is this guy calling a press conference?"

"Apparently the Chinese media has really gone overboard on this murder. They're writing stories saying this guy, Shen's boyfriend, is crazy. Saying he killed her. Guess he wants to tell his side."

Pan stood up and tapped a fork on a water glass. "Everybody listen, please."

But the reporters were still pouring in. Some of the camera operators were fussing over their equipment. "Hang on a second. We're not ready," one of them yelled. Pan stopped, took a drink of water, arranged the papers in front of him, adjusted his glasses, then started again.

"I am Selina's boyfriend," he declared loudly. "As you all know, recently there have been many newspaper reports about Selina's death and her boyfriend. To my knowledge, I can say here today that eighty percent of the reports is not truth or fact."

Pan paused, shielding his eyes as lights were turned on while he was speaking. "Sorry, I told you before. Please don't take pictures. I hope my privacy can be respected. Don't print my names on the papers or put my pictures on the television because I have to live in Toronto. I have endured enough personal attacks already."

Some of the reporters started to argue, but Pan sat down and refused to speak until everyone agreed that his name and his picture were not to be used. After several minutes of heated discussion, the photographers and camera operators agreed they would shoot only from behind or would block out Pan's face. Satisfied, Pan continued.

"Before I start, I have to say any rush speculation will only make things more complicated. I feel myself pushed to a public trial. Somebody has already imposed a trial by media on me. It's very unfair."

"Are you a mental-disorder person?" one of the Chinese reporters yelled out.

Pan scowled at her. "No! No! That is wrong. A mental-disorder person in this country would be sent to the mental institution because he is dangerous to other people. But I would like to clarify today that I am not a mental-disorder person, never in China or in Canada. I must clarify second thing. I have never been a surgeon, neither in China nor in Canada. Another thing I would like to clarify is that I never studied medicine in Canada before, not in Montreal nor in Toronto."

"But did you study medicine in China?" another reporter asked.

"Yes."

"What medical faculty?"

"I won't answer your question," Pan said, then went on to explain there were many types of doctors, including pediatricians, gynecologists, massage therapists, acupuncturists, and Chinese medical doctors. "During the Cultural Revolution in China, a barefoot doctor could also be called a doctor even though he hadn't studied medicine before. Once I studied medicine in China, but I wasn't a surgeon."

Pron came into the restaurant, two cameras around his neck. The back of his shirt was soaked with perspiration. He took out a handkerchief and mopped his brow as he got up on a chair, wobbling slightly, almost falling over as he positioned himself so he was facing Pan. He looked over at Donovan, grinned sheepishly, then banged off a few shots, getting down uneasily from the chair when he was done. Then he left.

A reporter from one of the five Chinese dailies in Toronto got Pan's attention and asked if he had been questioned by the police.

"I have never been summoned by the police before. Also I have never gone to any police stations."

The reporter persisted. "Have you talked to the police over the phone?" he asked.

"Naturally. The police have to know about the situation They want to know something about Selina before her death."

One of the reporters held up a clipping from the Toronto *Star*. "What about bitter argument?" she asked.

"I have legal proof that I had no argument with Selina."

The same reporter held up a recent edition of the *Star*, pointing to a large headline that read: VICTIM THREATENED TO EXPOSE IMMIGRATION SCAM, FRIENDS SAY.

"I was very surprised how the *Star* had got this information. Only the police knew she was the target of blackmail.

123

Not only was Selina the target of blackmail, I was also frightened."

Pan told the gathering he had received many threatening telephone calls. He said he gave taped conversations of the threats to the OPP.

Several reporters complained that Pan was being too evasive. Pan threw up his arms, stood up, turned away from the table, then wheeled back to face the reporters.

"I have talked a lot today. Perhaps the real killer is laughing and saying, 'Look, you have a scapegoat here.' The thing is, we have a lot of clues now. The police have told me the information I provide to them is very useful."

"Mr. Pan, if you really loved Selina," came another question, "why didn't you marry her and let her automatically be an immigrant so that no one could threaten her?"

"There are a lot of rumours saying that I used Selina by not marrying her. I had asked Selina to marry me in front of her mother." Pan looked down as he shuffled some papers. "I'm sure most of you know that Selina had many boyfriends before. I don't mind her past. I only wanted to marry her, let her change from wrong to right and start a new life."

A television reporter turned to Donovan and quipped: "Who is this guy? Does he work for the Salvation Army?"

"If you asked Selina to marry you," a reporter called out, "why didn't she agree?"

"Good question. In daily life people have unhappy things more than happy ones. Of course, there were reasons why Selina didn't want to marry me but I don't want to disclose them now. I sacrificed much for her, a lot of my friends left me. I had to bear many pressures. Now, this slander has damaged me. I have to eat crow for her."

Pan passed out slips of paper to the reporters. Donovan grabbed one. On the paper were three lines of neat Chinese printing. Pan translated. It was an excerpt of a letter Selina wrote to her mother, saying she would not marry him, but that everything was all right. Pan refused to say where he got the letter.

The questions turned to his relationship with Selina. Pan said he had met her through her sister and recalled what the sister had said about Selina that day.

"I request all of you don't print this in your paper. But she said, 'Whenever Selina meets a guy in the street, after talking to the guy for a short while, she will go home with him.' My response was to ask what the difference was between Selina and a prostitute."

"You seem to know about the killer. Is he one of Selina's boyfriends?" was another question.

"I don't know now," Pan replied. "Perhaps yes, perhaps no." Then he went on to explain that just before Selina left him, she didn't come home for several nights and refused to say where she had been.

Since Pan seemed to know so much about the mystery killer, was he getting police protection?

"Let him do harm to me," Pan replied, adding that he had been threatened as recently as the day before. "If he kills me everything is clear. Ever since I get involved with the Chinese democratic movement I don't regard my life as that important. Selina's death to me means the end. I lost interest towards everything. I lost hope."

Pan took off his glasses, wiped some sweat from his brow, and took a drink of water before continuing.

A reporter wanted to know if Pan had any clues that would help police find the killer.

"Yes, but please don't print it in your paper because I don't want to alert the real suspect. Bear in mind that this guy is a real mental-disorder person."

Pan said he only talked to Selina once after she moved out. "She called me at eleven P.M. I tried to keep her talking but she hung up the phone very fast."

He was asked if he had searched for Selina after she vanished.

Pan replied that he immediately told Selina's sister, Sophie, to notify the police. But the sister said she was too busy and it was none of her business. "Frankly speaking, there is no love between Selina and her sister. Her sister and her mother

125

have to bear a lot of the responsibility for what happened. They have to be blamed."

A huffing Nick Pron walked into the restaurant again, stopping in the doorway. His shirt-tail was sticking out of his waistband. His face was flushed. Donovan walked over.

"I'm getting too old for this shit," Pron said, wiping the sweat from his forehead with the back of his hand. "You're younger. How come I get stuck looking for the car?"

Donovan was smiling. "You volunteered. I take it you haven't found it yet."

"How do we know he drove here? Maybe he took a cab. What if he walked over? What if he lives in the building? For all I know, I'm killing myself for nothing."

"Just keep looking. The car's there. It's good exercise. Shouldn't be that hard to spot. How many blue Chevettes can there be with a missing front grill and a cracked windshield?"

Earlier that day, they had gone to the provincial licence bureau to see if they could get Pan's home address from his licence plate number, copied down during last night's chase. But the registered address was for Pan's Gerrard Street shop, not his home. They had decided to follow Pan again. They got to the press conference early and waited outside to see where Pan parked his car. But Pan, Wang, and Fang appeared suddenly around a corner and walked into the second-floor restaurant. They weren't sure if that meant he lived close by and had walked over, or if he couldn't find a spot in the always busy Chinatown and had parked several blocks away. Donovan and Pron needed to park their car close to Pan's or risk losing him in the maze of side streets in Chinatown. Pron said he'd find the car. But an hour after the conference started, he was still looking for it. And getting angrier by the minute. He grabbed a glass of water off a table and gulped it down.

"How's it going in here?" he asked.

"Think it's winding down. You got almost another hour to find it."

"I'll be dead in an hour," Pron replied, still puffing.

"I'm half your age. Let me go out and look. You're no good to me if you get a heart attack."

"Thanks for your concern. I have to keep going. You wouldn't know what streets I've checked." Pron glanced over at Pan, who was standing up, waving a piece of paper at the throng of reporters. "Looks like our man is a tad upset. I better get going."

The restaurant was on Dundas Street, and Pron had checked both sides for about five blocks in either direction. He had also walked up each side street on the north side of Dundas without any luck. There was still the south side to do. He went to a store, bought a can of Coke, and found some shade at the side of the building. He had just popped open the lid when a cameraman he knew came out of the restaurant, carrying his gear.

"Is it over?" Pron yelled at the balding man.

"Just about," was the reply.

"Great."

Pron guzzled the Coke as he started walking towards the first street south of Dundas. Cars were tightly parked on both sides of the street. Most of them were compacts. Pron checked his watch and started going from car to car.

Inside the restaurant some of the camera operators were putting away their gear as an animated Pan told the reporters how a Hong Kong newspaper's account of the murder had infuriated him.

"My friends and relatives read the story. According to the paper, the police arrested me, put me into custody, and then I disappeared. The report had done great damage to my family and on my own reputation." Pan patted down his hair. "My father had a heart operation last year and now he is very sick because of this."

A reporter for the *World Journal* asked Pan if he was going to sue any of the newspapers. Pan said yes, two of the Chinese papers. "They destroyed all my life, all my future, that's why I will law suit them."

Donovan stepped into the throng of reporters. "How come you never talk about how sad you are?" he asked.

"Beg your pardon?"

"You don't seem that sad."

"You go ask OPP."

"I'm not asking the OPP. I'm asking you."

"Many days have passed and my tears are dry. I cannot cry every time somebody says I should cry."

"I saw you less than forty-eight hours after you heard the news." Donovan moved closer to Pan.

"Beg your pardon?"

"I saw you less than forty-eight hours after you heard the news Selina was dead."

"Yes?"

"At that time you had no tears."

"No, that's not the truth. Even when she disappeared I just feel terrible." Pan's eyes stayed on Donovan. "I think now maybe she just ran away without leaving a note because she knew what was going to happen to her and she didn't want something bad to happen to me."

Pan started talking in Chinese. James Lin, a reporter with the *Sing Tao Daily*, translated for Donovan.

"He says somebody put a yellow paper with Chinese writing on the door of a house belonging to the man Pan believed was the suspect. He says the piece of paper is a spell that a person uses to drive the devil away if they know they've done something bad. He says he went to the house after Selina disappeared because he suspected Selina was there. The first day he went the spell wasn't there. The light was on but nobody answered the door. The next time he went, the spell was on the door."

The press conference was breaking up. Most of the camera operators were gone, and the few remaining reporters had formed a tight circle around Pan, drilling him with more questions.

Donovan walked to the door and looked out. It was rush hour. The long lines of cars on Dundas Street were moving slowly. A reporter from the Toronto *Sun* was watching him. He came over.

"Where did Pron disappear to?" the *Sun* reporter asked suspiciously.

"I was just wondering that myself," Donovan replied, glancing at the door just as a tired-looking but smiling Nick Pron walked in. He gave Donovan the thumbs-up sign, silently mouthing the words "Found it," as he walked past Donovan and the *Sun* reporter and over to Pan. Pron shook hands with Pan, nodded at Wang and Fang, then sat down and talked to them for a few minutes.

Donovan was waiting for him by the cash register when he finished.

"What lies did your buddy tell you this time?" he asked as they left the restaurant.

"He's really mad at you. What the hell did you ask him?"

"I hit him with the hard questions. I'm really getting sick of his bullshit."

"I had to apologize for you."

"You did what!"

"He was ready to go to the publisher and complain."

"Let him. I've got nothing to be afraid of."

Pron smiled. "You don't have to worry. I took care of it. Aren't you playing this bad-guy routine just a little too hard?"

"I don't believe in sucking up to killers."

"Somebody has to talk to him. And I still don't think he did it. I've seen nothing yet to convince me that he's the killer."

Pan's Chevette was parked on Grange Avenue, a side street two blocks south of Dundas. Pron had parked his car about a block in front of Pan's.

"You should have parked behind him," Donovan said as they got into Pron's car.

"I kill myself running up and down these streets pretending I'm a track star and all you can do is criticize me? Thanks a lot."

"What if he turns and goes the other way?"

"It's a one-way street, you bonehead. Don't you think I checked? Give me some credit."

"So what now?"

"We sit here and wait. He shouldn't be that long."

Nearly an hour later, Pan, Wang, and Fang, carrying armfuls of take-out food, arrived at the car. Pron and Donovan ducked low in the front seat as Pan's car drove by. Pron waited until a few cars passed, then pulled out of the parking spot.

Pan went west on Grange Avenue, driving slowly towards Spadina Avenue. One block, then two went by.

"Looks like nobody's on him," Pron said, speeding up a little.

A block from Spadina, a brown Corsica pulled away from the curb, cutting in front of Pron, forcing him to jam on the brakes. The two reporters lurched forward. Neither had on his seat belt. There was no way around the Corsica on the narrow street. Pron pounded on the horn.

"What's that about nobody being on him?" Donovan said. "Looks like the official car of today's chase is Chevrolet."

The driver of the Chevy was bald, just a few wisps of hair above the ears. Pron leaned out the window and yelled at him to speed up, but he kept driving slowly. Pan was nearing Spadina, signalling left.

"He's getting away," Pron shouted. "They've suckered us again."

Pron jammed on the brakes, put the car into reverse, backed up to the first side street, and headed down it. It was a one-way street, and Pron was going the wrong way. An oncoming van squealed to a stop a few feet from Pron's front bumper. The driver leaned out the window.

"You asshole! Watch where you're going!" he yelled.

"Hey, fuck you, asshole!" Pron yelled back. He turned the steering wheel sharply to the right and drove up the curb onto the boulevard, crashing through several garbage cans, sending them flying in the air, their contents spewing out. As they went around the van, Donovan reached up for the seat belt and snapped it on.

A car behind the van pulled to one side as Pron went roaring by. He turned right at the first street, which went west to Spadina, where he hoped to meet up with Pan.

"Watch out!" Donovan yelled.

A car had turned out of a laneway farther up and was coming towards them the right way on the one-way street. There was only enough room for one car. Pron wasn't stopping. The other motorist did, backing up the same way he had come, just in time to avoid being hit. When they got to Spadina, Donovan pointed frantically.

"I don't believe it," he shouted. "There he is!"

Pan's car was heading south towards Queen Street. Pron turned onto Spadina, keeping several car lengths behind Pan's Chevette. At Queen Street, Pan turned right. Pron followed, keeping his distance.

"This is easy, Donovan. I don't know how you lost him the last time."

They sailed along for several city blocks, keeping well back of Pan, until they got to Bathurst Street. Pan's car was the only one that got through the intersection before a streetcar went into a slow, ambling turn in front of them, making a horrible grinding noise. Pron hit the brakes, stopping inches away from the streetcar. He flung open his door.

"We're gonna lose him again," yelled Donovan.

"Fuck this," Pron yelled, jumping out. "You drive."

Donovan slid behind the wheel as Pron lumbered off, his long legs pumping like a fullback heading for the end zone. He ran around the streetcar and through the intersection, dodging several oncoming cars, banging his leg into the side of one car that had stopped at the last second to avoid hitting him.

"Hey, watch it, buddy!" the driver screamed, shaking an angry fist.

Horns blared at Donovan but he wasn't going anywhere. He folded his arms over the steering wheel, dropped his head down, shoulders shaking with laughter.

Farther up the street, Pron was still running flat out. He had to slow down when he came to a crowd of people gathered around a musician playing a lively tune on a saxophone. Pron elbowed his way through them. He bumped into a short, paunchy man who swung around and punched him in the shoulder. Pron kept running, weaving through pedestrians, for three more blocks. But he was getting tired. Pan's car had stopped at a street light. Pron got close enough to see Pan turn around, gesticulating at Fang, who was sitting in the back seat. But then the light changed and the Chevette sped off.

Out of wind, Pron stopped and watched it go. He slumped against the side of a variety store to catch his breath. There was a bike near the front door. He hesitated for about a second, then he grabbed it, hopped on, and headed off after Pan. The bike was too small, and his knees kept bumping into his elbows as he pedalled furiously along Queen Street. Just when he caught sight of the car, it turned right and vanished.

The car had turned down the second street past a park. Pron took a shortcut diagonally across the grassy field. He raced past a couple of men in lumber jackets who were lying on the ground, eating their dinner. One of them held up a can of beans in a mock salute. Pron exited the park and went down a back lane that ended at a residential street. Straight ahead a blue car was parked in a driveway. The hatchback was up. A man reached in for some boxes, then turned and walked towards the house.

Donovan was cruising slowly west along Queen Street when he saw a big man coming towards him wheeling a kid's bike along the sidewalk. Donovan pulled over, rolled down the passenger window.

"You don't look so good, guy," he said.

Pron just shook his head and grunted. His breath was coming in ragged gasps. Strands of hair were plastered to his forehead. He was limping slightly, favouring his right knee. There were grease stains on his pant legs.

"Can I say it?" Donovan asked. "This is easy. I don't know how you lost him last time."

Pron kept walking, ignoring the gibes.

"As for the bike, I understand. But will a jury?"

"That's it," Pron said, "just keep digging yourself deeper."

"Don't worry. We'll get his address. I'll check property tax records tomorrow."

"Do what you like, but I won't be there to help you."

"Why? You giving up?"

"No. I'll be a little busy."

"Oh?"

"I'll be staking out Pan's house. I found it."

Larry Edgar was furious. He had heard, through other witnesses, that Mrs. Chan was rethinking the statement she gave to homicide investigators about Selina Shen's reaction to the letter from Pan. Edgar sent Bradbury and McClelland to talk to the seamstress and find out what the hell was going on.

The Scotch Tape Gang reported back that Mrs. Chan had indeed changed her mind. She now seemed uncertain of Selina's reaction to Pan's letter. More than likely, said Bradbury and McClelland, a recent visit from Pan and Peter Wang had something to do with it. And that's what made Edgar so mad. While Pan was holding press conferences in Chinatown and telling the world his civil rights were being taken away, he was going around and harassing Crown witnesses in a murder case. Pan even got Mrs. Chan to sign a statement saying that Selina showed no reaction after reading the letter. The last person, other than the killer, to see Selina alive was now so confused that nothing she said about Selina's visit the Saturday she disappeared seemed to make any sense. And if all that weren't bad enough, Bradbury and McClelland said, those two *Star* reporters had been nosing around Mrs. Chan's house and would probably try to talk to her, and perhaps frighten and confuse her even more.

Edgar absent-mindedly twisted the CIB signet ring around his finger, something he did whenever he was nervous. There was not much he could do about the two reporters. It was a free country, and they could talk to whomever they wanted. And that's just what they had been doing. The tap on Pan's phone had picked up several of their conversations with him. It wasn't just the *Star* that Pan had talked to. He had also gone to the *Sun* and the *Globe and Mail*. He was worse than a damned politician at election time.

It was clear Edgar would have to do something to stop Pan from bothering Mrs. Chan, and other potential witnesses in the case. The time had come to quit pussyfooting around with him. Pan had been telling anyone who would listen that he was unfairly suspected of murdering his ex-girlfriend. It was time for the police to pay him a little visit and make it quite clear that he was indeed under suspicion, and that if he continued to talk to other witnesses it would not look good for him. In fact, Pan was a damned fine suspect. He had a good motive, the best there is — jealousy.

133

Michael Norton's report had made that quite clear. Pan had made all kinds of disparaging remarks about Fisher, and it seemed to Norton that he was very jealous of the man. He had pointed to the kitchen during the interview, saying to Norton that's where Robert Fisher and Selina had stood, as if the image was burned in his brain. But Pan denied there was any jealousy. He had told Norton that since his relationship with Selina was over, how could he be jealous? But a letter Pan had written to Selina a week after she moved out showed he still loved her and wanted her back. It was a love letter, dated February 13. Investigators had found it in Selina's room. Pan had stayed up late writing it, noting the time at the end: 4:40 in the morning.

"I miss you very much," it began, "every single minute. Have not seen you for several days—seems like ages. I have reserved the best table at your favourite restaurant for Saturday night. On Tuesday, your call came. I knew there was something going on. In life you cannot keep doing what you are doing, otherwise you will be a failure and a weakling. You have not solved your problem—your identity. You have no cars and no houses. You have to sleep with a lot of men to get all that.

"Don't give up hard work. We learn from mistakes. I hope separation can be peaceful. It remains a scar on our heart if we cannot control or decide our fate. We've been living together for three years. We met in the most difficult time. My feeling to you runs from pity to love. Life is cruel and you have sacrificed a lot. Why is life so unfair to you? You need someone who really loves you—takes care of you. I am not a perfect man. In three years we spent one thousand nights and days together. I can only relive my pleasure making love to you. When we were good—we loved to death. I don't care of the future. I won't forget the good times we had together. I will remember the love and the happiness.

"Tomorrow will be Valentine's day. Let's have dinner and just look at each other—forget worrying and suffering. I am ambitious and career-minded person. I am quite established now, so I have decided to take a break and enjoy life. 1988 will be a big breakthrough year. When I get my passport, I will travel, expand my businesses. You will perform at Seneca tonight. You have good potential — work hard at it. You are professional musician. We only live once — life is too short. I feel better after writing to you. Let me kiss you a million times, love you a million times.''

It was a passionate plea for Selina to return, thought Edgar. Pan still wanted her, and Fisher was threatening to take her away. Was the jealousy enough to make him kill? Perhaps the other letter, the one Selina had read the day she disappeared, would answer that question. He would have to try to get it.

CHAPTER ELEVEN

Clues and Alibis

The window was stuck. Detective Brian Kennedy leaned over the desk and jiggled it from side to side until it slammed shut, muffling the traffic noise from nearby Queen Street.

"There, Mr. Pan," he said. "We should be able to hear ourselves a little better now."

Kennedy and his partner, Gus Riddell, had gone to Rui-Wen Pan's house to talk about the murder. Although there were several room probes in the house, the ones in Pan's bedroom had been working the best. Edgar, who was listening in on the conversation, had told them to try to interview him in his bedroom.

Kennedy pulled up a chair. He was on one side of Pan, Riddell on the other. Pan was sitting on the edge of his bed.

"So you were saying, Mr. Pan," Kennedy continued, "something about your relatives coming to visit you?"

"Yes, they come soon," he replied.

"It'll be nice to have some family here, especially at a time like this, Mr. Pan," said Riddell, smiling. "It must be really tough. I mean, how does it make you feel that Selina's dead?"

"Of course, upset," Pan replied, brushing a lock of hair from his forehead.

"Oh, so you didn't throw her out?" asked Kennedy. "We thought —"

"No." It was emphatic.

"How did you feel about your relationship? Was it a good one, or was it rocky?"

"Very hard to say. First year we had the best time. She did everything and work hard and study hard perfectly. Because she knows that she did something terrible and she really want to correct it and start with her new life."

Kennedy shot Riddell a glance. "Oh," he said. "So you didn't fight at all then?"

"No, if I can use one word it was *perfect*. But since her mother came here the end of last year, everything totally change."

"Okay. So did you start to have arguments then, like most couples have arguments?"

"No. We have several arguments but it was useless. We could not resolve the problem. Maybe I said, 'Okay, we should marry each other.' After we have family, have children, maybe everything settle down. But she refused."

"Did you love her?"

"In the beginning, to be honest, I didn't love her at all."

Riddell edged his chair closer to Pan. "Oh, you didn't?" he asked.

"No, I didn't love her at all, but there was no choice for me. During that time she says, 'I know I'm a dirty girl, I'm not pure, I'm the worst girl in all the world. But since I told you this I feel much better.' So after that my feelings go from pity to love."

"Do you think she loved you?" Kennedy asked.

"I think so, but just in the beginning. Our relationship, the best times, were destroyed by her mother and her sister."

"What do you mean by this 'worst girl in the world' business?"

"Well, even this morning someone just called me and we discussed her whoring. Like every time when she went out she never let me know where she went."

"What, you mean she would bring friends in?"

"No," Pan replied, jabbing a finger in the air, "she never introduced her friends to me. Some days, somebody would drive a car to our place and pick her up and I would say,

137

'Why didn't you invite them in for a cup of tea?' But she would never."

"That's strange, isn't it," said Kennedy. "I'd find that a little disheartening if my wife did that and didn't introduce me to her friends."

"Yeah, that's why —"

"Yeah, I can imagine that kind of hurt a bit," said Riddell.

"I mean last New Year's for example. We were supposed to go to a party. I was waiting for her till late in the evening but she never came back till seven o'clock in the morning."

"Excuse me, Mr. Pan," Kennedy said, tapping his right ear. "This is embarrassing but I've got this problem with this ear and you're such a soft-spoken man. I wonder if you could just speak up a little louder."

"Oh, yes," Pan said apologetically. "Very sorry I speak low. It's just that I . . . I don't feel so well. I haven't been able to eat or sleep. I'm sorry."

"That's okay, Mr. Pan," Riddell said, patting him on the shoulder. "You're doing just fine."

"Now, Mr. Pan," Kennedy started. "Some of our questions may seem a little bit pointed but you must understand we need the answers to help us solve the case. You and Selina lived together for three yeras. Did you have any children?"

"No, but she has a child. A daughter. Maybe four or five years old now. Father is a black guy. She knew him for six months. She didn't even know his name but she went to bed with him. This was before I knew her. I can't believe this."

"Women are hard to understand," Kennedy said, with a wry smile. "They can sure turn a man inside out at times. I know."

"Like another time, she only saw this guy, Taiwan soldier, she just saw him once on a streetcar and they went to bed together. This is, I mean, this . . . is, this is like a prostitute."

"Okay, did she like to sleep with a lot of other men? I know that's a pretty pointed question."

"Yeah, I think so." Pan folded his arms across his chest and gave the detectives a knowing nod. "But I don't really understand why. I mean, I try to figure out the purpose. I wonder, does she sleep with them for money?"

"Some women just like to sleep with a lot of men," Kennedy noted. "They need to fulfil themselves or something."

"That must be her problem. I don't understand why she has to sleep with them."

"I know," Riddell said, nodding. "I know."

Kennedy paused before asking the next question. He glanced at the bed. "Did you and Selina have a normal sex life?" he asked. "Were you content, or did that cause any problems?"

"There was no problem."

"Did she ever express that she felt there was a problem? Any inadequacies with either of you?"

"No. But in recent times I got a new store. And I was really busy. And so I thought that even though I was working hard and was tired, I told Selina we could go to England or to Europe and go travelling. But she said, 'No, I don't want to go anywhere. I have something to do.' "

"Now, you've been telling us she'd been seeing other men in the past. But was she seeing any men while she was living with you?"

"Yes," Pan said, his voice dropping. "She had somebody she was involved with. Another guy. And I think I can give you some evidence very useful to help you with this."

"May we have his name?"

"I don't know his name. But I know his wife's name." He got up and went over to the desk, wrote something down on a piece of paper, and gave it to Kennedy. On it was the name Anna Leung Fisher, along with a telephone number.

"I can't tell you exactly, but this woman's husband," Pan said, sitting back on the bed, "I have a strong feeling about."

"We're open to anything," said Riddell. He and Kennedy already knew about the Fishers, but they wanted to see if Pan had any new information. "What do you know about this guy?"

"Well, Toronto Mayor Art Eggleton had a cocktail party at City Hall and that's where I met Miss Anna Leung. She is a young Chinese artist. So after I invited some people and her to our place. She brought her husband, a professor. I only talk to him three to five minutes. But Selina, she talk to him

139

almost all the night. Standing in the kitchen while everyone else was in the living room. This is just before she disappear."

"Well, this was your house," Kennedy said. "Your girlfriend. Did you say anything about it to him?"

"No, I just go in. Talk to him briefly about general things. Then two days later this professor called me around midnight, said thanks for the party but can I speak to Selina? She was sleeping but she came to the phone. They talk almost one hour."

"Was she impressed with him? Did she like him?"

Six kilometres away, in a soundproof room at OPP headquarters, Detective Inspector Edgar pressed the earphones closer to his head. The lines on his forehead deepened as he strained to hear Pan's answer. The technician seated beside him adjusted the sound board, then looked at Edgar, who nodded.

"I think she did like him," Pan said. "I think maybe she fool around with this guy. Next day when I was in my store this professor call my place again. I get a strange feeling from talking to him. He says that maybe he can help her, help Selina. But I was really mad. I said, 'Nobody can help her except herself.' He says, 'Maybe she has problems with her mind?' I said to him, don't call again."

"That's right, Mr. Pan," Riddell said, punching the air with a fist, "be tough."

"Well, then, several nights she never come back home. I ask her, 'Where were you last night?' She says, 'I was at my sister's place. Besides, it's none of your business.' But later, I ask her sister and she say, 'No, she wasn't at my place.' "

"So then what did you do?" Riddell asked.

"I went to see Miss Anna Leung, the professor's wife. I said I have some very important news. I told her that there is great shame about your husband and shame for me about Selina. And she is very sensitive and knows what I mean that her husband is with another woman. And then she starts crying. I told her that you should divorce this guy. That he's not good for you. She says she did everything for him and got nothing back. She says she feels cheated and that the same thing happened last year when her husband fool around with two Chinese ladies and another lady from the south."

"This professor," Riddell said with a smile, "he's quite the boy."

"Like he says to these women, 'I can help you study English and go to university.' Then he just fool around with them all the time."

"With Selina seeing this professor, did that hurt your relationship, make you jealous?" Kennedy asked.

"No. That's her problem. Not mine."

"Well, I can tell you're very upset. I really think you loved her very much."

"Let me just say that for three years there are many young girls I could have gone out with, but I always refused and I never go out with another girl. And she knew this." He crossed his legs, folded his arms, and turned to look out the window.

Riddell loosened his tie. "Getting a little warm in here."

"I could open window," Pan suggested

"No, that's all right," Kennedy said quickly, glaring at his partner, who smiled. "It's my ear, Mr. Pan. This darned ear. I have trouble hearing at times."

"To be quite honest with you," Riddell continued, "I'm finding this quite interesting about this professor. I guess it was not too long after she met him that she left you. Did she ever leave you before?"

"Yes, two times. Those times she left in front of me, went to stay with her sister, then called me and came back the next day. But this time it was different. She left and didn't come back." He paused. "I loved her. I tried to save her. The only thing she needed was love and somebody to protect her. In the past she did a lot of things that were very bad to me and she felt very bad because she did some cheating. I knew she was very weak and soft. But I still tried to help her. Sometimes she even tried to jump out of a window and kill herself. And still I try to help her. Because of her I lost all my friends. They said, 'Rui-Wen, you are living with a dirty garbage girl.' "

"So, I guess you were ashamed to be with her?" Kennedy asked.

Shaking his head, Pan replied: "No, I never feel shame. I tried my best for her . . . and she left me."

"I guess you weren't too bothered by her past?" Riddell said.

Pan's face softened. "There is a Chinese proverb," he said, his voice suddenly very calm. "When you marry dark, you have to marry dark for all of your life."

Kennedy moved his chair so that he was directly in front of Pan. "Mr. Pan, we're going to ask you some blunt questions right now. Did you ever feel you could kill Selina?"

"No. Never."

"Did you ever threaten to kill her?"

"No."

"Now, Mr. Pan, some men, if their women go out and screw around on them, they become very . . . upset."

"Yeah, I understand what you mean. Maybe in Western country this happen. But not with me. I was always ready to accept her. I knew what kind of person she was, and I just wanted to dedicate my life to save her."

Riddell flipped back a few pages in his notebook. "From our investigations," he said, "Selina was last seen on February 20, 1988. Is there anybody who can say they were with you around that time? A good friend? Somebody who could vouch for you?"

"Yeah, I have many. I was selling my house right after she disappeared. I can give you names of people who came those days to see my house. But you should look into these other people, like the Taiwanese army soldier. She told me this guy went into her bedroom, tried to rape her all night. There was another, an Italian, he came around the store all the time and bothered her. Asked her for a date, but she refused."

"These guys," Riddell said, "are they still in Toronto? Do you know their names?"

"I don't know."

"Does Selina have any pictures around that might have these people in them?"

"I don't have any so far. When I find out, I give you that," Pan said.

Kennedy stood up. "I want to make one thing very clear to you right now, Mr. Pan," he said, straightening his jacket. "You must be fully aware at this time that we are treating you as a suspect, as well as her other friends. We're going to have to look into you very deeply."

"Okay," Pan said. "No problem. I—"

"And we're going to look into your brother very deeply."

"Yeah."

"And while we're conducting our interviews, anybody else who comes to our attention, anyone who even looks slightly suspicious, we're going to do a very deep and thorough investigation into them."

"Okay, no problem. I understand."

"Anything that you've done in the last ten years, or while you've been in Canada, we're going to know about it."

"Okay, I understand."

"And we're not going to quit looking until we know exactly everything."

"I understand."

"Are you sure you understand?"

"Yes, of course I under—"

"So while we're doing this you're probably going to hear some rumours because we're going to be talking to people you know and these people are probably going to start some rumours. And these rumours are going to get back to you, you understand? Now we're not going to be telling people what we find out. So if the information gets out, it's because we've spoken to people and we can't stop these people from telling you all about that."

Pan shifted on the bed, rubbing a hand over his chin. "I understand. I understand."

"If I stand and talk to you today on the corner and people know I'm a policeman, it's going to be all over town by next week that you were talking to a policeman. But we are going to look very deep into everybody. So if you can supply us with somebody who's tangible, somebody who is a suspect, or who could be responsible for her death, we will look into them very deeply. Now what was the date you last saw Selina?"

"I think it was before she run away. It was early February, a Saturday, I think it was the first Saturday, the fifth or sixth of February."

"And you haven't seen her since the fifth or sixth?"

"That was the last day. But on a Tuesday or Wednesday after that, she called me."

"Who?"

"Selina called me. I spoke to her, and that was the last time."

"Did you ever speak to her after that?"

"No."

"Well, I'm going to go down and I'm going to have detectives go all around that area, okay?"

"Okay, not any problem."

"These investigators are going to speak to all the people down there, around your shop. And they're going to ask these people if anybody has seen you down there with her during the month of February. So what you're telling me is that February sixth is the last time you saw her?"

"Yeah. I swear."

"And she has never been with you since that time?"

"That's right. Even if you find anyone who says I was with her together after that day, I would take the legal responsibility."

"What you're saying is that you would take all the legal responsibility?"

"That's what I told you. You think that I am a liar?"

"Are you responsible for this? Have you killed her?"

"No. I told you no. She run away. If you find out anybody who saw me with her together after February, after she run away, that means I told you a lie, that means I am not an honest person. I take all the responsibility. I told you, that is the last time I saw her."

"Okay. If I have somebody, if one of my investigators comes up with somebody who saw you on, say, the fifteenth, that means everything you are telling me now is a lie."

"Yeah, that is right."

"So you understand what I am saying? Because if somebody says that they saw you with her between the sixth and twentieth, I am going to come down here, Mr. Pan, and I am going to arrest you for murder. And I am going to take you in. And I am going to question you. That is why I am making this very clear."

The phone rang. Pan picked it up, said a few words, then handed it to Kennedy. "It's for you."

It was Edgar. "That's enough," he said. "Get the hell out of there."

CHAPTER TWELVE

The Shadow Men

The scrubbing sound of bristle against pavement jerked Harvey Loxton out of that dreamy state that comes just before deep sleep. He opened his eyes wide then squeezed them tightly shut, creating a row of deep furrows in his forehead. With his thumb and middle finger, Loxton rubbed his eyelids, trying to coax them to stay open. He reached for the box of tissues on the front seat beside him, tore out three in rapid succession, and bunched them together in his calloused hands. Pinching one nostril shut, he blew the other one clear of mucous, repeated the procedure with the other nostril, then wadded the soggy tissues into a ball and threw it on the floor of the passenger side of his car, joining about ten of its cohorts on the rubber mat. Loxton rolled his head from side to side, massaging the nape of the neck as he followed the progress of the street sweeper as it passed his car, shooting water into the gutter, swooshing around the slushy mess of dirt, cigarette butts, chocolate bar wrappers, and other assorted road trash, before it all got sucked into the big yellow machine's cavernous bowels. Loxton shook a cigarette from his pack of Winstons and stuck it in the side of his mouth, not lighting it.

Loxton hated being the point man. It meant he couldn't go for a coffee, get something to eat, or even take a leak. Just hours of staring, which tonight meant watching a shabby, two-storey row house in Toronto's west end. There was a rule among the "shadow men" who did police surveillance work: never drop the eye on your target. If you did, if you just looked away or dozed for a few seconds, your target could take off, and you'd be "smoked." Loxton had to make sure that never happened. The six others on the surveillance team had the luxury of doing some free driving, holding to a general position nearby, waiting for the point man to radio that the target was on the move. Four team members "boxed the compass," each taking a quadrant around the object of the surveillance project. A fifth officer was the road boss, the one who ran the operation. Number six was the floater, always on hand in case someone got spotted by the target, burned. He was the note taker, the person who kept a running chronology of what happened in their twelve-hour shift.

Ordinarily, the surveillance officers took turns being the point man, switching off every two hours. But they were short this night because two were off with the flu, and Loxton, drowsy from some antihistamine pills, was well into his third hour as the eye. He was dying to light the cigarette, but under the strict rules of the shadow men he wasn't supposed to smoke because the red glow could give away his position. He rolled the cigarette back and forth over his bottom lip, tapped it on the dash several times, put it back in his mouth, took it out and tapped it again, then jammed it back in his mouth.

"Aww, fuck it!"

Loxton took out a match and lit it, inhaled deeply, and slumped in his seat as he slowly blew the smoke out his nose. He wasn't worried about being spotted. It looked as if everyone was asleep inside the house. It had been that way since Loxton parked his Chevrolet Corsica in the alley across from the house. The officer he'd replaced had been parked a block away, but Loxton didn't like staying that far back because he didn't trust his eyesight in the dark. He'd been smoked once following a bank robber, and he didn't want it to happen again. The road boss drove by along Shaw Street. Loxton's two-way radio crackled.

"Butt out" was the short, terse message.

Loxton took one last drag, sighed, and flicked the cigarette out the window. "Fuck you," Loxton muttered. He was getting tired of being a shadow man. His back was aching, he was hungry, he wanted to keep smoking, and he was desperate for a piss. There were times when it was real fun working for the squad. Like when they tailed bookmakers, for instance. Those guys were always on the move, forever darting in and out of buildings, always "spinning," or changing direction unexpectedly, stopping at phone booths for quick calls. That was fast-paced, exciting work.

Rui-Wen Pan, however, was boring. He didn't do much, just drove from his home to one of his stores or out to a restaurant, then back home. Loxton longed to get back on the streets, doing some real police work, like, for example, arresting people. This being a shadow man was a younger man's game, not for an old veteran with a weak bladder. After seven years of it, he was sick of skulking around, hiding in his car, watching people from darkened doorways or roofs of buildings, listening and following but never interfering. Maybe if he could just hassle somebody for a few minutes, stop a motorist and ask for his identification, making him squirm in front of the badge, he'd feel better. Or maybe he was just fed up with being a cop. Twenty-eight years of pounding a beat, rousting whores from fleabag motels, busting dope heads, and now following people around had added up. So what if he did have a stack of commendations in his file, it was the two failed marriages and the bad liver he would remember most when he finally retired.

"Two minutes, post five," his radio said. That was the road boss, telling him his replacement was in position, and he'd be free to go at 2:30 A.M. sharp. He noted the time in his memo book, flipped it shut, and snapped the elastic band around it. Just as he was pulling out of the lane, a fire truck went full tilt along Queen Street.

"All right, who got burned?" somebody quipped over the radio.

It was a standing joke with the shadow men. Even though Loxton had heard the line a million times he still smiled. He turned west onto Queen, nodding to the woman who shared the deserted street corner with him. She had stiletto heels, black mesh nylon stockings, a tight purple skirt, a bomber-style mink coat, and a sad look. Before this assignment was over, he was going to take that hooker out and buy her a drink. Prostitutes, like cops, worked lousy shifts and were always getting fucked by the public. She looked as bored with her work as he was with his. As he drove off, Loxton caught the flare of an approaching car's headlights in his rear-view mirror. The car slowed at the street corner. Maybe she'd make some money after all.

Loxton had driven several blocks when he noticed the same distinctive headlights in his mirror. The beam on the left was shooting higher than the right. He spotted an all-night pizzeria and parked in front. The car with the funny headlight pulled over to the curb about a block back. Loxton got out, went into the store, placed his order, used the washroom, then walked up to the lone clerk.

"I don't exist," Loxton told him, flashing his badge. He ducked out the back door.

The car with the funny headlights drove slowly past the pizzeria, made a U-turn, and parked on the other side of the street. There were two men inside.

The passenger went into the pizzeria.

"What happened to the guy who came in here?" he asked the clerk.

The clerk shrugged. "You want pizza?"

The man went outside, looked at the one driving, raised his arms in exasperation, then walked into the alley beside the pizzeria. It was pitch black. He walked tentatively into the darkness. Behind him, a man stepped from the shadows.

"Are you Mr. Pron or are you Mr. Donovan?" the man asked.

Donovan turned with a start.

"You didn't just shit your pants, did you, son?" Loxton asked, striking a match and lighting a cigarette.

The flickering light revealed droopy eyes underneath bushy brows joined in the middle. The nose was pushed in like a boxer's. The cheeks were pock-marked and crisscrossed with the tiny red lines of broken blood vessels. The tired face needed a shave.

"Ah, I'm Donovan."

"You fuckin' cocksuckers must think you're really shit hot, following me around, playing amateur private dicks. You know what kind of dick you are?" Loxton grabbed his crotch. "This kind of dick." He stepped closer to Donovan. "Just what the fuck do you think you're up to? Do you realize you're fucking around with a policeman? I could have you on charges right now. Get that fucking Jolly Green Giant partner of yours over here. I want him to hear this, too."

Donovan hurried into the street and waved Pron over. Loxton was sneering at Pron as he walked into the alley. He jabbed his finger at Pron's chest.

"Okay, Mr. Hot Shot, you wanna follow people around, get that fucking headlight of yours fixed." He turned towards Donovan. "And you, you slimy little runt, get that fucking taillight on your greaseball car fixed and stop running reds and driving up on curbs. You guys think you know about surveillance, you don't know shit about doing obs on somebody."

"We found you," Donovan said.

"That's 'cause I let you. Every time we fucking turn around, you guys are there with your noses up our ass. Do you realize you're fucking around with a homicide investigation?"

"We're just doing our job," Pron offered.

"Does your job include being a fucking asshole? If you guys keep doing your job this way, you're both gonna end up with a gunshot in the back of the head. When it comes to reporters, that's what I call dying of natural causes."

Loxton mashed his cigarette into the pavement. He lit another. "Just what are you fuckheads up to?"

Pron took out his cigarettes and patted his pockets for a light. After a moment's hesitation, Loxton handed over his matches.

"We're trying to find out if Pan's the killer," Pron said.

"Pan? Who the fuck is Pan? I've got a frying pan at home."

"Isn't he the guy you're following around?"

"Who says I'm following anybody around? I'm not following anybody. I'm being followed around by you two dickheads!"

"What about all those cop cars around here?"

"Cop cars? Cop cars have red lights on the roof. I don't see any fucking cop cars around here. There's gonna be a fucking ambulance around here if you two pussies don't go home."

"So why were you outside Pan's house all night?"

"I still don't know who this Pan guy is."

"That alley, you were parked in the alley across from his house for a long time."

"I was having a smoke, what business is that of yours?"

"Pretty long smoke," Donovan ventured.

"Maybe I was doing some of this." Loxton cupped his right hand and moved it rapidly up and down. "You two are gonna stick your nose into the wrong place and get it blown off. I got no time for this shit."

He walked out of the alley and into the pizzeria, paid for a slice, then headed for his car. Pron and Donovan followed him over.

"You guys deaf or something? Read my lips. Get the fuck out of here!!" He opened the door to get in.

"We ran your licence plate and —" Donovan started to say.

"You did what?" Loxton looked angrily at Donovan.

"We wanted to see who you were, so we checked your plate."

"You fuckheads. Don't you realize that I'm gonna get in shit if that gets back to my boss?"

"Well, I, ah . . . I didn't know."

"That's the trouble with you amateur dickheads. You're messing into things you don't know nothing about."

"We, ah, we know a lot about Pan. We talk to him all the time. I guess we were hoping you could tell us more."

"I can't tell you fuckers nothing. I'm even seen talking to you I could get fired."

"Maybe we could meet somewhere sometime and talk?"

Loxton took a bite of his pizza slice, got into the car, and closed the door. He started the engine. Pron and Donovan stood by the door, watching through the closed window as Loxton finished his dinner. Finally, he lowered the window.

"Look, give me a number. Maybe I'll call you. Then again, I probably won't."

CHAPTER THIRTEEN

Tribute to an Ill-Fated Lover

Rui-Wen Pan stood alone before the makeshift altar, head bowed, face buried in the palm of one hand. He glanced up at the picture pinned to the black curtain at the front of the high-school auditorium. It was an enlarged snapshot of a smiling Selina Shen, taken by him when they had vacationed on the west coast of Canada three years ago. On either side of the picture four vertical scrolls bearing Chinese funeral symbols hung from the ceiling to the floor. There could be no casket at this service. Selina's body parts were in cold storage at the city morgue.

Pan gazed at the picture for a moment, then bowed his head again. To his left, Peter Wang placed a circular wreath of yellow irises and gladioli on the floor to one side of the altar. A white banner with black Oriental script ran across the front of the wreath. Andrew Fang scurried up and down the auditorium stairs taking picture after picture with his thirty-five millimetre camera of the lone mourner who seemed oblivious to all that was going on around him.

Outside the auditorium people were arriving for the memorial service. But none ventured inside. They waited in the corridor, milling restlessly about near the main door, a few peering down at Pan standing alone in the pit of the sunken amphitheatre, like an abandoned child standing forlornly on some street corner. His silent, solitary tribute finished, he wiped a hand across his eyes, then turned to Wang and Fang waiting a respectful distance away. He nodded at them, and the trio left quickly by the side door.

As soon as they were gone, the mourners — former class-mates, teachers, Selina Shen's young students, and their parents — filed solemnly in, filling the auditorium. Pan's wreath was hastily moved away from the altar and hidden behind a loudspeaker. Four potted white daisies were put in its place. A beefy-faced man with a brush cut moved to the centre of the altar, tapped on the microphone, satisfied himself that it was working, and introduced himself as Wei Fu, the parent of one of Selina's students.

"Thank you for coming here today. This is a very sad time for all of us. We have lost a close friend, a beautiful person whose most unfortunate tragedy strikes to the bottom of our hearts." Wei Fu looked sideways and motioned for a young, man to turn on a video recorder hooked up to a large television monitor. "I would like to play a tape for you. After you have watched, I would ask you to stand for a moment of tribute."

It was an excerpt from Selina's last performance. She played some Mozart, then switched to a more lively Chinese arrangement. The upbeat melody seemed out of place in the darkened auditorium, amid the sobs of her friends. When it was over, Wei Fu stepped up to the microphone.

"To those of you who took classes with Selina here at Georges Vanier Secondary School, she was known as a tire-less worker. She gave of herself to teach the music that she loved. To all of us who knew her, she was a gentle soul whose tragedy is a great loss to the community. She came to Canada to build a good life, knowing that Canada, a country built by immigrants, would help her succeed. And she was succeed-ing, working, learning, becoming a good Canadian. There are many of you who called Selina friend, and I know you all did your best to find her when she was missing. I want to tell you something that you can all take comfort in. Selina was a Christian and believed, as good Christians do, that the soul is immortal. When Selina, up in heaven, finds out that her friends and colleagues did so much to find her, even though we failed to help her, her soul will be given a deep comfort.

I ask God to grant her eternal peace and console her family."
He paused a moment. "We all loved her dearly. May she rest
in peace."

Pron stood at the rear of the auditorium among the television cameras. He had arrived early, before the other reporters,
in time to speak with Pan. He had forgotten to charge the
batteries for his camera, and he worried the flash hadn't gone
off when he photographed Pan at the altar. But where the
hell was his partner? He looked towards the door just as
Donovan walked in. The next speaker was Keith Davies, principal of the Scarborough Christian School.

"We have lost, in the prime of her life, a woman who could
have done so much. The news that Selina was dead was
almost impossible for us to bear. When I first met Selina, I
was struck by the potential for great joy in her life. When I
heard she had been murdered, I wept in my room, alone, for
her sister in Canada and for the parents in China who have
lost so much." Davies took out a handkerchief and dabbed
at his eyes before continuing. "Though we have suffered so
much, we must all remember that life must go on. There will
be many inquiries, questions, and newspaper reports that we
will have to endure. Just remember, no matter what is said,
that we all knew nothing but good of Selina."

Davies lowered the microphone and a small girl, one of
Selina's students, brought a violin to the front and began to
play. Pron edged past the television crews and sat down
beside Donovan.

"What happened to you?"

Donovan grinned. "You'll never guess who called."

There was a full moon that night. Its light glittered off the
lake, turning the grass of the park a ghostly white. It was
nearly one o'clock. Pron and Donovan had been waiting for
two hours, their car parked against a line of wooden railroad
ties separating the small parking lot from the treeless, grassy
area.

"Are you sure he said Fourth Street?" an uneasy Pron
asked. "Maybe he said Fourteenth Street?"

Donovan said nothing.

"Maybe he meant the other end of Fourth Street?"

Donovan sighed. He picked up the next day's *Star* off the seat. Opening it to page sixteen, he read again the story they had written after the memorial. The headline read: FRIENDS MOURN MURDERED MUSICIAN. There was a three-column picture Pron had taken of Pan at the memorial service. Donovan folded the paper and tossed it into the back seat.

"He'll be here."

"You think he'll tell us anything?"

"He's not going to come all the way out here in the middle of the night to talk about his mortgage."

"Tell me again what he said on the phone."

"He didn't say much. Spent about a minute talking about how there was no way he could talk to us. Then he spent another minute saying we were both fuckheads and that we were interfering in a police investigation. Then he said that maybe, if we were down around the Fourth Street park tonight, he might show up."

"Maybe!" Pron said, his voice rising. "We've been waiting two hours on a maybe? You never said he told you maybe."

"Didn't I? Sorry."

Donovan elbowed Pron, nodding to a car's headlights coming towards them on Fourth Street. It headed into the parking lot, then onto the grass, made a U-turn, and stopped with the rear end of the car to the lake. The driver killed the lights. Nothing happened for several minutes. Then the flare of a match lit up the interior of the car, followed by the steady glow of a cigarette.

"That's got to be him," Donovan said. "Only a cop would be arrogant enough to drive into a park." He reached for the door handle. "Let's go. We're not going to do this by mental telepathy."

The moon had disappeared behind a cloud, leaving the lakefront park in darkness. Pron and Donovan walked slowly towards the black car, about thirty metres of open space away. As they got close, the driver lowered the window, took a long, last drag, and flicked the butt in their direction.

"Aren't you boys up past your bedtime?" Harvey Loxton said, exhaling. "Hope one of you guys got some smokes. I'm fresh out, and I don't feel like talking unless I've got another butt.''

Pron took out a pack and offered him one. Loxton lit it, took a few puffs, studied them, then glanced around the park.

"You fellows wouldn't be wired, would you?''

"No tape recorders, just notebooks. See,'' Donovan said, opening his trench coat, trying a smile.

Loxton glared at Donovan. "Listen, shithead, I carry around something a lot worse than your scribbler, so don't go fucking with me. Get in.''

For a few moments it was quiet in the car. Loxton puffed away on his cigarette, glancing from time to time in his rearview mirror at the two occupants of his back seat. Pron kept shifting his long legs, trying to get comfortable in the cramped space. Donovan dug around in his pockets, taking out a roll of wintergreen-flavoured candies. He flicked one free with his thumbnail. It fell out of his hands, bounced off his knee, hit the rubber floor mat, and went under the front seat. Donovan reached a hand down and started fishing around for the candy.

"What the fuck are you doing?'' Loxton had swung around.

"Ah, looking for something I dropped.'' Donovan sat up, looked at Pron, grinned sheepishly, and blushed. Pron stared straight ahead and said nothing. "I had this mint and, ah, it fell under the seat and . . . I —''

Loxton turned to Pron. "How do you work with this guy?''

"It's tough. Sometimes it's really, really tough.''

"You know, I read your stuff, and on some of it you're not far off. But then I see you fuckers in action and I wonder how you could tie your fucking shoelaces.''

"Look,'' Donovan began, ''all you do is shit all over us. Is that why you called, to take another shot? If that's what's going on'' — Donovan reached for the door handle — ''I'm leaving. I don't need some cop with a grade-eight education dumping all over me.''

"Take it easy. Get back in the car.'' Loxton smiled. It played over his face briefly, not a lot of humour behind it. Loxton took another cigarette from Pron, lit it, and let the smoke out slowly. "The first time I ran into you guys, I though you were the worst pricks in the world. But I've been thinking about it and what I've come to is this. If we don't tell you anything, you're just going to go out and find it on your own. Some of it will be wrong but you'll write it anyways. But whether it's right or wrong, we're the ones who are gonna end up looking like a horse's ass.

"You guys have been bang-on with some of what you've written. Everybody thinks you've got some kind of a mole in the force, somebody giving you the inside track. But you guys are such assholes that no cop in his right mind would talk to you."

"So why are you talking?" Pron asked.

"I'm not. You got that straight? I don't want to end up back in uniform pushing a patrol car."

Donovan leaned forward. "Why can't you just tell us if Pan is the chief suspect? Just one simple question."

"It's never just one question with you fucking reporters. If I answer one, it leads to another, and then another. There's no end. Look, I shouldn't even be here, but there's something about this murder that bugs me. I've seen a lot of murders. People get killed and, sure, it's bad, but there's nothing you can do about it so you just do your job. But this one has really bothered me for some reason."

Loxton reached into the side pocket of his windbreaker and pulled out a neatly folded page from the *Star*. It was a story Pron and Donovan had written about the murder, the one with the picture of Selina playing the violin, her shadow in the background.

"How could somebody take a loving, trusting woman like that, kill her, and cut her up into pieces?" Loxton said. "You know why this country's fucked up? We give a guy life and he doesn't get life. He's out in eight or ten years. The guy who did this to her, he should be put away forever. We need laws like in them Muslim countries. Over there, you steal and you get a hand cut off. Every week they line the thieves up, some big guy comes over with a sword and it's whomp whomp whomp. A dozen hands are gone. Sure, they still have crime over there, but at least people know that if you do something wrong you're gonna pay. Here, you commit a crime and they put you in a nice jail, feed you and clothe you, and in a few years you're out.''

''We didn't come here for a lecture on Arab crime,'' Donovan said. ''What can you tell us about Pan?''

''You guys should be doing some investigating,'' Loxton said.

Donovan slapped his hand on the car seat in disgust. ''This is investigating! Getting people like you to talk is investigating. This is Canada, not the United States. People don't just hand us official reports when we ask for them. Nobody has to tell us anything. I mean, we don't even know how they identified her body.''

''Why don't you just go ask the chief coroner?''

Donovan threw up his hands. His knuckles rapped against the roof. ''Exactly my point. We did go to the chief coroner. He told us to screw off. That's why we've got to be sneaky.''

''Why don't you just wait for the trial, if there ever is one?''

''Because we want it now,'' Pron said. ''People are really fascinated with this murder. For example, the forensic stuff is probably the most basic information but we can't even get that. If you can't tell us about Pan, then why can't you at least give us some of the forensics? I don't see how that could screw up the investigation.''

Loxton took some tissue from an inside pocket of his windbreaker and blew his nose. ''This damn cold,'' he said, balling up the tissue and throwing it on the floor. He motioned towards Pron. ''Gimme another smoke and let's talk about your friend, Mr. Pan. What have you fellas found out?''

''Why should we tell you what we know, when you won't tell us anything?'' asked Donovan.

''Let me ask you this,'' said Loxton. ''How closely have you checked Pan's background?''

''We've asked around,'' replied Donovan.

''But did you go to Montreal? Did you talk to his uncle?''

''Should we?''

''What you do is your own business.''

''I've got a question for you,'' said Donovan. ''Selina was last seen around Pape and Gerrard, near one of Pan's stores.''

"That's right."

"We know she probably wasn't seeing Pan because they had split up."

"A reasonable assumption."

"So who was she seeing?"

"All you reporters are the same. I answer one question, then it turns into another and another, and before I know it I'll say too much and they'll bust me back into uniform and stick me in some office adding up parking tickets. Let me put it this way, what did Selina do for a living?"

"She worked for Pan," replied Donovan.

"Okay, but what else?"

"She gave music lessons. What are you saying? She was giving a music lesson near Pan's store?"

"I didn't say that."

"But that's what you are getting at. How about giving us a hint as to where?"

"From what I hear, you guys have already been there."

"Of course," Pron said, snapping his finger, "the seamstress."

"You didn't get that from me," said Loxton.

CHAPTER FOURTEEN

Mystery Letter

The big blue truck lumbered to a stop in front of the grocery store. A teenager with a dopey look on his face reached into the rear of the truck for a bundle of newspapers, then tossed it towards the store. The papers landed with a thud against the door. The kid rapped twice on the side of the truck with his knuckles and the driver sped off. A sour-faced Pron watched it go.

"This is stupid, Donovan," he said, glancing across the street at the darkened seamstress's shop. They had been parked in front of it all night, waiting for first light before trying for an interview. It was not Pron's idea. "We could have gone home, got some sleep, and come back at a decent hour to talk to the woman. Why are we here now? Why do I keep letting you talk me into doing this? Staying up all night. I've got a wife and a family. And they're at home. And that's where I should be. At home. Home. H-O-M-E. But when I work with you on these stories, home becomes this stupid car. I think I've finally figured it out. I'm the one who's stupid."

The police scanner in Pron's car, silent for the past several hours, was coming to life. "Alarm bells ringing, 480 University," said the female police dispatcher. "Units 5204, 5208, 5214 attending. First unit on the scene please advise."

"What's your problem?" Donovan said, grabbing his mug from the dash. "We've got coffee, the prospect of a good interview, and now we've just had home delivery of the morning paper. I'll be right back."

He walked over to the store, bent down beside the bundle of that morning's *Star*, and, after glancing around, used the edge of his car keys to tear through the yellow plastic band around the bundle of papers. He picked up a paper, glanced at the front-page headlines as he fished through his pockets for loose change, threw some on the bundle, and wandered back to the car, stopping first at the seamstress's shop, which was still dark.

"Not long now," he said cheerfully to Pron as he got in. Pron grunted.

They read silently as more calls came over the scanner. A police officer reported that the call to University Avenue was a false alarm. A story tucked away at the back of the paper caught Pron's eye. It was a newswire story out of Beijing, the capital of China. The report said a "glimmer of democracy" had crept into the country's National People's Congress. For the first time in decades, dissenting views were argued in the glare of international media coverage, it said. A female delegate had started it off in a vote on membership in a legislative committee. She abstained from the vote and had the audacity to question the selection of the committee chairman, an election that was always rubber-stamped. A few minutes later, the story continued, a second delegate joined in the dissent, while television cameras raced to record the historic incident. Pron showed Donovan the story.

"Wonder what Pan would have to say about this?" he asked.

"Be his usual modest self," Donovan replied, after skimming through the story, "and try to take all the credit. Say it was his magazine that brought about the change."

The police scanner got noisier as dawn came. Along Gerrard the street lights were snapping off, traffic increasing. A police call went out for a violent domestic fight on College Street. Complainant was the ten-year-old daughter of the combatants. Another police call for an insecure door on Lansdowne. There was a person having a heart attack on St. Clair Avenue. A car ran into a pole on the southbound Don Valley

Parkway. Some gas was leaking at a house on the Lakeshore. Woman with slashed wrists on the Danforth. Diabetic in seizures on Seymour Avenue. And a naked woman running along Queen Street.

Pron quickly locked in the channel on that last call. The woman was in her thirties, the first policeman on the scene radioed, and she was running after a streetcar. A policeman, who said he was carrying a blanket, radioed that he was joining in the chase. The radio was silent for several moments, then a huffing police officer's voice came on the air. He was trying to sound sombre, but not having much success. He said he had caught the woman and wrapped her in the blanket. He said he was taking her home, to the Queen Street psychiatric hospital. Just then the lights went on in the seamstress's shop.

The faded green curtains that had been drawn tight across the shop's picture window parted slightly, revealing the face of an Oriental woman with droopy eyelids who looked to be in her late forties. It was the same woman who a few days earlier had been questioned by the investigators. The face was there for a moment, then disappeared. Pron and Donovan went over and banged on the glass door. The woman cautiously opened the door just a crack.

"What you want?" she asked suspiciously, craning her head upwards at the two strangers. She drew her robe tighter around her neck.

"Can we talk to you about Selina Shen?" Donovan asked, sliding a foot into the doorway.

The woman shrugged. "Who? Who is this Selina? I don't know Selina."

"Selina Shen," Donovan repeated, pushing slightly against the door. "She taught music to someone in your family. We want to talk to you about her."

"No talk," the woman said, pushing against the door, which stopped at Donovan's foot. "No talk to Selina. She gone."

Donovan eased the door inwards a bit. "We know Selina's gone," he said. "We want to talk to you about her. We want to ask you some questions."

The woman pushed on the door, but it didn't move. Donovan had his foot firmly wedged against it.

"Can we talk to you about Selina?" he repeated.

"Are you police?"

Pron took out his *Star* identification. It looked like a police badge, and when he showed it to her, she stared at it silently, somewhat confused, but said nothing.

"I already talk with police," the woman replied.

"Just a few more questions," said Donovan, "about Selina. We're doing our own investigation."

"Please, I know nothing," the woman said.

"You're Mrs. Chan, aren't you?" Donovan said, pushing the door a few inches. "Mrs. Eng Siew Chan?" They had looked up her name in the city directory. "We just want to —"

"Hey!" Pron suddenly shouted.

His arm shot out through the doorway, pointing at something inside the shop. The woman tilted her head, staring at Pron's outstretched arm, which was about a foot over her head. Her gaze travelled along his arm to what he was pointing at.

"That music stand over there," Pron said, barging past the startled woman, who scurried to get out of his way. He went into the shop and grabbed the stem of the silver stand and lifted it off the ground, brandishing it triumphantly in the air. "Selina's! Is this Selina's?"

The woman started yelling in Chinese and went hurriedly towards him, motioning frantically with her hands. She yanked the stand away from Pron and put it back on the floor.

"Go away," she said. "Leave, please. I told everything."

Pron rested his hand on the stand. "So Selina was teaching here," he said. "Just before she disappeared. You must have been the last person to see her alive. Other than the killer, that is. All her friends are cooperating with us. They want to find out who is this madman that did such a thing. Everyone is so upset. They've all helped us. You must, too."

"I scared," the woman said. "Not want to talk. Selina is gone. No one can help Selina now."

"The killer is still out there. What if her killer goes after someone else? How would you feel then?"

"Please go."

"We write stories," said Donovan. "Sometimes newspaper stories help police. Police like lots of publicity, you know, good for the investigation. Do you want her killer to go free?"

"I tell everything to police. Everything. Even about letter."

"Letter?" asked Pron, glancing at Donovan. "What letter?"

"Letter," she repeated.

"Letter to Selina, you mean?"

The woman looked down. "From him," she said.

"Who do you mean?" Donovan asked. "Pan?"

"Letter make trouble." The woman picked up a piece of cloth from one of the tables and twisted it nervously in her hands. "Now you two make trouble."

"Yes, we make trouble," Pron said, "and we're sorry. We don't mean to bother you. And we'll go right away. But first can you tell us more about this letter? Was it a love letter?"

"I can't say. I scared."

"Scared of who? Pan?"

"Yes. Pan."

"He was the one who wrote the letter?"

The woman looked down and shook her head.

Pron put a hand on her shoulder gently. "Was it Pan? Was he the one who wrote the letter?"

"Yes. Yes, it was Pan."

Donovan stepped forward. In an even gentler voice he said, "This letter, when did Selina get it?"

The woman's eyes were reddening. She wiped the corners with the cloth.

"Did Selina get this letter on that Saturday, the day she was giving the lesson?"

The woman nodded.

"Did you see the letter? Did you read it? Can you tell us what was in it?"

"Pan wrote letter."

"Yes, yes. You said that. But do you know what was in it?"

"He came in from his store. Gave me letter to give to Selina."

"On the last day she was seen, right?" Pron asked.

"Last day I saw Selina, Saturday. She came to give my son a lesson. I gave her letter. She read it. Read it again. Her face change."

"Changed? How?" asked Donovan.

"Unhappy. She read in a very quiet manner. Then she leave. No lunch, no talk, very short lesson." The woman dabbed at her eyes again.

"What was in the letter? What did it say?"

The woman shrugged.

"You didn't read it then?"

"Selina not show me. She take letter with her. Never see her again."

"Did you ever ask him what he said in that letter that got her so upset?"

"A few days later Pan came here. He told me Selina was missing. He didn't know where she was. He gave me another letter, tell me to give it to Selina." The woman rubbed her eyes again with the cloth. "But no Selina to give letter to."

"A second letter?" asked Pron. "Did you say there was a second letter?"

The woman didn't answer.

"This second letter, do you have it? Can we see it?"

"No. No. No more questions."

"Where's the letter, the second letter? It could help us find out why she disappeared."

"I give letter back to Pan. No more questions. Please go now. I don't want to be seen talking to you."

"Didn't you read it? Didn't you want to know what he said to her?"

"Just go." She pointed to the door. "Please." She walked over to it and held it open. "Please leave me alone."

The newsroom was nearly empty when they got to the office. Bob Burt, the assignment editor, was having a coffee and reading the morning papers. He liked their angle about the letters. Could they do the story for the next edition? It wasn't a request. The story was easy to write. It was above the fold in the first section. The headline read: SLAIN VIOLINIST GOT MYSTERY LETTER.

After they filed it, Burt waved them over to his desk. He congratulated them for doing a good job on the murder. The news desk was pleased with what they had uncovered. It was a nice little murder mystery. He really liked the way they had been beating the opposition, especially the *Sun*, the tabloid rival that was supposed to be the blood 'n' guts paper. Yes, he was quite happy with their work. But there was just one small problem.

They'd worked on the story together for more than a week, and that had left him in a bit of a bind. He was short of staff, and there were a lot of other things going on in Metro. Sure, it was a nice mystery. Good-looking victim, lots of intrigue, and plenty of gore. Is that true she might have been alive when she was cut up? he wondered. Why did the boyfriend want to keep telling the world he was innocent of something he had never even been charged with? He had to be guilty. If that was the case, how much more could they write on it? The police must be close to an arrest. Didn't they risk getting in the way of the investigation?

"Isn't that the whole point of doing this?" Donovan asked, facetiously.

"Now here's my problem," Burt began, his voice sounding tired. The Economic Summit was coming up, and the paper was going all out to have the best coverage. They were planning a special supplement. People had been pulled off their regular beats to help out. The annual meeting of the leaders from the top Western nations was going to be on the front pages for weeks. The *Star* would be going head-to-head with some of the best papers in the world. They did not want to get beaten on a scoop in their own backyard. Did the paper really need two senior reporters to cover a murder that was already getting to be old news? Could they not just keep tabs on it while they went on to other assignments? "Now don't get me wrong here, fellas," Burt stressed. "We're pleased with what you've done. You're really sticking it to the opposition. There're just other things out there to cover."

"I told you, Donovan," an angry Pron said as they walked away. "It's the same every time. I just knew this would happen. First they want us to get as much as we can on the murder, and then, just when we're getting somewhere, bang, they pull us off. They can't expect us to work this hard on something, then drop it. I know what's going to happen. I just know it. My first really important assignment, a 'must cover' event, will be an after-dinner speech for some fat politician."

"There's one thing to be thankful for," said Donovan.

"How's that?"

"If it were winter, you'd probably get stuck with a lesbian ice-skating party at City Hall. Look, nobody said we couldn't keep going."

"Yeah, great. On our own time."

"Well, what have we been doing up till now?"

"Donovan, I'm tired. How long we been going on this? Five, six days? Maybe we have done enough. I'm not going to write another word about it. They want me to drop it, I'll drop it. If the *Sun* beats us tomorrow, too bad. I don't care. I'm going home to bed."

It was dark when Pron awoke. He got out of bed quietly, trying not to disturb his wife. But as he moved towards the door, he stumbled on a hammer. His house renovations had been going on for what seemed like years, and there were tools everywhere. Limping to the stairwell, he cursed his home renovations, the *Star's* office renovations, renovations in general. Why had he ever moved out of his downtown Toronto penthouse into an endless nightmare of construction? He made his way to the darkened kitchen, bumping into a sawhorse set up next to the stove. He opened the fridge door, rummaged around for several minutes. Nothing caught his interest.

"Aw, to hell with it," he said, and got dressed. Before he left the house, he called Donovan and left a message on the answering machine. Pron figured Donovan was probably out with yet another woman.

Half an hour later, Pron was parked in front of a row house in the west end, eating a slice of pizza and listening to the police scanner. Around midnight, a blue Chevette with a missing front grill pulled into the driveway. Three men got out and started unloading boxes from the car, carting them into the house. They worked quickly, quietly in the shadows. Pron watched them for a few moments, finished off his pizza, then got out of the car and walked over.

CHAPTER FIFTEEN

Five Ways to Say Murder

Andrew Fang was having trouble with his load of boxes. The cartons were piled past his chin and he could barely see over the top. As he made his way into the house, he stumbled on the first step of the porch and almost dropped the load. After he regained his balance, he nudged the screen door open with an elbow, then coaxed it the rest of the way with his toe, just wide enough to squeeze sideways through the opening. Once he was inside, he let the door slam behind him, right in Peter Wang's face. Wang, also laden down with cartons, immediately started to yell in Chinese at his co-worker. Fang turned, swung out a foot, and kicked open the door, but he did it too hard and the door banged into Wang's arm, jarring loose one of the cartons he was carrying. Muttering softly, Wang bent over, fumbling with one hand to pick up the carton. Finally he slid it up the side of his leg where he held it as he walked stiff-legged into the house, manoeuvring around Fang at the doorway, who was balancing on one leg as he held open the door with the other. Nearby, just a few feet away, standing beside his battered Chevette, watching silently, was Rui-Wen Pan.

Pan took his briefcase out of the car and waited by the front steps for Wang and Fang to finish their work. Although it was nearly one in the morning, Pan's day was far from over. There was the accounting to do. He still had to go over the books from his three east-end variety stores. He had kept the shops closed in an extended period of mourning, and the bills were beginning to pile up. Then there was the correspondence to finish, the letters he had to write to his family and business associates in China, which he planned to visit later that year. And, if he wasn't too tired, there was his own writing to do. Despite all that had happened, he had to keep up his writing. The closing of a car door across the street caught his attention. He turned to see a familiar face walking towards him, and he frowned.

"Working late, Mr. Pan?" Pron asked, extending his hand.

Pan ignored the outstretched hand. "How did you find my house, Mr. Nick Pron?" His tone was brusque. Pron left the hand out. Reluctantly, Pan shook it. His grip was weak, the palm cold, the gesture almost meaningless. "You have no business coming to my house to bother me. My home is private. That is why I gave you my number, so you could call me. I do not go to your house. Why do you come to mine?"

"I was in the neighbourhood, Mr. Pan," replied Pron. "Thought I'd drop by, see how you were doing." The truth was, Pron wasn't sure why he was there.

"Did police tell you to come here? I think so. You and Kevin Donovan are working with police. Of this I have legal proof. Kevin Donovan is policeman, and police and media are working against me. I have nothing to say to you. I have obliged you with comments before, but no more. Please go away. I have nothing more to say."

"Sorry you feel that way, Mr. Pan. By the way," Pron said, reaching into his pocket and pulling out a newspaper clipping, handing it to Pan, "did you see this article in today's paper?"

"What is this?"

"It's about the Chinese democratic movement. I thought you might know something about it."

Pan studied the article. He took his time answering. Jia-Wen came out of the house, just long enough to sneer at Pron, say something to his brother, then leave, watching them from the shadows of the front verandah.

"Yes, this is very true," Pan said finally. "My magazine will have big story on this."

"Is that the *China Voice*? Or is it *China Spring*?"

Pan didn't answer. He reread the article before handing it back to Pron. "My magazine is distributed about the world, Mr. Nick Pron. Did you know that?"

"No."

"Your Toronto *Star*, how big is it?"

"Circulation? About half a million. More on the weekend."

Pan started nodding in a smug sort of way. "This is nothing. Your newspaper is seen only in Toronto. My magazine has circulation of four million people around world. Many people in many countries will read this. Stories of democracy in my magazine over past year have helped to cause this in actual fact. This I tell you, Mr. Nick Pron, but it is not for publication."

Wang and Fang had finished unloading the car and stood silently beside it, awaiting further instructions from Pan. He dismissed them with a curt wave of his hand.

"Like you, Mr. Nick Pron," Pan continued, "I am a writer. A very accomplished writer. I write daily. How many stories do you write in a day?"

"I don't know, two, three. Something like that."

"And how long?"

"The stories? Ten, fifteen paragraphs each."

"And that is how many words?"

"Three, four hundred words maybe. Sometimes more, sometimes less, depending upon how busy it is."

"Each day I write at least ten thousand words. Do you understand how much more that is than what you write? Sometimes I write well into morning. Do you ever write that much, Mr. Nick Pron?"

"Not enough room in the paper."

"You write stories about nothing, about garbage. I write stories for a purpose, to help my people. I write stories of democracy. I am number-one pioneer of the democratic student movement in this country. I want to bring reforms to China. You are educated man, Mr. Nick Pron, but do you know anything about my country?"

"Some. A little."

"You understand nothing. Everything you take for granted, freedom, rights of individual, rule by law, my country has none of that. I want to bring these changes to China. When I was a little boy, China erupted. Do you know about the Cultural Revolution? During that time there was no rights for anyone. That was big disaster of my country. It destroyed everything. There is no human rights. No democracy. No liberty. That is what I want to change. When you write something about murder, you hurt my plan. I am not a killer. I did not murder Selina Shen. For her death I take no responsibility."

"I never said you were the killer."

"But you write stories blaming me. You are trying to put me into hell, Mr. Nick Pron. I ask myself, 'What is your purpose? Why do you try to destroy me? I am not your enemy. Did I do something bad to you? Do I owe you something and not repay?' "

"But you hold press conferences, and you keep talking to the media."

"I am afraid to talk to you, but I am also afraid not to talk to you."

"What does that mean?"

"I am afraid of what you represent. You have great power through your newspaper. Your stories are read by many people and they believe what you say, even if it is wrong. They are read by Chinese papers and translated as fact. That has caused me much damage in my community. I ask myself, 'How could such a thing happen in democracy?' "

"I think we're right most of the time, Mr. Pan."

"Lies!" he suddenly blurted out. "You write lies! Eighty percent not truth and fact! All wrong, eighty percent!"

Jia-Wen opened the screen door and motioned for his brother to come inside, but Pan shooed him away with a flick of his hand and continued, his voice getting louder.

"I am afraid of you," Pan said, "I am afraid of what you write. I am afraid of your questions."

"Don't answer them."

"If I say nothing, people say, 'Look. He's afraid to speak. He must be killer.' If I speak, people say, 'Why does he have to defend himself if he is innocent?' You see, I cannot win going alone against the mighty Toronto *Star*. Every time you make another story, you ruin my reputation."

"We never used your name in any stories, other than the press conference."

"See? Press conference. That is another promise you break. Other papers, like *Sun*, they pledge not to use my name. But my name appears in Toronto *Star* and everyone knows I am boyfriend."

"It was a public meeting. We had every right to name you."

"I said not to. That was my condition of press conference. See, you do not respect anything. You have no morals. No scruples. You promise not to use my name, then you use it."

"I never made such a promise."

"Your stories have hurted me. Hurted me deeply. You should check your facts more carefully before you put such . . . such . . . garbage, such lies in paper!"

An old man's face appeared in a bedroom window of the neighbouring house. The face was gnarled and sleepy. The man yelled something in Chinese at Pan, who stared back contemptuously, as if he was the one who had been disturbed.

"I want you to remember one thing, Mr. Nick Pron. It is a Chinese proverb. As you brew, you must drink."

"What is that supposed to mean? Is that a threat?"

"Just remember what I have said, Mr. Nick Pron."

The man at the bedroom window kept yelling at Pan, who finally shouted something back. Pan then took Pron by the arm and led him towards the sidewalk in front of his house. They stopped under a flickering street light.

"People like that," Pan said, pointing towards the bedroom window, "they know nothing. They are uneducated."

Pron took out a cigarette and lit up. He looked down the deserted street at the row of parked cars. There were yellow slips of paper stuck under the windshield wipers of each one, put there by the squadron of green-uniformed parking control officers who zipped nightly around Toronto, tagging illegally parked cars. One car at the end of the row didn't have a ticket. Pron couldn't be sure, but there seemed to be something hunched behind the steering wheel. Harvey Loxton?

"What are you staring at, Mr. Nick Pron?" Pan asked, suddenly looking in that direction.

Pron quickly butted out his cigarette. "Uh, nothing. Nothing," he replied.

"I am sure I am being watched," Pan said, glancing around the street. "As boyfriend I am Number one suspect of police. Of course. This I know. I have to be so careful what I say. Careful not to make any mistakes. Everyone is trying to frame me."

"I'm not trying to frame you, Mr. Pan."

"If you were any good, you would find the real killer of Selina Shen. I cannot go out in public. People point at me and say I am killer. I cannot show my face. My friends do not call me. I cannot do business. You have caused me all this trouble, Mr. Nick Pron. If you are sincere, you will help me catch the killer, help me resolve this case."

"I need names, somewhere to start."

"I, too, am looking for killer with police. I will never give up the idea to catch the killer. People who are framing me are hiding the real killer."

"These people you keep talking about, who are they?"

"This information I have given to the police."

"Can you tell me anything?"

"Go ask OPP. They will tell you. Go ask Larry Edgar. He is one top of guy who is investigating."

"Police aren't talking to us, Mr. Pan. In fact, they hate us."

"Then ask Kevin Donovan. He is working with police against me."

"You know something? You really got a one-track mind."

"I beg your pardon?"

"Forget it."

"There is something I can tell you. The person who is responsible, he is man of very great power."

"This is the killer you're referring to."

"He's like a lawyer, or a professor. This man, I know who he is."

"What's his name?"

PICTURE OF INNOCENCE: Selina Shen with a bouquet of flowers from Rui-Wen Pan. (Inset) Selina Shen's 1983 student picture. Shen interrupted her studies in music and English two years later to have a baby with a man from El Salvador.

POSTCARD ROMANCE: Rui-Wen Pan and Selina Shen on a trip to Niagara Falls the year before her death. The popular tourist attraction was one of Pan's favourite spots.

FACING THE MEDIA: Rui-Wen Pan vigorously defends his innocence at one of two press conferences he held before his arrest.

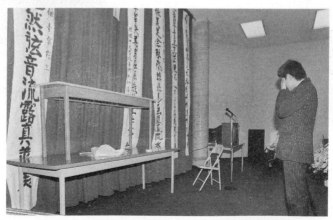

LONE MOURNER: Rui-Wen Pan bows his head and cries at the memorial service for Selina. Several hundred of her friends waited outside for him to leave before starting the service.

LAST MOVEMENT: Rui-Wen Pan's variety store at 1044 Gerrard Street East, one of three he ran in Toronto's east end. Selina Shen was last reported seen alive at a shop two doors away after giving a violin lesson on a Saturday afternoon.

A GRISLY FIND: One of Selina Shen's severed legs was found in a green garbage bag thrown over the embankment of the Thousand Islands Parkway at Rockport.

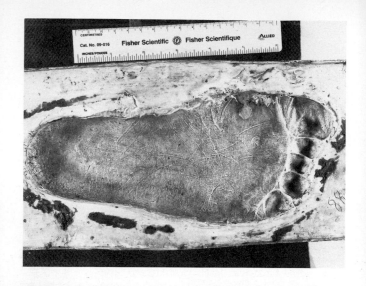

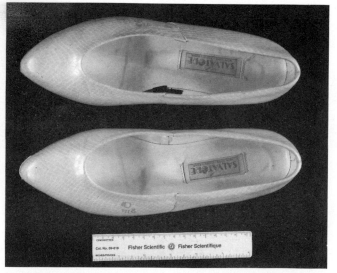

SOLE PROOF: The footprints left in a pair of Selina Shen's size eight and a half shoes matched plaster casts of the feet found on the Thousand Islands Parkway.

THE KNIVES: The paring knife, meat cleaver, and three butcher knives that Rui-Wen Pan threw into Lake Ontario at midnight, the day after the body parts were identified as Selina Shen's.

CULTURAL PARANOIA: The pier in Toronto's Beaches area where Rui-Wen Pan threw the knives and cleaver into Lake Ontario. Pan claimed that an ingrained fear of police persecution made him dispose of anything that might incriminate him.

DINNER IN CHINATOWN: From left to right, Nick Pron, Rui-Wen Pan, Kevin Donovan, Andrew Fang, Peter Wang, at a late-night supper several months after Selina Shen's murder. Pan's brother, Jia-Wen, took the picture.

TAKE-DOWN: Ontario Provincial Police Detective Garnet Rombough (left) and Detective-Inspector Larry Edgar escort Rui-Wen Pan to jail after his arrest for first-degree murder.

THE PROSECUTORS: Crown prosecutors Gary Clewley, standing, and Bob Ash handled the second trial.

THE DETECTIVES: From left to right, Special Constable Stephen Tsai, Detective-Inspector Larry Edgar, and detectives Brian Kennedy and Garnet Rombough.

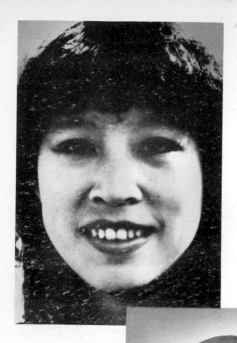

MASK OF DEATH: A skull pulled from the Cataraqui River was identified as Selina Shen's through several forensic tests, including one where a picture Rui-Wen Pan took in Vancouver was superimposed over the skull.

"Once when he called Selina and she cried on the phone, I took the phone and he also threatened me. I tape recorded everything," Pan said, nodding smugly.

"Can I hear the tapes?"

"This I have given to police. You must talk to Larry Edgar to get this."

"Once more, can you tell me the name of this professor, or is he a lawyer?"

"I am writing a book about this. In my book I will tell all. You will be very unhappy. Very surprised."

"What do you mean by that?"

Pan didn't reply. He just smiled.

"Can I at least read your book? Have you written it?"

"You must be patient. In time you will see. Yesterday I wrote much, but only four thousand words," Pan said. "I work very hard, twenty hours a day, seven days a week, both on book and at stores. I think you are also hard worker, Mr. Nick Pron. I think we are much alike. To get anywhere you must work hard. Selina did not want to work hard. I will tell you something about Selina," Pan said, his voice dropping as he leaned forward slightly, in a conspiratorial fashion, "something I never tell anyone before. But this not to put into paper. Agreed?"

Pron nodded.

"Selina liked nice things but she did not want to work for them. People told me she was using me." Pan gazed absently into the distance and for a moment seemed oblivious to Pron's presence. "Selina took advantage of me," he continued. "She took advantage of men. But I always forgave her." He paused, smiled briefly, then looked at Pron. "I have just remembered something about her. When she was young, she suffered greatly. She was most unfortunate person. Ill-fated. I will explain everything in my book. It will make you cry. It will let the public decide who should take responsibility for her death. In my book I will tell my true feelings. The book will move you deeply. It will also explain the cultural shock that Chinese students face when they come to Canada. This book will be read by all my countrymen before they come here."

"Do you have a publisher?"

Pan opened his briefcase, showed Pron a sheaf of handwritten pages. Pron reached for them, but Pan snapped the top shut.

"The book is in Mandarin. You would not understand."

"I'll get a translator."

"Mr. Nick Pron, you should be looking for the real killer. The media can do things the police cannot do. It is the job of the media to find the killer."

"It is the job of the media to write stories."

"You are wrong. The media has tremendous power in this country. The media can ruin people if it chooses. Look at what it has done to me. It has ruined my reputation."

"Let me read the book and I'll write a story about it. Maybe that will help you."

"Book! Book! All you ever ask me about is book!"

"Well, I'm interested."

"You should write one yourself."

"About this case, you mean?"

"I will tell you something but it is not for publication. I have already written a book."

"Oh?"

"It is a mystery story."

"Like in murder mystery?"

Pan took a while to answer. "It was a long time ago," he said finally. "I even forgot about it until now."

"What's it called?"

"*The Affair by the West Lake.*"

"Tell me more about it."

Pan shook his head. "That is past," he said. "I am more concerned about what is happening now. All this pressure on me. Everybody saying I am killer. People want to know how I can stand the pressure. They want to know why I have not committed suicide. I am under so much pressure I could have committed suicide. At one time I thought I might. But I know now that is wrong. Because if I killed myself, people would think I am the killer. They would say, 'Look, he is deranged. He killed himself. He must be the killer.' But I am not deranged." He touched his forehead. "Selina was the one who had mental problems."

"No one else ever said that."

"Then you should check your facts. This is correct."

"We talked to a lot of her friends. No one ever said anything about her being ill."

"My poor little girl, I feel so sorry for her. I wanted to help her but she would not let me. This new book I write I will dedicate to her. I will call it . . . *Tragedy of Love.* Yes, that is title. You can help me with this book, Mr. Nick Pron."

"How?"

"I need research for my book, which will show that police sometimes wrongfully accuse people with murder. This will help get police going on the trail of the real murderer. I need newspaper stories. The OPP recently say a man was a serial killer who was not. Also I heard that in Quebec, many years ago, man was executed for murder. Years later another man came forward to say he did it."

"Yes, I've heard of those cases. That one in Quebec was the Coffin murder case. I can get that information for you, Mr. Pan. But you've got to do something for me. I want to hear those tapes."

"Check your files on something else, Mr. Nick Pron. This murder of Selina has received more publicity than any other murder of Chinese person in Canada. Is this not so?"

"There have been a lot of stories."

"I will say so in my book, but I want you to check for me first. I consider you my good friend, Mr. Nick Pron. We will talk again. But please do not bring Kevin. I do not ever want to see him again. He acts like an uneducated person. Like someone from the lower class."

They shook hands. This time, Pan's grip was firm, confident.

Pron got in his car and drove down the street, slowing in front of the last car in the row, the one without the parking ticket on the windshield. As he approached it, the driver rolled down the window and leaned out. Pron pulled his car up alongside, rolled down his window.

"How was your little chit-chat with the killer?" asked Donovan. "I thought you were going to drop this."

"Went out to get a slice, just kept going. You been here the whole time?"

"Most of it. Looked like you guys were having a pretty good session. Still think he's innocent?"

"He talks a good argument for being framed."

"Sure, but did he give you anything to work on?"

"Well, he did say something about knowing the killer. A guy who's either a lawyer or a professor."

"That narrows it down," Donovan said, "to about ten thousand suspects." He reached over and picked up two pieces of paper from the seat beside him. "And you believed him?"

"He's doing a book on how he's being framed. Wants me to help him with the research."

"Great. Both of you can write it from a jail cell."

"He said it's our job to find the real killer."

"That's what I've been doing."

"Oh?"

"I've got something here you might like to see," Donovan said, handing Pron the papers he had been holding.

Pron flicked on his roof light to get a better look. There were two photocopied pages. Two lines of Chinese writing ran across the top of the first page. In smaller type below were two columns of Chinese characters. Beside each of the Chinese characters was a word or phrase in English.

"What is this?" Pron asked.

"Just start reading."

" 'Political offender, culprit, swindler, poisoning, espionage, rape, criminal law, accomplice, first offence, arsonist, strongly suspected person, material evidence, circumstantial evidence, war criminal, subversion, testimony of a witness, warning, summons, a wanted notice. . . ' " Pron looked at Donovan. "What the hell?"

"Keep going."

" 'Offender caught red-handed, arrest warrant, custody, at large under a wanted notice, to put under surveillance, penal discretion, judgement, to be convicted of, prisoner, to

detain, life imprisonment, death penalty, stay of execution.'
Is this a page out of the training manual for the Chinese
mafia?''

''There's more.''

'' 'Murder . . . Homicide . . . Murderer.' Donovan, there're
at least five different ways here to say murder in Chinese.
Mind telling me what this is?''

''See those two lines at the top? Roughly translated they
mean, 'English words Chinese students need to know.' ''

''Need to know for what? When they get arrested? Is this
a translation guide for criminals?''

''It's the first article . . . from a magazine.''

Pron smiled.

''A magazine about democracy.''

''Let me guess, *China Voice*, Pan's magazine about
democracy.''

''Still think he's innocent?''

CHAPTER SIXTEEN

Child's Play

Andrew Fang was driving the Chevette that day. He saw the pot-hole but couldn't swerve in time and hit it with a front tire. The car bounced sharply, then there was a clunk and the back end lifted slightly, as if the tire ran over something. Fang glanced in the rear-view mirror just as a black object went cartwheeling into the gutter. He pulled over to the side of the road and stopped.

"What is it?" Rui-Wen Pan wanted to know from the back seat. Seated beside him was Sandy Hui, a friend who owned a dress store beside his shop on Broadview Avenue. The fourth person in the car was Peter Wang.

"Why did you stop?" Wang asked.

"Something came off the car," replied Fang.

They all swung around to look at the object lying in the gutter. It was about the same size as a pound of butter. Pan was the first out of the car. He bounded out the door and hurried over to the black thing lying in the road. He stared at it for a moment before picking it up. His face broke into a smile as the others crowded around him.

"See," he said, holding up the black box for the others to look at, displaying it proudly like a big game hunter showing off a fresh kill. "This is tracking device. Those bastard policemen are following us around."

They all turned, almost in unison, to stare at a man carrying a bag of groceries who happened to be passing by on the sidewalk. The man with the bag of groceries stared back but kept walking.

"We must always be on our guard," Pan continued, as he inspected the black box. One side was crushed in. There was a tiny antenna at one end, but half of it was missing. "There is a possibility police have an instrument like this in our house. We must be careful what we say."

Pan handed the black box to Fang to look at. He in turn passed it to Wang, who gave it to Sandy Hui.

"We must always be on our guard," Pan said, taking the black box back. As the foursome walked to the car, each was scanning the street, looking for something or someone connected to the police. They saw nothing. Pan threw the black box on the floor of the car as he got in. He was still shaking his head as they drove off.

Farther up the street, a lone motorist was slumped behind the wheel of his parked car. He had been watching the foursome in his rear-view mirror, waiting. He let the Chevette and several other cars pass before he pulled out. There was a two-way radio on the seat beside him. He picked it up, held it in his lap, then pressed the transmitter switch.

"Target found the bird dog. He's on to us. Be careful."

The shadow men had to wait until just before dawn to do the job. Pan was always the last one to go to bed. They waited an hour after the light went out in his second-floor bedroom before making their move. There was no debate over whether the deed had to be done. It was more a matter of pride than anything else. Bad enough that the tracking device had been found. That was just plain sloppy. The black box had been put behind the fender, but the bump had jarred it loose. There must have been some rust where the magnet rested against the metal. That didn't matter now. What the shadow men didn't want was to have the black box used against them somehow, whether it was traced to their unit or, down the road, used by some defence lawyer in court to embarrass them. Defence lawyers took a special delight in embarrassing cops on the witness stand. That was the bonus part of the job.

A dummy had been made that resembled the original bird dog. They got a technician to slap together a mock-up, a realistic look-alike with no identifying marks on it. If it came to that, they could always blame it on the Canadian Security Intelligence Service, CSIS. The Canadian spy agency had opened a file on Pan, who had often bragged to friends that the United States Central Intelligence Agency wanted him to work as an agent, spying on Chinese groups in North America. The fake bird dog was stuffed with old batteries to give it the proper weight. The next part was trickier.

The two shadow men who would do the job parked on Queen Street, just around the corner and out of sight of Pan's house. One of them was carrying a flat shaft of metal with a notch at one end. He held it close to his leg as they walked around the corner and up to the car parked in the driveway. The shaft, known as a Slim Jim, was a tool popular with locksmiths, tow truck drivers, burglars, and, on this night, police officers. The big tool was easy to use. Quick. The notched end went in first, sliding down like a cobra inside the door panel at the window. The notched end hooked underneath the locking mechanism, at the point where the vertical bar from the door button was attached to the horizontal bar for the lock. A quick flick of the wrist brought the bar up, popping the lock. It took all of eight seconds. But there was something wrong.

"Shit," muttered the man who had broken into the car.

The black box he had picked up from the back seat of Pan's car was crushed. He held it close to the one his partner had, which was in perfect shape.

"Now what?" asked the man who had broken into the car.

His partner looked at the broken black box in one hand, the undamaged replacement in the other, and snickered.

"Simple," he said, dropping the good one to the ground and smashing it with the heel of his shoe. Then he picked it up and handed it back.

"There," he said, "couldn't even tell the difference myself."

The broken black box was put where the other had been found, the door of the Chevette was quietly closed, and the two men left quickly, headed for their car, and drove off into the night.

The big blue Chevrolet Caprice was the lead car, Detective Inspector Larry Edgar behind the wheel. It was a ten-minute drive from his office by the waterfront to the row house in the west end of Toronto that had been the focus of so much attention. Edgar made a right off Queen Street then an immediate left, turning sharply into the driveway where a blue Chevette with a battered front grill was parked. Edgar parked the big Caprice right behind the Chevette, so close that the bumpers touched. The driver of the Chevette would not be going anywhere for at least the next several hours, and maybe a lot longer. The tiny hatchback with the missing front grill looked like a toy car in comparison to Edgar's full-sized, four-door sedan. The grey van from the forensic lab pulled up on Edgar's left. An unmarked OPP car skidded to a halt beside it, kicking up some dust from the gravel driveway. The last car in the convoy was a Metro police cruiser. It rode up on the sidewalk and screeched to a stop. There wasn't enough room left in front of the row house to park a bicycle.

Almost in unison, car doors flung open. Edgar was the first out. He marched smartly up to the fence in front of the house and threw open the gate that barely came to his knees. He walked up three rotting wooden steps and into the enclosed porch, then knocked loudly on the front door as all policemen do. There was a small window in the door. Edgar peered inside. It seemed nobody was at home, but he knew that wasn't so. He glanced around the verandah, at the rows of cardboard boxes with Chinese lettering crammed into the tiny room. Christ, he thought, it's going to take hours to go through all of those. Edgar knocked again. A man appeared in the kitchen and started walking towards the front door. The big detective reached inside his suit jacket as the door slowly opened.

"Rui-Wen Pan?" Edgar asked, although he knew who it was.

The man standing in the doorway nodded.

Edgar held out a thick packet of papers, the corners stapled together. Pan reached slowly, somewhat hesitantly, for the sheaf. He read carefully what was written on the front page, then flipped through the rest of the documents, glancing up from time to time at Edgar, who stared impassively, the corners of his mouth curled down in a tight frown. As he read on, Pan glanced around Edgar at the phalanx of big men behind him, some crowding into the sun room, others standing on the steps, while the rest gathered in the driveway. All of them were staring at Pan, while they waited patiently to get inside his house and go about their job, the job of tearing his home apart.

"That paper," Edgar said, pointing to what Pan was holding, "is a search warrant. A legal document signed by a judge. It gives us the right to search your house."

The investigation had been going on for five months, but this was the first time Edgar had met Pan face to face. For a few moments the two men were framed in the doorway, the detective towering over the chief suspect in his murder case. Edgar did not identify himself. That was intentional. He didn't want the man who had dogged his thoughts day and night these past months to know who he was, at least for the time being. He wanted to be just another nameless cop that day. This was a good chance to study Pan, to watch him closely while his house was being ripped apart. Edgar's investigators had told him Pan wanted to meet him, had constantly talked about how much he respected and trusted Edgar. The detective wanted to keep it that way for now. What they were doing that day was sure to upset Pan, and Edgar didn't want that anger focused on him. If he arrested Pan for Shen's murder—and there didn't seem to be anybody else with the means, motive, or opportunity to murder her—he wanted to be on good terms with him. That might make it easier to get a signed confession out of him.

Up until now Edgar had relied on his investigators to draw him a picture of Pan. But he needed this, a direct encounter, a chance to talk to the man whose voice he had heard and whose thoughts he had read on what had seemed like an endless number of wiretaps and surveillance reports. Edgar needed to form his own opinion, to get his own gut reaction about the man who was telling the world he was innocent. There was a good reason for all that. When the investigation was through, the decision whether to make an arrest would be his and his alone. He wanted to make damn sure he had the right man.

Edgar scrutinized Pan's face as he read the warrant, then glanced at his hands, which were trembling. That wasn't surprising. Edgar wondered what it would feel like to see yourself referred to as a killer. And that's what it said in the search warrant; it named Pan as a suspect in the murder of Selina Lian Shen, on or about February 20, 1988.

"Go ahead," Pan said to Edgar, handing the search warrant back and stepping to one side, "do whatever you have to."

Edgar was mildly surprised at Pan's composure. A dozen burly men barging into somebody's house without notice could be a pretty traumatic event. You never knew what sort of reaction to expect, but it was usually tense, at least at the start. But Pan was so calm it almost seemed that he had been waiting for them. Maybe he had even laid out a little spread for them to nibble on while they went about their work? This was not a man who was likely to break down and blubber out a murder confession.

The others, Jia-Wen along with Wang and Fang, were in the kitchen. Their expressions showed they weren't quite sure what was happening. Good, thought Edgar, as he made his way along the dingy corridor towards them. That confusion would work in his favour. They wouldn't offer much resistance to what he had planned.

Edgar glanced around at the rooms on the main floor, which were small, untidy, in the sort of shape one might expect of a place where four bachelors lived. A pungent odour of cooking oil filled the kitchen. There was a fish aquarium in one corner. The sink was filled with dirty dishes. The first thing to do was to get them all separated. Two officers, along with a translator, took Wang and Fang aside, directed them into the living room. The two seemed to be very loyal to Pan. Well, now was the time to test that loyalty. He wanted to make damn sure Wang and Fang knew they were involved in a murder investigation—maybe even put a little fear into them, show them that the police meant business. He was pretty sure they didn't know anything, but if they did, and were covering it up, he wanted there to be no doubt in their minds that hiding something from the law would definitely get them into trouble.

Edgar had something special planned for Jia-Wen. He wanted his investigators to get a statement out of Jia-Wen, but not at the house. He wanted him away from his brother. Detectives Brian Kennedy and Gus Riddell took Jia-Wen to OPP headquarters, leaving Pan by himself. But if being alone bothered him, Pan didn't show it. He watched silently as the procession of police officers trooped in and through his house.

The officers fanned out. Edgar's brother Clare, a Metro homicide detective, started poking around in the living room. Although the murder was an OPP case, Pan lived in Toronto. Police protocol required that a Metro officer accompany the search team. When Edgar notified Metro of his intentions, he asked for his brother to come along. Ray Higaki, a blood specialist from the Centre of Forensic Sciences, went straight to the basement, where he began to swab the walls, floors, and drains, hunting for minute traces of blood. Edgar still didn't have a crime scene, the place where Selina was murdered. His detectives had scoured the countryside where the body parts had been found, searching everywhere for the scene of the crime. They had found nothing. They had even checked dozens of rental lockers, especially those with refrigerated units, the kind used by hunters to store meat. Edgar didn't think Selina had been killed at the house, but even if she had, the chances of getting blood scrapings at this late stage were slim. Edgar had brought along Brian Dalrymple, the OPP's crime lab expert, to help out in the search. Dalrymple went upstairs with several technicians. They rummaged through clothing in drawers and closets. The uniformed officers who were part of the team stood watch by the door.

As the slow, tedious job of going through Pan's belongings dragged on, Larry Edgar was dying for a cigarette. But when you were tearing someone's house apart, it seemed in bad form to butt your ashes onto his floor. The detective stood in the hallway, back to the wall, arms clasped in front of him, twisting the detective's ring on his finger, while his men went about their work. He was watching Pan, who had been roaming around the house.

Edgar had faced a dilemma in going ahead with the warrant. He knew he could not put off searching Pan's house and stores any longer and still hope to find something. But the search put his investigation into a new phase. It officially notified Pan of what it seemed that everyone in Chinatown was saying, that he was the man who killed Selina Shen. Although the bird-dog incident had let Pan know that the police were on to him, it was not the same as reading a court document naming him as a killer. He was bound to be more cautious. But at the same time there was a chance that having his house torn apart would upset him enough that he would say something incriminating, and it would be picked up by the room probes.

Edgar hoped the search would also stop Pan from harassing people who could end up as Crown witnesses against him. The detective was still furious that Pan had tried to intimidate Mrs. Chan, the seamstress who was the last person to see Selina the day she disappeared. Several days after the body parts were identified, Pan had shown up at Mrs. Chan's with Peter Wang. Pan had grilled her on a story in the *Star* that quoted Mrs. Chan as saying that Selina's face had turned ashen upon reading Pan's letter, and that she had cut short the lesson, then disappeared. Pan had recorded Mrs. Chan's answers and had practically forced her to sign a statement denying Selina had been upset by the letter. Pan's visit had frightened the hell out of the seamstress, and she was starting to backtrack on her original story. Her statement that Selina was upset by the letter was a vital piece of evidence against Pan. Edgar didn't want any other witnesses harassed.

Pan was one cool customer, Edgar thought. He didn't seemed bothered at all as the officers started carting out boxes and boxes of his belongings, everything from magazines and photo albums to his letters, writings, and personal effects. There were dozens of cassette tapes everywhere, and since

Pan said he was always taping calls, those tapes were taken as well. The officers even took videotapes. There were several videotapes that left some of the officers quietly chuckling. They were movie tapes of the great Chinese detective, Charlie Chan. If Pan was upset by the horde of intruders picking through his most personal belongings, he didn't show it. He even tried to make small talk with Edgar.

"How long have you been a police officer?" he asked the detective.

"Twenty-one years," replied Edgar.

"And you've always been a policeman?"

"I was in the military before that, for five years."

"This thing," Pan said, nodding at the officers, "I have lived through this before."

"Oh?"

"Yes, in my home, in China, there was a time of great tragedy. Do you know this?"

Edgar didn't reply.

"It was called the Cultural Revolution. All rights were taken away. Many people died in this time. Millions."

"I see."

"I lived through this. Police just come into any home they choose."

"We have a search warrant. Did you want to see it again?"

"Yes, I know. But during this time in my country police did not need this . . . this, search warranty. They had the power to do whatever they chose."

"Your parents, Mr. Pan," asked Edgar, "they still live in China?"

"Yes. My parents are old. They do not know of this business."

"Your mother, I understand she's a medical doctor?"

"Who told you this?" Pan challenged.

Edgar didn't reply.

"You should check your information. My mother play piano. She has never touched a surgical knife. Where you hear this? This is not truth and fact."

"Oh? Well, maybe it's your father that I meant. He's the doctor in the family."

"What my father does has nothing to do with this matter," Pan replied tersely.

"But he is a doctor?"

"My father is retired."

One of the officers came into the kitchen and whispered something to Edgar. Edgar followed the officer upstairs, where Ray Higaki was examining some of Pan's clothing.

"What have you got, Ray?" Edgar asked.

"A small stain," replied Higaki, pointing to a spot on Pan's undershorts. "It could be blood. Can't be sure. I don't think there's anything I can do with it, though."

Edgar looked around the bedroom, idly wondering where the technicians had planted the bugs. He knew it had to be somewhere close to the bed because of some of the intimate conversations the probe had picked up. Edgar wandered around the upstairs for a while. When he went down, Kennedy and Riddell had just returned with Jia-Wen, who seemed to be in a very vile mood.

Edgar had figured the older brother to be a bit of a hothead. He was taller than Pan, with a sturdier build. His nose was shaped like a boxer's, and Edgar wondered if it had been broken in a fist fight. Jia-Wen had been in the country for two years, during which time he had worked and lived with his brother. He had stayed with Selina and Pan at their Scarborough home, but by all accounts it had not been a happy threesome. Jia-Wen never got along with Selina, complaining that she didn't do enough housework. There were rumours of a love triangle between the two brothers and Selina, but that's all it was, just rumours. A few weeks before Selina disappeared, Jia-Wen had packed up and gone home, apparently fed up with the constant bickering. From the wiretaps, Edgar knew Pan had called Jia-Wen soon after Selina's body parts were identified, asking him to come back to Canada.

Jia-Wen said nothing as he sat down at the table. But Edgar knew his short fuse was already burning after being questioned by Kennedy and Riddell. Jia-Wen was barely able to control himself while the police officers went through the house. Edgar wanted to use that to his advantage, to work Jia-Wen, get him so mad that he might say something, either now or after the police left. With a little prompting, Jia-Wen might erupt. There was a knife on the kitchen counter. Edgar pointed to it.

"Is that yours?" he asked Jia-Wen.

Jia-Wen muttered something in Chinese, angrily shaking his head.

Edgar called out to one of the officers, telling him to seize and bag the cleaver for testing. He didn't really think it was the murder weapon. He was just pushing Jia-Wen, who watched in silence. At least, at first.

"What right do you have to be here!" Jia-Wen blurted out as he jumped to his feet.

Edgar stared at him but said nothing.

"You have no business doing this!"

The yelling brought everyone into the kitchen, including Pan, who walked over to his brother.

"It's all right," he told his older brother. "Let them do as they want."

But Jia-Wen pushed his brother to one side and angrily approached Edgar.

"What right have you got to do this?" Jia-Wen repeated. "Where is your badge?"

Edgar took it out and showed it to him.

"You shouldn't be here. You have no right."

Edgar slowly reached into his pocket and took out the search warrant. He unfolded it and held it in front of Jia-Wen's face.

"This gives me the right," he said.

Edgar had hit the right buttons with Jia-Wen. Could he push him a little harder? He wanted the two brothers talking after they left the house. If Jia-Wen knew his brother killed Selina and was covering up, he hoped the brother might blurt that out. If he did, it would be picked up on the room probe. Edgar turned to Dalrymple, who had just put the meat cleaver into a cellophane bag.

"Take that man's fingerprints," he said, pointing to Jia-Wen.

Since he couldn't force Jia-Wen to be fingerprinted because he wasn't being charged with anything, Dalrymple had to ask first for Jia-Wen's permission. After a few minutes of arguing with his brother, Jia-Wen grudgingly agreed to let Dalrymple take his fingerprints.

A defiant Jia-Wen stared right into Edgar's eyes as Dalrymple took each of his fingers in turn, pressed the tips into the ink pad, then rolled each over the allotted space on the fingerprint card. When Dalrymple was finished, Jia-Wen grabbed a towel and carefully wiped the blue ink from his fingers, the whole time sneering at Edgar. Later, when the two of them were alone in the kitchen, Edgar turned to Jia-Wen.

"I know you didn't do it," the detective said.

"Then why do you fingerprint me?"

"It was your brother," Edgar said.

"What do you mean?"

"We know your brother did it. But you can still get into trouble if you hide what you know."

Jia-Wen stared, his eyes hooded with anger, and said nothing.

"You can go to jail for ten years."

"If I didn't do it, why take fingerprints?" Jia-Wen wanted to know.

Edgar didn't tell him the real reason. "Just remember what I said."

The officers had been at the house for most of the day. The search was winding down. Gradually, one by one, they returned to the kitchen to get further instructions from Edgar. There was still Pan's store on Gerrard Street to search.

Finally they were done. Pan and his brother watched them go. Their argument started almost as soon as the door closed.

"Why did you quarrel with him?" Pan demanded of his brother. "There was no alternative anyway. Let him take it. If he wants to take the knife, let him. But he has no right to take your fingerprints. When it gets to court, he will be finished."

"He'll arrest you and send you back."

"To shout like that, really detestable. I told you to let him take it. I would not feel easy if he did not take it. I was worrying that he would not take it."

"Why would he?!' asked Jia-Wen.

Pan, voice rising, said: "I am not guilty! Never! Never!"

"I was only saying what he said."

"I took it out and read it," Pan said, referring to the search warrant. "It said that I killed Selina Shen on the twentieth of February in the year 1988. I said just take whatever you want, I don't care, right? Now he has come to a conclusion, he has positively concluded that I committed the crime. What things they took, I feel it is also laughable. He took a picture of me as a student in white working clothes. 'What is this? What are you doing?' I said. Then I said, 'Do you want more? I have several hundred photographs in mainland China.' "

"Yeah," Jia-Wen said.

"You tell me, how could I kill a person? They will not be able to find anything, then I will talk again. Whatever I say now is superfluous. He has no right to enter court, no right to take your belongings, has no right to take your fingerprints. It is useless. He was stupid, just stupid. Just let him take it. Having taken it, in due course, he would be totally finished. I will be watching. I will see."

"He told me," Jia-Wen said, "you were the one who did it."

"He is saying that I was the one who killed Selina Shen?"

"He said that I didn't do it. It was you. But if I didn't do it, then why take the knife?" Jia-Wen wondered.

"He is saying that I did it?"

"He said to me I would be sentenced to ten years."

"To say one wrong word can be critical," said Pan.

It was Jia-Wen's turn to yell. "What did I say wrong?" he demanded. "How critical can it be? The facts are here."

"It is useless to talk to you. Do not tell him even one word. Do not tell him a sentence. What am I afraid of? I can stand my ground. Now he has nothing at all. Did he take the kitchen knife?"

"Yeah. He took one."

"All useless. You think I am a fool. Yeah? After he has finished this trick, he has no more to play on me. He said that I did it? Arrest me. Have me put in the trial. If they prosecute, let them prosecute," said Pan. "I prepared myself long ago. Therefore, I told you not to talk to them today. It is useless for you to say anything now."

"Whatever he took, he should have asked us to sign. If anything is taken, it has to be listed. I said, 'Why are you taking these? Why should I sign that for you to take away?' "

"Eventually he has to register whatever is taken. That is the way. He gave me a list and then he took those things," Pan said.

"A big mess," said Jia-Wen.

"Just use your head. I let them in. Opened up the room. 'Just do whatever you want,' I said. Some time ago that wife of Canadian prime minister Pierre Trudeau, they said she was selling narcotics or something. Later on she got off on a technicality. The police were all wrong. All along this was improper behaviour, pure and simple. Taking advantage of us Chinese."

"Forget it!" Jia-Wen said.

"Forget it? Why should I worry about them? Forget it. Let me tell you, no matter what happens, don't tell anyone. Second, don't pay any attention to them. That is, don't even say a word. Don't quarrel. It is useless. Don't even say an extra word."

"What if they take you away?" asked Jia-Wen.

"How can they take me away? Let me be taken away. What are you afraid of? After I have been taken away, be sure you do not get all anxious. You just do your business. Don't worry about me, okay? I knew it was going to be like this then. I will give you two numbers, my lawyers'. It costs money to find a lawyer. I am fucking broke. Just hire one. I tell you, they are acting blindly and rashly. Let them do whatever they want. Am I afraid of him? I only have to say one sentence and they will be speechless."

What the hell did Pan mean by that? Edgar wondered, sitting in his office at OPP headquarters. Say one sentence? Speechless? That was the trouble with these eavesdropping devices.They could get you the most intimate conversation of a murder suspect, but then they could leave you guessing as to what he was really talking about. Although Pan spoke volumes, what did he really say? Was he deliberately talking in riddles? Or was that just the way of the Chinese? Never to be direct, always to talk around a subject. There were times when Pan came tantalizingly close to saying something really incriminating, only to stop short, as if he knew the police were listening in and he wanted to tease them. It was at those times Edgar felt like stepping into the conversation to ask Pan what he really meant.

The transcript lying on his desk, labelled Communication Number 23, was the most aggravating of the huge batch of wiretaps that he had read through. It was a recording of the conversation between Pan and Jia-Wen right after his house had been searched. His tactic of baiting Jia-Wen seemed to have worked, because the two brothers did have the argument he had been hoping for. But the transcript of their heated discussion seemed to raise more questions than it answered. There was a line on page twelve that he kept reading over and over again.

"I knew it was going to be like this then," Pan said to Jia-Wen, imploring him not to worry.

What the hell did that line mean? Was Pan admitting he was the killer and always knew he would be arrested? Or was he saying he always knew he would be arrested because he was Selina's boyfriend, and boyfriends were always the first suspects in domestic murder cases? Maybe the answer lay in a section of the tape marked "inaudible," right after that sentence.

Edgar had enlisted the help of a full-time interpreter to translate the mountain of wiretaps from Mandarin to English. Stephen Tsai, a government security guard at the coroner's office who had been sworn in as a special constable for this case, certainly had his work cut out. Translating the sheer volume of wiretap evidence was a daunting enough task, even without all the glitches.

The room probes at times missed key words, either because they were spoken too fast, too softly, or were distorted by the classical music Pan often played on the radio. Tsai had to replay some segments of the tape more than a dozen times just to get one word. There was one potentially key section that highlighted this problem. Tsai had replayed this segment over and over again. But it was just too faint. He couldn't make it out. Edgar turned to page three. It began with a comment from Jia-Wen right after Pan had remarked on how the search warrant named him as the killer. It started off with something inaudible. Then Jia-Wen said:

". . . killed. Yeah, hit a person . . . and killed that person. Killed that person . . . killed . . ."

"So what to kill a person . . .?" Pan replied.

"Now . . . we both are . . ." Jia-Wen's last word was inaudible.

Edgar lit a Player's cigarette, swung around in his chair, and gazed out his office window at the expressway. He repeated the line in his head.

"Now something we both are something," was what Jia-Wen had said.

Did he mean, "Now they know we both are guilty"? Or was it, "Now you've told me, we both are guilty"?

Edgar swung back to his desk and butted out the cigarette. You could go crazy trying to figure out what Pan and his brother had said. There was a second conversation that took place soon after their search of the house. It was between Pan and Peter Wang. Pan was complaining about being tired. It was quite obvious the pressure was getting to him.

"Just now I was turning over and over and couldn't get to sleep," said Pan.

"Yeah," replied Wang.

"I had just fallen asleep, thinking, 'Forget it. Go to sleep.' I looked at the time and it was thirty minutes, forty minutes, two hours, and I still could not fall asleep. When the phone rang, I was in real difficulty."

"You were just about to fall asleep?" asked Wang.

"It is not like it used to be. First of all, once I wake up, I can't fall asleep again. The second is, after falling asleep, whether or not I can get up. This very cruel business. He said it was me. If you think there is something, just arrest me. We are in a country of law. If you say it was me, then it was me. I have accepted the situation long ago."

"Yeah," said Wang.

"I have so many things to do. I am not a mental case. I will be turned into one, yeah. If you think that I did something wrong, that I committed a crime, then bring evidence. Just charge me. All I have to say is one sentence — and it will be over. If I am very cruel, would I have been able to treat Selina Shen the way I did? I would not say that I loved her, because she let me down. She let me down in her lifetime, let me down numerous times, still let me down after her death, right?"

"Yeah."

"The police had no idea of what they were doing. Ten billion people in mainland China to look at the dark and dirty aspect of the Western countries. This is a case of, under heaven, all crows are equally black. He said that my mother is a medical doctor. How stupid. My mother teaches piano. What my father does has nothing to do with this matter. Even if my father was the authority on anatomy in the whole world, or in China, so what?"

"Therefore they are talking nonsense," Wang said.

"How can the police solve the case? They are miles off course. They are so stupid. The one stood beside me during the search, like guarding me, right? How can you depend on him to do these things which need the use of a brain?"

There was Pan's arrogance again, Edgar thought. Maybe Pan thought he was outsmarting the police, but this game was far from over. While Edgar respected Pan's intelligence, it was pretty obvious Pan didn't think too much of their grey matter. The next section reaffirmed how little Pan thought of the police.

"Nothing but child's play," he said to Wang near the end of the transcript. "If he is really so careful, then how could he forget such a big thing? What they really need to investigate about me, those that are the most important, those are here and they didn't even touch them."

Edgar thought about that line as he drove home that night. He mulled it over all through supper. It was still on his mind when he went to bed. What was the big thing they had missed during the house search?

"Those that are the most important," Pan had said. "Those are here and they didn't even touch them."

What could they have missed? He had watched the officers tear apart the house. They had done a thorough search. How could they have missed anything? Was Pan playing with him? What was that expression he used with Wang? Child's play. Is that what he thought this was? A game for children? Did he know the police were eavesdropping? Was he taunting them? Throwing out little fake clues? No, that was too easy a way out. Edgar was convinced his team had missed something during the search of the house. Something incriminating. But what? They had gone through everything. What could it be? He couldn't stop thinking of that line.

"Those that are the most important, those are here and they didn't even touch them."

Edgar repeated the line over and over to himself. He worried that he might never find out what it was that he had missed. And that bothered him. He did not sleep very well that night.

CHAPTER SEVENTEEN

Billboard Justice

There was a telephone message waiting for Pron when he reported to work for the evening shift in the radio room. It said a Chinese man called but didn't leave a name.

"He phoned several times," Carol Coles, the editorial assistant, told Pron as he thumbed through the small box in which the messages were kept. "Said he didn't want to give his name because his phone was being tapped. You sure deal with some weird people. Has this got anything to do with the murder of that violinist?"

It had been more than five months since the murder, and several weeks since the last story had appeared in the paper. Although all the attention and interest around the newsroom was focused on the Economic Summit, the annual meeting of leaders of the top Western democratic nations, people in the newsroom were still asking questions about the body parts case. It was an unsolved murder mystery, a whodunit. Was it the boyfriend? Had any more of her body parts been found? When were the police going to make an arrest? Those who had seen the message for Pron, and that included Lou Clancy, the city editor, wondered if it was Pan who had called.

"Sounds like Pan," Pron said. "I wonder what he wanted?"

"Nothing much, just your home phone number," Coles said.

"Christ! I hope you didn't give it to him."

Coles smiled. "No. I gave him Donovan's because he never buys me coffee."

"Oh . . . ah, cream and sugar?"

"Thanks. Your Chinese friend seemed eager to talk, like he had something important on his mind."

"If he does call again, can you put him right through? I'm in there," Pron said, nodding towards the police radio room. "Dr. Frankenstein has returned to take care of his monster."

Much to his chagrin, Pron was back in the Box. It was a room he had helped to create, suggesting to senior editors that the only way to ensure thorough coverage of police news in Toronto was to have as many scanners as the *Sun*. So the paper had gone from one scanner in the newsroom to nine. It was advice Pron was starting to regret.

Shelley Page, the reporter in the radio room, threw up her arms in jubilation, like one of the converted at a religious meeting.

"These things are going nuts," she said, as she quickly gathered up her notebooks and papers, sneering at the police scanners. "I just can't stand it in here. They should hire a cop to do this. How can anybody understand anything? There's a fire on the Danforth, somewhere around Main Street. I checked with the fire department, but they had nothing for us yet. Bad crash on the Don Valley. Car into a truck, I think. Or was it the other way around? There's something about a missing kid in Etobicoke. The Emergency Task Force are checking out a report of a man with an Uzi somewhere on Bloor. Other than that," she shouted over her shoulder as she hurried from the room, "really nothing going on. Except for the Summit, of course."

Pron took off his glasses and rubbed the corners of his eyes with his thumb and forefinger. He looked around the Box. There was a plate of half-eaten French fries, bathed in gravy and ketchup, next to the computer, a napkin tossed on top of the food, as if to hide it from the fruit flies buzzing over top. Sections of that day's paper were scattered around the desk and on the floor. The waste-basket was overflowing with newspaper. Someone had pulled a batch of police sheets from a drawer, then dumped them on the floor.

"Can you turn those damned things down?" one of the copy editors shouted from his desk. "We can't hear ourselves think over here."

Pron sat down at the computer terminal to sign in. Just as he did, the screen went black. The terminal in the overloaded, antiquated system had been taken off line. He called the computer room to get it turned on. The line was busy.

"Any more on that fire on the Danforth?" It was Bill Lennon, one of the photo editors, who had walked into the Box.

"I haven't got a clue," Pron replied. "I just got in."

"I need to know fast how bad it is if we hope to get a camera there in rush hour. Any idea how many people hurt?"

"I said I don't know! I just got here."

"Geez, you're sure grouchy today."

Assignment editor Bob Burt came into the room. "The radio's got an item about a fire on the Danforth," he said to Pron. "Any idea how bad it is? Jesus, what a mess in here."

"Gimme a minute. I'll find out," Pron said. "But first, is it okay if I take off my jacket?"

Lennon turned to Burt. "He's in a lousy mood," he said, talking about Pron as if he wasn't there. "Guess I would be, too, if I had to work in here. What a pigsty!"

"Can you check with the cops about a protest at the Summit?" Burt asked, glancing around at the garbage. "Radio stations are saying something about pickets outside Thatcher's hotel room. We might need more bodies over there. Let me know as soon as you can, okay?"

It was about two hours before things finally settled down. The big blaze on the Danforth turned out to be a burning pot on the stove. The protest outside the British prime minister's hotel room was four skinheads waving placards. There were about twenty specially trained security officers circling each protester. The missing kid was found watching television at his friend's house, unaware that half the police force in Etobicoke had been combing the streets for him. There was a man carrying an Uzi on Bloor all right, but it was the plastic kind that squirted water. The only thing that checked out was the accident on the Don Valley Parkway. Five people went to hospital. The photo desk didn't want to hear about it. They already had a good accident picture for the next day's paper. All the other space was taken up with shots of Summit leaders, in a group, singly, with their wives, more shots of just wives, and so on. Pron was about to go for coffee when Carol Coles buzzed him on the intercom.

"Caller for you on line one, Sounds Chinese. Could be your man. And, by the way, thanks for that coffee."

"Right after this call, I promise," Pron said, picking up the phone.

"What's all that noise on the phone?" the caller asked. "Are you tape recording this call, Mr. Nick Pron?"

"Hello, Mr. Pan," Pron said, turning down the scanners.

"I have to be so careful what I say to you," Pan continued. "Because if you put it in the paper, you ruin my reputation. You have caused me much trouble. I was just reading one of the stories you and Kevin Donovan put in the paper."

"Which one was that, Mr. Pan?"

"You said Selina left after bitter argument. There was no bitter argument. Who told you such a lie?"

"Everyone says that, Mr. Pan. Everyone we talked to."

"You must be more careful what you write, Mr. Nick Pron. These stories have caused me great harm. Your stories are quoted as fact in Chinese papers even though eighty percent of what you write is not truth and fact. Eighty percent all wrong. All lie, eighty percent."

"Then complain to the Bureau of Accuracy. Do you want the number?"

"I wanted to law suit you, Mr. Nick Pron. But my lawyer says you are too clever in what you write."

Pron glanced around the Box. "I'm not that clever, Mr. Pan," he replied.

"I beg your pardon?"

"That search you wanted, Mr. Pan. It's ready. Is that why you called?"

"I have something to tell you. It is very important. This will help police to solve the case. The Chinese papers who say I am killer, they will have to show their evidence. They will have to say who told them such things. I will tell you something, but this is not for publication. I am law suiting two

Chinese papers. They will have to tell my lawyers where they got their facts. Then I will know who is telling these lies. This information I will give to the police and Larry Edgar. He is responsible policeman who works hard. These people who are trying to frame me are hiding the real killer. My lawyer says these papers have no evidence that I am killer. He says they just get information from Toronto *Star*. They take Toronto *Star* stories and put in their paper. Tell me, Mr. Nick Pron, who did you talk to? These people are the ones trying to put me in the frame-up.''

''I talked to a lot of people. None of them wanted their names used.''

''They are liars! If you print what they say, I will law suit you, as well. You must check your information. You must not use gossip. Do you understand, Mr. Nick Pron? Kevin is working with police to frame me, and now I think you are helping him. You are putting me on the public trial. Your stories are giving the public the wrong attitude. You are trying to put me into hell. But I am laughing at you. You must be careful what you write, Mr. Nick Pron. You must be very careful.''

''That sounds like a threat.''

''I am not giving threat. But just remember, Mr. Nick Pron, as you brew, you must drink.''

''Yeah, so you've said before.''

''Whatever people tell you about me, it's all slander, rumours, lies. Today I have given the police most helpful information about the case.''

''And what was that?''

''For this you must ask the police.''

''Was it the tapes? The ones you keep talking about? The ones where that man threatens Selina?''

''For this you must ask Larry Edgar.''

''He's not returning my calls.''

''I was just reading a newspaper story. In *Globe and Mail*. Very important case. Donald Marshall. Do you know this case?''

''The Indian out east who served eleven years for a murder he didn't do? Yeah, I know it. Why?''

"Because I want you to help me, Mr. Nick Pron. This is very important case. It will be in my book. I want you to get me all the newspaper clippings you can on Donald Marshall. Can you do that for me, Mr. Nick Pron?"

"I'm a little busy."

"If you do that for me, I will do something for you."

"What's that?"

"I will make you most famous person."

"I don't want to be famous."

"I will tell you at dinner. I will even pay. The other times we meet you always pay, so this time I will pay."

"Good. When? How about tomorrow?"

"It must be later in evening. You know I spend many hours at my business. I am very hard worker. Yesterday, for instance, I work all day and night and then come home and write four thousand words. I am very tired. I will meet you in Chinatown. Do you know Dragon Centre?"

"I can find it."

"Meet me there at eight o'clock. There are many good restaurants close. I like you, Mr. Nick Pron. You are my friend. But people tell me, 'If he is your friend, why does he not invite you to his house?' You have been to my house, Mr. Nick Pron, but I have not been to yours. I would like to meet your lovely wife and family. You make a promise that you would invite me but you forget. You have memory problem. My friends, they ask me what happened to the invitation. I tell them that Mr. Nick Pron forget to invite."

"Wait till I finish my renovations, Mr. Pan. My house is a mess right now."

"See, Mr. Nick Pron, you do not trust me. This is what people say, 'If he trusted him, then he would invite him to his house. He must think he is killer if he does not trust him.' Maybe you will give me invitation one day. I will see you tomorrow. But don't bring Kevin Donovan. He works for the police. I don't want to see him ever again. He is very bad person. This I have heard."

After he finished his shift that evening, Pron stopped off for a beer at the Monarch on his way home. The Monarch was a cozy little west-end bar that was a hang-out for cops and crooks. It was known for its big glasses of draft beer, thick veal sandwiches, and meat platters. The bar was also famous for something else. Newcomers to the Monarch usually had to go through an initiation, just like the hazing faced by first-year university students. Pron's had been particularly embarrassing. Peter, the waiter who did the hazings, had crept up behind Pron, plunked a giant dildo on his shoulder, and sprayed a stream of water into his lap. Then he rinsed off the dildo in Pron's beer and wiped it clean in his sports jacket. Peter had then dropped to his knees in front of Pron, loudly proclaiming that he was going to give him oral sex while the other patrons in the bar looked on, hooting with glee.

The dimly lit bar was crowded that night, but Pron didn't recognize anybody. After he had a couple of drafts he got up to go, stopping first at the washroom. He was standing in front of the urinal when a man stepped up to the one beside it. He was wearing a lumber jacket torn at the elbows. His beard was bushy, unkempt, and his hair looked as though it hadn't been combed for days.

"Working on anything good lately?" he said to Pron.

Pron turned to the man and looked more closely at his face. "Sid?" he asked.

The bearded man smiled briefly. He was an old police contact Pron hadn't heard from for years. The last time he had seen him, Sid had been in uniform and sporting a brush cut.

"Don't even ask what I'm working on," Sid replied.

"Let me guess. Drugs?"

"I've been hearing some things about you lately. None of them good. You and that Donovan are pissing off a lot of people."

"What do you mean?"

"You still working on that Pan case?"

"Yeah."

"That's what I mean."

"I haven't done a story on the murder for weeks."

"I'm only hearing this third hand, but I gather you're getting too close. You two just won't leave it alone."

"But he keeps calling me."

"Take some advice. Don't talk to him. You still think he's innocent?"

"He says the cops are framing him, along with the media."

"What about the incident down by the pier? How does he explain that one?"

"What incident? What pier?"

"You don't know about the night by the pier?"

"What are you talking about, Sid?"

"You're a reporter. Why don't you do some investigating and find out?"

"Talking to guys like you, that is investigating."

"Gathering information with your dick hanging out is not what I call investigating. Look, I can't say anything more," Sid said, moving to the door. "Just keep in mind what I said."

Sid was sitting at a table with several other men who all looked like the kind of vagrants who sleep on warm air grates. Pron passed by the table on the way to the exit, but Sid made no motion to invite him to sit down.

There were two of them, troop-carrying size, green in colour, and as the helicopters hovered over the Art Gallery of Ontario, the whump-whump-whump from their rotor blades was deafening. The seven heads of state from the leading Western nations were to meet that afternoon in the heart of Chinatown to discuss world affairs. Ringing the art gallery, looking uncomfortable in the hot sun, were two hundred police officers, decked out in black. Black baseball-style hats, black overalls, black boots. Holstered at their waists were 9 mm handguns, also black. On the rooftops of every tall building around the art gallery were more men in black, these equipped with high-powered rifles and scopes. The men on the ground, the sharpshooters on the rooftops, were all part of the new Metro Police Public Order Squad, specially formed for the Summit. Their job was simple. Make sure no one bothered the seven heads of state. And right now their attention was focused on a crowd of about sixty men and women milling about in the intersection in front of the art gallery, carrying signs that called the world leaders a band of terrorists.

The day before, a group of women had taken off their blouses, bared their breasts as a show of protest to the Summit gathering. As he glanced at the fully clothed female activists in front of him, Donovan was disappointed they had decided to be more modest in their act of civil disobedience. With nothing happening on the Shen murder, Donovan was on general assignment, covering protests, fires, public meetings, and whatever else caught the assignment editor's fancy. Like Pron, he hadn't covered any of the main events at the Summit. An afternoon protest was as good as it was going to get. He stood midway between the cops and the protesters, waiting for something to happen.

"Arrest the G-7! They're all killers!" one demonstrator shouted, holding aloft a sign with a caricature of President Ronald Reagan riding a nuclear warhead, a big grin on his face, and a cowboy hat on his head.

"Stop the starving! Stop the suffering! Stop the seven!" shouted a woman with a ponytail, her face taut, red with anger. She was in her mid-thirties and wore torn jeans and a T-shirt with a peace sign on it. She moved towards the solid wall of police, a dozen of her cohorts following close behind. The human barricade didn't budge.

"We have arrest warrants here for all seven leaders," the woman leading the protesters shouted, shoving a piece of paper in the face of one of the police officers. "You are officers of the law. I am asking you to honour these warrants."

The solid line of men in black parted slightly, and a police officer stepped forward. Although he was dressed like the others, he was much older and grizzled looking. He was obviously the man in charge.

"I must ask you to back up to the sidewalk!" he ordered. "The motorcade is on its way, and this street must be clear."

The woman with the ponytail thrust the paper into his hands. He peeled off his damp cap and rubbed his arm across his sweaty forehead as he studied the document. The crowd of protesters pressed tighter. Several television crews moved in.

"These mean nothing," the grizzled-looking cop said, handing the papers back. "I will not execute these warrants.

You have ten minutes to move away or we will arrest all of you on charges of breaching the peace."

And with that he turned smartly, the black line parted slightly, and he disappeared behind them. The protesters started yelling, waving their placards in the air. Then, in unison, they sat down in the middle of the intersection. Some of them drew peace signs and antiwar slogans in chalk on the sidewalk. One wrote the words *Metro Police* and drew a large Nazi swastika beside them.

Donovan stooped to get a few quotes from the woman with the ponytail. When he stood up, he noticed a tall, white-haired man, wearing a dark blue business suit, approaching. A television crew trailed behind him. His name was William McCormack, and he was the deputy police chief of the Metro force. He nodded to the protesters, even waved to one of them, a big smile on his face, then he disappeared behind the line of officers in black. A few moments later he reappeared, the grizzled-looking officer by his side.

"I want you all to know that I have no problem with you staying in this area," McCormack told them. "This is a free country. But you must move back thirty yards. You are welcome to carry on your protest from the sidewalk." He pointed across the street. "Over there."

One of the protesters shouted: "We don't care if we're jail-cell bound, gonna let no SWAT team turn us around." They all linked arms, crossed legs, and stayed put.

McCormack, still smiling, turned to the officer at his side, jerked his thumb over his shoulder.

"Do 'em," he said. Then he turned to the crowd of protesters, smiled, and walked away.

Moments later, a fleet of police paddy wagons pulled up to the intersection. The officers in black broke ranks and waded into the crowd of protesters, grabbing people and trying to pull them up. The protesters screamed but refused to move. As they were lifted to their feet, the protesters kept their legs crossed, their bodies swaying awkwardly in the air as they were carried to the paddy wagons. They had expected to be arrested. Many had on wrist bands to stop the handcuffs from cutting into their skin. Not far from the intersection, in the shade of a building, a man eating a hot dog appeared to have more than a passing interest in the spectacle of the mass arrests. He seemed to be studying what was happening, taking mental notes of the events. Donovan walked over and said hello. The man eating the hot dog was one of Toronto's top Crown attorneys.

"Slow day in court?" Donovan asked.

"Just wanted to see who was going to be on the docket tomorrow morning," the Crown attorney replied. He pointed to a scrum of reporters shouting questions at President Ronald Reagan as he walked into the art gallery, Prime Minister Brian Mulroney close on his heels. "Shouldn't you be over there?"

"I'm here for the real action," Donovan replied, looking at two policemen struggling to get a woman into a paddy wagon.

"You've been writing stories on that Shen murder, haven't you?" the Crown attorney asked, after finishing his hot dog.

"Not lately. Nothing much to write about. Boyfriend keeps saying he's innocent. Cops keep saying they're investigating. I think they're waiting for some big clue to turn up."

"That might help the case."

"Oh? So they are having trouble."

The Crown attorney smiled. "Well, I'm heading back to court," he said, picking up his briefcase, turning to go. Donovan walked with him.

"So who is the killer?" he asked casually, not really expecting an answer. "Pan?"

The Crown attorney took his time answering. "Probably," he said finally. "Least, that's what the cops think."

"Then why hasn't he been arrested?"

"Little thing called evidence. They don't have enough of it."

"What are they missing?"

"Her head, for starters. Nobody knows how she was killed. Maybe it will tell them."

"So, if they find out how she was killed, then can they arrest Pan?"

He turned and scowled at Donovan. "You're sure interested in this case."

"Just asking questions."

The Crown attorney stopped, put down his briefcase, and took out a pack of cigarettes. "Maybe too many questions," he said, lighting one up.

"You know how it is. You've got to ask fifty questions to get one answer."

The Crown attorney puffed on his cigarette. "Look," he said finally, "you might as well know this now. You'll probably hear it later anyway. The cops are claiming you guys have been getting too close. They say you're screwing up their investigation. Getting in the way. Talking to potential Crown witnesses. That sort of thing."

"So? The cops are always getting mad at reporters."

"No, I mean really mad. Mad enough to get legal advice about what to do."

"What do they want to do, sue us?" Donovan asked, laughing.

"No. Charge you."

Donovan stared at him, a worried look on his face. "You're kidding."

"I think they call it obstruction of justice."

"For asking questions? They'd never be stupid enough to arrest us on that."

The Crown attorney smiled.

"Would they?"

"Kevin, you might like it in jail. Lots of time to write."

"Are you serious?"

"Damn right I'm serious. They wanted to know if they had grounds to charge you two."

"What did you say to them?"

He looked up at the circling helicopters. "I told them to go fuck themselves. You guys are just doing your job."

The electronic billboard high atop the Dragon Centre shopping mall was telling passersby in English and Chinese to give to the Salvation Army, a message that was flashed roughly fifty-five times every hour. It also urged the pedestrians, again in both languages, to give blood. In between pleas for money and blood, the billboard flashed headlines from news stories.

Rui-Wen Pan stood on the sidewalk at the base of the billboard, staring at the messages. A steady drizzle was falling that night. Pan took off his glasses and wiped the raindrops from the lenses. One of the arms of the glasses was broken, held to the frame with thick, black tape. Pan checked his watch again, looked over to where his brother was window-shopping with Wang and Fang.

Pron and Donovan had arrived early and were across the street in a restaurant having a beer, watching Pan from their window table. They took their time finishing before walking over. Pan was annoyed at being kept waiting. He was even less pleased when he saw Donovan.

"You two have been drinking," he said, eyeing them suspiciously after everyone had shaken hands.

"Here are your newspaper clippings," Pron said, handing a brown manila folder to Pan.

He barely glanced at it before giving the package to Wang to carry. Pan said he had made reservations at a restaurant just up the street. As they walked that way, Pan took Pron aside while the others went on ahead.

"You lied to me, Mr. Nick Pron," Pan said. "I told you not to bring Kevin Donovan. I do not want him here. He is policeman."

"He's a reporter, just like me, Mr. Pan. Don't be so paranoid."

"I have to be careful. They're all conspiring against me. I have proof of this. You see that sign," he said, pointing down the street at the electronic billboard on top of the Dragon Centre. "Messages on there are from Chinese newspaper. They say boyfriend is mentally deranged. Boyfriend is killer of Selina Shen. There, in flashing messages. This I have seen with my eyes. In a country ruled by law, is this justice, Mr. Nick Pron?"

"They're not naming you, are they?"

"I am most famous person in Chinatown. Everyone know I am Selina's boyfriend. They are saying Selina killed by boy-

friend. I have something to tell you, but only if you promise
not to put in your paper. These newspapers that I law suit,
the ones that say I am killer, they have no proof of anything.
My lawyer saw what they had as evidence and he just
laughed. 'What's wrong with their lawyer? If that's all they
have, then they're in real trouble,' he told me. Before I was
ninety-nine percent certain I was going to win law suit. Now
I am one hundred percent.''

Pan nodded smugly as he stared at the electronic billboard.

''You'll be a rich man, Mr. Pan.''

''The money that I win,'' Pan replied, ''it is not important
to me. I do not want a single penny of it. I will use the money
to build a statue to Selina, my beloved. I will build two stat-
ues. One at Scarborough Christian School, the other in
China. But that is not for paper. After I win law suit, then
you can print.''

''The tapes, Mr. Pan. Do you have those tapes you made
of the man who threatened Selina?''

''Why do you always bother me for tapes?''

''If you want me to help you find the killer, that might not
be a bad place to start.''

Pan looked ahead to the restaurant, where the others were
waiting patiently. He started that way.

''Do you have those tapes?'' Pron asked again.

''Who told you about tapes?''

''You did. I think you're the one with the memory problem,
not me. Where are the tapes?''

''I was looking for tapes just other day.''

''And?''

''I cannot find. These tapes . . . I lose.''

Two stone lions, painted gold, red, and blue, stood guard
at the entrance to the yellow brick restaurant. The maître d'
who greeted them knew Pan. They spoke for a moment, then
the maître d' seated them at a large, round table near a stage
on which bands usually played for the entertainment of the
diners. Instead of a band that night, there were two carpenters on the stage, building a set for a play. Large snakes were
painted on each flat. To one side was a huge papier mâché
snake, painted green.

211

"It is for Chinese New Year," Pan said. "It is Year of the Snake. If you knew anything, you would know that."

Pan ordered for everyone, and was the only one not to have a drink. He leaned back in his chair and was quiet, almost sullen, as the others clinked glasses and toasted the Year of the Snake. Soon the table was filled with steaming plates of rice, beef, vegetables, chicken, shrimp, and soup. Everyone dug in, except Pan.

"You're not hungry, Mr. Pan?" Pron asked.

"I cannot enjoy food since Selina died. I lose much weight. People tell me, they say I should forget about her and take care of myself. They do not understand. My life is finished without Selina."

The waiter put a tray of beef in front of Pan. He picked up a strip with his chopsticks, put it on his plate, then looked around the table for something. He saw the knife. It was beside Pron's plate. Pron was the only one at the table using a knife and fork, in fact, about the only diner in the restaurant that night not using chopsticks. Donovan nudged Pron as Pan held the meat in place with a chopstick, then started slicing through the meat with the knife. He cut the meat into four neat strips, cutting each piece slowly, carefully, so that each piece was the same size. Then he picked up one piece with his chopsticks and started to eat.

"Nice cutting job," Donovan whispered to Pron, but not softly enough. "Why don't you ask your pal there if that's the way he cut up Selina?"

Pan turned sharply towards the two of them, as if he had heard. "What did he say?" he asked Pron.

Pron was stuck for an answer.

"I'll tell him," Donovan said, leaning around Pron to face Pan. "That the way you cut up Selina? Nice and neat."

Pan turned to his brother, said something to him in Chinese. Jia-Wen shrugged. Pan leaned closer to Pron.

"How can he say this thing?" he asked. "I invite you to dinner and he says this. I think he must be mentally unbalanced to say such a thing. I have no more appetite to eat."

He put down his chopsticks, leaned back in his chair, folded his arms across his chest, and stared ahead silently. The waiter brought over more drinks. The restaurant was starting to empty. Donovan picked up his drink and wandered over to the stage, struck up a conversation with one of the carpenters.

"I do not know why you are seen with him," Pan said, staring at Donovan. "He brings shame to you. I am a writer, you are a writer. We are educated people. But him" — Pan motioned towards Donovan, who was sitting on the papier mâché snake, laughing at something the workman was saying—"he is lower class."

The waiter brought a plate of fortune cookies along with the bill. Pan picked up the bill, glanced at it briefly, then put it back on the tray. He broke open a cookie, took out a tiny strip of paper. He smiled as he read it, then handed it to Pron. It said: "The laws sometimes sleep but never die."

The waiter hovered around the table, glancing from time to time at the bill as he shuffled plates around. He left with an armful of dirty dishes, but was back a few moments later. He made a big show of picking up the unpaid bill, looked at it, cleared his throat noisily, looked around at the diners before putting the bill back on the tray. Pan remained motionless, leaning back in his chair, his arms folded across his chest. Donovan was the first to realize what was happening.

"Your killer friend intends to stiff us with the bill," he said, loud enough for Pan to hear.

"I don't think I have enough to cover the bill," Pron said, reaching into his pocket, taking out a five and three one-dollar bills. "Have you got any plastic?"

Donovan took out his American Express card, tossed it on top of the bill without even wanting to know how much it was, and sneered at Pan. The waiter, who suddenly remembered how to smile, bowed politely at Donovan before hurrying off with the card.

"So much for believing anything Pan tells you," Donovan said, signing the bill when the waiter returned.

Donovan got up and made a point of shaking hands with Wang, Fang, and Jia-Wen, but not Pan.

"Thanks for the dinner, Mr. Pan," he said. "Hope you enjoyed it. Food's not as good in jail."

As they were leaving the restaurant, Pan took Pron aside.

"I will tell you something that will help you catch the killer. I have told police this and they are working on it. It is very important that you find out where she worked after she left me. In this period I think she had trouble. I think she met someone who hurted her."

"How do you know that?"

"This I know. I cannot tell you exactly but I tell police. You find out where she was before she disappeared and you will find the real killer."

"You have to give me more than that. You said she worked. Where?"

"A restaurant downtown. Maybe Jarvis. Maybe on Yonge."

"Where on Jarvis? Where on Yonge? They're big streets."

"All I know is that she worked in restaurant. You find this restaurant. She meet someone there, someone who might have done her harm."

"That's not much to go on, Mr. Pan. I hope you told the cops more than that."

"See, Mr. Nick Pron. I am helping you solve this case. If you do this, you will be most famous person. You do this to make up for all the trouble you have caused. I trust you. You are my friend. Maybe if you solve this case, you will invite me to your house. I think then you will trust me. If you forget to invite, maybe I will have to come over . . . on my own."

Pron was silent on the drive back to the *Star*.

"Still mad about getting stiffed on the bill?" Donovan asked. "I'm the one who should be mad."

"He wants to come over to my house," Pron replied.

"Who? Pan?"

"He's convinced I'm his friend. He says if I trusted him I wouldn't be afraid to invite him over."

"Of course you have no intention of doing that."

Pron didn't answer.

"You're not going to, are you?"

"Well . . ."

"Pron, the man's a killer!"

"We don't know that for sure."

"Figure it out. Who else is there? Pan had the means, Pan had the motive, Pan had the opportunity. You don't think the cops are going to waste all that money following him around if they didn't think he did it. Of course he killed her. There's no one else."

"But what if there is someone else?"

"Okay. Okay. If you think he's so innocent, then why not invite him to your house? Have him over for dinner. Introduce him to your family."

"He might confess."

"Sure. Of course. Maybe while you're sitting around the dinner table. What the hell, it's a reasonable risk. I mean, what are you gambling with? Just your family's safety."

Pron was silent as he stared at the crowds of evening shoppers in Chinatown. And then, suddenly, he shouted: "Stop the car!"

"Huh?"

"Right there." Pron pointed to a phone booth. "Pull over right there."

Pron got out, hurried into the phone booth, fumbled through his pockets for a quarter, then dialled a number. He let it ring.

"C'mon. C'mon," he said, slapping a hand against a leg. Finally someone answered.

"Hi. It's me," Pron said to his wife. "Is everything okay?"

"Of course," she replied. "Why shouldn't it be?"

"Oh, nothing. Nothing. Uh . . . is the front door locked?"

"I don't know, I guess so. Why?"

"Could you check?"

"I will."

"No, I mean right now. Could you check the front door right now to see if it's locked? Just to be sure."

"What's wrong? What's going on?"

"Nothing. Just check it. Okay? I'll hold on."

"Are you sure nothing's wrong?"

"No. No. Everything's fine. Just try the door. I'll explain in a minute."

"All right." His wife put the phone down and was back a moment later. "It wasn't locked."

"But you locked it, right?"

"Yes, I locked it. Now do you mind telling me what this is all about?"

"Oh, well, I was just . . . I was just talking to this cop. And he was saying that . . . that there was, uh, a drug addict and he was breaking into homes in our area, looking for money to get dope. I just got a little worried, that's all."

"Are you sure that's all? You sound kind of funny."

"Look, I won't be late tonight. But don't answer the door if you're not sure who it is. Promise?"

Pron gave Donovan a weak grin when he got into the car.

"What was all that about?" Donovan asked.

"You're right," Pron replied. "Even thinking of inviting him over to my house was a stupid idea. Let's invite him over to your house."

The *Star*'s cafeteria was crowded with the evening shift workers, most of them the blue overall-clad men and women who ran the paper's giant printing presses. One of the few editorial staff waiting in the cashier's line was Pat Dolan from the art department.

"I haven't seen anything in the paper lately about that awful murder," she said to Pron. "Do they still think the boyfriend did it?"

"He looks like the best suspect," Pron replied.

"There's one thing I don't understand," she said, as they walked up to the newsroom. "Why were all the body parts dumped in that one area?"

"Remote, I guess."

"There're a lot more desolate areas around the province than that. It's almost like he wanted the police to find her."

"What are you getting at?"

"Just curious about why he picked that area. Can you show me on a map where it is? I was just up there. My husband and I were thinking of getting a cottage around there. But I don't want to find an arm on my front doorstep. How dreadful."

Dolan took out a map of eastern Ontario and spread it over one of the artist's tables. Pron pointed out the places the body parts had been found, each one south of Highway 401, the main link between Toronto and Montreal.

"He probably just got off the 401, maybe took Highway 33," Pron said, tracing a finger along the road. "At that time of year, the road would be deserted."

"Didn't you tell me before Pan had written a book, something about a lake?" Dolan asked.

"It was called *An Incident*, or something like that, *Beside West Lake*."

"Did he ever say what it was about?"

"Never mentioned it again."

"Have a look at this," Dolan said, pointing to a spot off Highway 33.

Pron was quiet as he stared at the map. "Well, son of a bitch," he said loudly, slamming his fist down on the table.

"It's just too much of a coincidence."

Dolan had pointed to a small inland body of water around the area Selina's remains had been found. It was just off Highway 33, and almost directly south of the place that Andy Borisenko had found her torso inside a garbage bag. The body of water was called West Lake.

"I think I've got to find that book," Pron said.

CHAPTER EIGHTEEN

A Murderous Affair

"I was scared," Sophie Shen said. "That's why I didn't tell you the whole story before."

"Scared of what?" asked Larry Edgar. They were in his office at OPP headquarters, Edgar, Sophie Shen, and Constable Gus Riddell. "Or should I say who?"

"Scared of Li Ling, I mean, Rui-Wen."

"Why?"

"If I said things about him, I was afraid he would hear. Afraid he might hurt me."

Gus Riddell, standing to one side of Edgar's desk, loosened his tie. "But we told you," he said, pulling up a chair beside her, "there was nothing to worry about. We'd protect you."

"You do not understand. So much was happening at the time. He was always talking to people. He would have found out from someone that I was helping you. And then I might have been hurt. Maybe like Selina."

Edgar opened a folder on his desk and took out a picture of Selina.

"It's because of what happened to Selina that we need to know everything you know. A dozen police officers have been going day and night trying to find out who murdered your sister." Edgar pushed the picture towards her. "We need your help, and we need it now."

Sophie looked at the picture for several moments before picking it up. Edgar watched her closely. His detectives had talked to Sophie many times before, but she always seemed to be holding something back. Being scared could explain only part of that. Edgar suspected there were other reasons.

"Okay," Sophie said, putting the picture down, "I will answer your questions."

"Good," Edgar said. "There're a few places you could help us. Her baby, why didn't you tell us about her baby? We knew she had a child. From a South American fellow. Why didn't you tell us? Were you embarrassed because Selina wasn't married?"

"At first, when she was pregnant at school, I didn't even know. One time I even told her she should go to an exercise class, because I thought she was getting fat. She wouldn't tell me. She was ashamed, I guess. And she wouldn't talk about it. Just put the baby up for adoption. So it was a family secret. I didn't think it was important to tell you."

"But don't you see that the father of the baby could have been crucial to our investigation?" Riddell asked. "As it was, when we finally tracked him down, we determined that he was in the clear. If we hadn't known about him, that could have hurt us down the line, if this ever gets to court."

Sophie seemed to be on the verge of tears. "Also, I think I didn't tell you because Rui-Wen seemed so angry about the baby all the time. He would ask 'Why did she go with that damned black? Why did she have a baby with that El Salvador? Why was she always going disco dancing, drinking in bars, showing off?' Because he was so angry about it all the time, I was scared he would hurt me for telling you about these things."

Edgar picked up the picture of Selina and put it back in the folder. "Okay. Some of the questions we're going to ask you may be going over old ground, but we just want to make sure we get everything straight. Now, you told us before that you lived with Pan before your sister did, right?"

"Yes."

"But not for very long."

"Just three months."

"That's not very long. You told us you moved out because Mr. Pan favoured your sister. I'm wondering, was there something else?"

Sophie didn't answer.

"Other people have told us there was trouble," offered Edgar.

"Yes," Sophie said finally, "there were problems."

"Tell us about it," Riddell said. "It could be important."

"Well, I think I told you before that he always wanted to know where I was. But it was more than that. He took away my freedom. He was old-fashioned Chinese. No respect for women. Like sometimes, he would go to the piano store I worked at and bother my boss, ask her where I was going and what I was doing. Always checking up on me. One night I came home late. The lights were off and I didn't think he was home, so I went to bed. I was just drifting off to sleep when the lights suddenly came on and he was there beside the bed. I was scared. He must have been in the house all the time, waiting for me in the dark. That is when I decided to leave him. I couldn't keep up the relationship. He told me if I left he would make my life insufferable. But I had to get away. I wanted Selina to stay away from him, but she said she was falling in love. So I asked my ex-husband to find me a place to live, someplace secret. Someplace Rui-Wen couldn't find me. I did not even say goodbye. I moved out when he was not there, just left his key under the doormat. The only one who I gave my telephone number to was Selina. When Rui-Wen asked, she gave him the number. That made me very mad at her. He started calling me, asking if I was coming back. I said I would not. He kept calling. Sometimes he was nice, but most times he was rude."

"He just wouldn't leave you alone, would he?" said Edgar.

"Then he found my house and came there late one night. Soon after that happened I moved out. Then he kept calling me, so I had to change my number."

"Did he ever threaten you?" asked Edgar.

"Once, before I moved out, he told me that if I want to leave, he won't let me leave. If I want to die, he won't let me die."

"Was he with your sister by this time?" Edgar asked.

"Yes. But that didn't matter. He still followed me."

"Did Mr. Pan ever hit you?"

"Not me, Selina. He hurt Selina."

"What do you mean hurt?" Riddell asked.

"I think I told you before that they argued a lot, and Selina moved out several times. But what I did not tell you is that Rui-Wen beat my sister up."

Edgar nodded.

"One time," Sophie continued, "she told me that they were fighting, yelling, I mean. They always fought about small things. When Jia-Wen moved in, they fought even more. They had been fighting over who was to do the laundry and the cleaning and the cooking. I think Selina did it most of the time, but they did not think so. So this time I am telling you about, Rui-Wen was yelling at her and he punched her in the stomach. Hard. Then he kicked her legs, made many bruises. Selina told me that he pushed her from corner to corner, hurting her."

"When was this?"

"Maybe a year before she died."

"Did she report this to police?"

"No."

"Was she afraid to go to the police?" asked Edgar.

"Rui-Wen knew she wouldn't. Selina was afraid she would lose her immigration status. Rui-Wen would always bring it up. Always. Hold it over her. Like a threat. He would say that she would be sent back if she ever complained." Sophie wiped away a tear. "Rui-Wen said she would be sent out of the country and never allowed to return."

"That's okay, Sophie," Riddell said. "We know this isn't easy. It just seems strange to us that she put up with him for so long."

"My sister did not want to go back home. Rui-Wen knew that and he used that to keep her. Even when she moved out she always went back."

"Mr. Pan must have been pretty upset when Selina moved out the last time and never came back," Edgar said.

"On Monday, the day after Selina never showed up for dinner, I called Rui-Wen at his home. As soon as he heard my voice he said, 'It is all your fault. She has left me to live with some Canadian guy.' I was not sure what he meant, so

I drove over to his home on Puma Drive. When I was getting out of my car, he came out the front door and met me in the driveway. He would not invite me in, said he was in a rush to get to an eleven A.M. appointment. He seemed kind of nervous, but would not tell me why. I told him I could not reach Selina. He said to come back that night at ten and talk to him."

"Did you?"

"Yes. I was scared, though. I brought my friend Ela Mu with me. She followed me in her car and waited while I went inside."

"Who was in the house?"

"Just Rui-Wen and his brother."

"And they were eating dinner?"

"Yes. But there was something else I just remembered. Something I didn't tell you before. Rui-Wen was eating with a spoon, not chopsticks. He was using his left hand to hold the spoon even though he is right-handed. His right hand was resting on the table. It looked as if the hand was injured."

Edgar gave Riddell a quick glance. "Why didn't you tell us this before?" he asked Sophie.

"I don't know. I guess I forgot."

"His hand, did you get a good look at it?" asked Edgar.

"The palm was bruised. It was swollen," replied Sophie. "It was like a purple bruise."

"And this was the right hand?" asked Edgar. "You're sure of that?"

"Yes. Because I thought it was odd that he was using a spoon and holding it in his left hand."

"Did he say what happened?"

"He said he hurt it moving stock in his store. He could hardly move his hand. I told him he should go to a doctor. He said it was only a minor injury. 'Why should I go to doctor when I am a doctor?' he told me."

"This is very important information, Sophie. You noticed he had an injured hand on Monday, the day after your sister didn't show up for dinner?"

"That's right. And later when we were driving in my car, he had to use his left hand to open the door when we got out."

"Let me get this clear," said Edgar. "On Monday, the day after Selina didn't show up, you noticed that Pan's right hand was badly injured. Is that right?"

"Yes."

"And it was so badly injured that he was using his left hand to eat. And later, in the car, you noticed he had to open the car door with his left hand, not his right. Since he was the passenger, he should have used his right hand to open the door."

"He had to reach across his body with his left hand to get to the handle."

"And when you were in the car with him, how did he hold his right hand?"

"He held it in his lap, always with the palm up. That's the way he held it at the dinner table, with the palm up."

"Did you see Mr. Pan before that weekend?"

"No."

"What I'm getting at here is whether you noticed his hand before the weekend your sister disappeared."

"I only saw him after," replied Sophie.

"So you wouldn't know if his hand had been injured before that weekend?" asked Edgar.

"No. But it looked like a recent injury," added Sophie.

"Why would you say that?" asked Edgar.

"The way he was holding it, like it bothered him. And I could see the bruising. You will arrest him, won't you? I know he killed her."

"Sophie, you've been a great deal of help. This information on the hand is very important. I can promise you that we will solve this case, we will make an arrest. I want to thank you for coming." Edgar stood up, extended a hand. "Thank you again. Gus will see that you get back home."

The man approaching their table was walking slowly, dragging his feet like a condemned prisoner going to the gallows.

He had the tired look of someone who has worked too hard all his life. His body was emaciated. His pants hung loosely around his waist, his skinny arms dangling lifelessly by his side. He greeted Pron and Donovan with a suspicious, unfriendly gaze, ignoring their invitation to sit down.

If Pan had really written a book, nobody seemed to know anything about it. None of his acquaintances had ever heard of *The Affair by the West Lake*. There was no such title listed anywhere in the reference library. If the police knew about it, they wouldn't comment. Pan might just have been bragging about writing a book, but they had to check. Selina's body parts had been found near a small lake in eastern Ontario called West Lake. Was there any connection between the book and the murder? Did the book title refer to a murderous affair? If they could get a copy of that book, it might explain a lot about Pan and the murder. Donovan had come up with a possible lead. The wife of one of Pan's former friends had given him the name of a Montreal man in whose house Pan had lived when he first came to Canada. Both had some time owing at work and early the next morning they were on the road to Montreal.

Jony Mark was Pan's "uncle," she said. He was the owner of La Maison D'Egg Roll, a restaurant on the outskirts of Montreal. Pron and Donovan were the first customers in the restaurant when it opened that day. But it took a bit of coaxing to get Jony Mark to leave his kitchen and come over to their table.

"Can we talk to you about your nephew, Li Ling, or Rui-Wen Pan?" Donovan asked Mark, who still wouldn't sit down at their table.

"I don't know anything," he said.

"But he is your nephew?" Donovan persisted.

Jony Mark shook his head. "I'm sorry you came all this way for nothing." He turned to go. "I must go back to the kitchen to prepare for lunch."

The restaurant was starting to fill up. Pron and Donovan ordered beer and drank slowly. Two police officers came in for lunch and sat down at a table near them. Every now and then Jony Mark appeared from the kitchen and looked their way. He went over to the table where the policemen were sitting and said a few words. On his way back to the kitchen, he stopped a waitress and said something to her. In a few minutes, steaming plates of rice and chicken were on Pron and Donovan's table.

"We didn't order anything," said Donovan.

The waitress nodded towards Jony Mark, who was standing by the kitchen, watching them.

"Tell him to take a break and come over," Donovan told the waitress. "Tell him we want to buy him a beer."

The noon-hour crowd was almost all gone before the thinly built Mark came over to their table.

"You have talked to Rui-Wen?" he asked, fumbling through his pockets, as if looking for a cigarette. Pron gave him one and lit it.

"Many, many times," Pron said.

"You think he killed that girl?"

"He says he's innocent," replied Donovan.

"He wants us to find the real killer," added Pron.

"Are you really his uncle?" asked Donovan.

Jony Mark pulled up a chair from a nearby table and sat backwards on it. "Not real uncle. He just call me that. Not related. I was good friend with Rui-Wen's father, Boo Chi Pan. When Boo Chi wanted his son to go to Canada, he called me and asked me to help. To be sponsor. I filled out all the immigration forms, paid the money."

"You and his father are good friends?"

Jony Mark shook his head but didn't explain.

"Rui-Wen stayed with you?" asked Donovan.

"Upstairs. He sleep in room with my children."

"Did he ever work in your restaurant?"

"No. Never. Except just once. He worked in kitchen cutting chicken but he hurt his hand. His hands were too soft. He got a blister cutting chicken with butcher knife. After that, he threw down the knife and never worked again. All the time study. He said, 'Uncle, I don't want to go back to China. I want to learn Canadian ways.' "

"His English is very good. Could he speak it when he came here?"

225

"No, nothing. He learned himself, clipping newspapers and reading articles. All night he read stories. Trying to improve his language. He kept my children awake at night. Always talking to himself, learning to speak English."

"That must have been quite a hardship for you. Taking somebody in and paying for him. You and Rui-Wen's father must be good friends."

Jony Mark didn't answer at first. He lit another cigarette and said something to one of the waitresses. She brought him a bottle of beer, and he drank from the bottle.

"I came to Canada in 1957," he said. "I worked for $17.50 a week. I saved for years to buy this place. I worked six and a half days a week, cooking, cleaning tables, washing dishes. When Boo Chi ask favour, I still have six kids living at home, four boys and two girls. I am not rich man. I still have family in China. They want to come here. Boo Chi very important man in China. Very important doctor. He was doctor to big shots in government. I remember one time a big government man hurt his arm. He was going to lose it but Boo Chi saved it. He wanted his son to come here. He asked me to sponsor him once when I was back in China visiting. So Rui-Wen comes here and lives with me."

"Did he ever tell you he was a doctor?" asked Donovan.

"Many times. He said he learned in China but could not be a legal doctor in Canada unless he went to school. He went to Concordia University. But he never talked much about it and then moved out."

"How long did he live here?"

"Eight months. After he moved out, he never came back. Never called. But then once I got a call. It was from jail."

"Tell us about that."

"It was collect call from Rui-Wen in jail in St. John, Quebec. It was something to do with immigration. He went to New York for something. On way back he was stopped at border. No papers. Police arrested him. Then they sent him to Montreal detention centre. My wife and I went to see him. He was very embarrassed. He would not look me in the face. He only spoke to my wife. 'Don't worry, Uncle," he said. 'I will be okay. I will get out.' He wanted us to bring copies of his magazine with us when we came again.''

''*China Spring.*''

''Yes. I had not even heard of magazine, but he said he had founded it with another man.''

''Did you bail him out?''

''I offered to help. He said, 'No, Uncle, don't worry about me. People I know from my magazine will come and help me.' I was mad at him because I had promised his father I would look after him. And now he was in jail. He told me his trouble was his business. He told me to go away. So I went away. I have not talked to him since.''

''That's gratitude. Do you ever remember him saying something about writing a book?''

''He was always writing. I never asked him what about.''

''Is there any of his stuff still here?''

Jony Mark shook his head. ''Will he be arrested?'' he asked. ''Policeman who come here, he say maybe.''

''But that policeman,'' asked Donovan, ''he didn't say when?''

''I just thought real soon.''

Donovan turned to Pron. They were both thinking the same thing. Great time to be out of the city if there was going to be an arrest.

''So you don't remember anything about him writing a book?'' Donovan asked again.

''No. But he said he worked for a newspaper.''

''Chinese newspaper?''

''Something like *Chinese Press.* But I can't remember for sure.''

The offices of *China Press* were in the heart of old Montreal, on the edge of the city's Chinatown. The editor, a balding Chinese man in his late thirties, knew of Rui-Wen Pan. He remembered Pan had written for the paper six or seven years ago, around 1982. As for Mr. Pan writing a book, he wasn't sure. He hadn't been around at that time. Could they look through back copies? Unfortunately that would be impossible. There had been a fire at the newspaper offices in 1985. All their files, records, and back copies of *China Press* had been destroyed in the blaze. But there was somebody who might know. He reached for the index box on his desk.

The woman who came to the door at the house in the east end of Montreal had long, shiny black hair. Vcrinza Tong smiled as if she knew them, explaining as she invited them inside that the editor of *China Press* had just called. She said she had also heard from other people that the two had been asking questions about Selina Shen's murder.

"I'm surprised such a large paper as the Toronto *Star* would care about somebody like Selina," she said.

"We've heard that one before," said Donovan.

"I don't know if there's anything I can tell you," she said.

"How well did you know him?" Donovan asked. "The guy at China Press said you and Pan dated." Vcrinza Tong laughed. "I knew him but not as his girlfriend. We were just friends, not even that, more like acquaintances."

"He wrote for your newspaper?" asked Donovan.

"That's when we were just starting out. I think it was 1982 or 1983, about a year after he came to Canada. He showed up one day and said he wanted to write for *China Press*. Now, in those days, *China Press* was desperate for articles, stories about the Chinese community. We published weekly and we didn't have much advertising so there was plenty of room for articles. I told Li Ling—that's what he said his name was—I couldn't pay him too much. He told me that didn't matter. He said his parents were so wealthy that he didn't have to worry about getting paid." She hesitated, smiling.

"What's wrong?" asked Pron.

"I was just remembering what he looked like when he came into the office. He had on shoes with really high heels. You know those shoes, the ones that make you look taller."

"You mean, elevator boots."

"Yes, that's what he had on. He was trying to look and sound really important and he had on elevator shoes. I wanted to laugh but I didn't want to embarrass him. And he was wearing these sunglasses, they had big oval frames, just like a woman's sunglasses. It was like he didn't know how to dress."

"Was his writing any good?" asked Donovan.

"We took anything. There wasn't much editing. I thought he was going to write about the community. But he wrote political stories. About democracy, and how bad things were back in China. He was always writing stories about how Chinese people in Canada could help change things back home."

"Was he really that serious about this democratic movement?" asked Donovan.

"I just remember him being very emotional whenever we talked about it. There was one time, shortly after I met him, we were out walking and we had just bought sandwiches, smoked meat sandwiches at Schwartz's, and we were sitting on a park bench eating them. Li Ling started talking about the democratic movement and how he was going to bring democracy to his country. That was one time I remember that I really did like him. He said so many nice things about China. About how it was a great country that could be better off if all the young Chinese would work and struggle hard for democracy. He got tears in his eyes at one point and asked if he could hold my hand while we talked. I let him. Maybe somebody saw that and thought we were dating. Or maybe he just told people we were dating."

"Did you go out with him very much?" asked Pron.

"In the first week he started writing articles, Li Ling told me he couldn't possibly come around the office anymore because if he did, he would fall in love with me."

"What did you tell him?" Pron asked.

Verinza Tong smiled. "I told him fine. You had better not come around. Just mail in your articles. Actually, I kind of got mad at him for that. I think he was trying to trick me, pretend he loved me, so he could get his special articles published."

"What special articles?"

"The first one he wrote was about a man named Bingzwang Wang, a man with a doctorate at McGill University who was supposed to be the Canadian leader of the Chinese democracy movement. Have you heard of him? He's someone you should talk to. I think he lives in New York. Anyway, I have a suspicion that Bingzwang and Li Ling set me up."

"How?"

229

"Well, I think that Bingzwang wanted a big story done about himself and the democratic movement, and about a magazine Bingzwang was publishing. I think he and Li Ling made a plan that Li would join *China Press* and write stories about Bingzwang and how great he was and how great the movement was. I'm sure that's what they did. Later on, I found out that Li Ling was working with him on the magazine. It was all a big set-up to get free publicity. After that, I wouldn't let him write any more for the newspaper."

"What about books?" Donovan asked. "Did he ever write books?"

Vcrinza Tong shook her head. "I don't think so. His writing wasn't that good."

"We think he may have written a book. We're trying to find it. It's called *The Affair by the West Lake.*"

"This book, what is it about?"

"We don't know. That's what we're trying to find out."

"When did he write it?"

"We think around the time he was here, in Montreal."

Vcrinza Tong thought for a moment. "Well, there was something," she said. "But I have to make a phone call."

She went into the kitchen and was on the line for several minutes. When she came back, she explained she had called a man known as the Librarian.

"He used to work for us. He has back copies of all the newspapers. This story, this book, I think he might know something."

The phone rang and she answered. She talked for a few minutes, then joined them again.

"That was the Librarian. He doesn't have the copies, but he remembers the story," she said. "It was like a short book, like a . . . a . . . I can't think of what they call it."

"You mean, like a novelette," said Pron.

"That's it. That's what it was. When I called that man up, he remembered. It was a long time ago. I had forgotten."

Pron and Donovan leaned forward.

"Can you remember anything about it?" asked Donovan.

"We ran it over several editions. I think four or five."

"You mean, you serialized it?"

"Yes. The story was too long for one paper. But we almost didn't run it."

"Why?"

"It was very . . . sexy. I was the one who edited it. I remember parts of it being very erotic. Not the sort of article our paper usually ran. We were pretty conservative. A lot of older people read the paper. I can remember being afraid to run it, afraid of getting criticism."

"What was it about?"

"What did you call it?" she asked.

"The Affair by the West Lake," answered Pron.

"I remember the title being something different. Like . . . uh . . . *Murder by West Lake.'*"

"Really," said Pron. "Tell us more."

"It was a story about an army officer. Very dashing, good-looking. An officer from a good family from the north of China. He met a woman at a party. She was from the south of China and she belonged to a wealthy family. The first time the officer saw her she was coming down a big staircase wearing a beautiful gown. It was low cut in front. The woman was very . . . very . . ." Vcrinza Tong hesitated, motioning with her hands in front of her chest. "You know."

"Voluptuous?" offered Donovan.

"Yes. That's what I mean. She was very buxom. So buxom the dress couldn't hide her figure. Everyone was looking at her. She was beautiful, or so he wrote in the story. After this party they fell in love. But there was a problem with that."

"What do you mean, a problem?" asked Donovan.

"The officer. He was married already. But they kept seeing each other anyway. They had an affair."

"The officer, this woman," asked Pron, "can you remember their names?"

"No, it was too long ago. I just remember he was very handsome and she was very beautiful. And she was always wearing this gown he bought for her."

"Not white, by any chance, was it?" asked Donovan.

"How did you know that?"

"A lucky guess. Go on. What happened?"

"He wanted to break off the affair, but she kept pleading with him not to. Finally he did. She was upset. She kept calling him. She wanted to get back together but he wouldn't see her anymore. Finally, I think, she threatened to tell his wife about the whole affair unless he saw her."

The phone rang and Vcrinza Tong, who was a real-estate agent, excused herself while she hunted up a house listing for the caller. Pron and Donovan paced about her living room, trying not to look impatient, but not having much success. She got off the phone, but it rang almost immediately. This time when she talked her voice was louder, almost angry. She looked peeved when she came into the living room.

"That was my boyfriend," she said. "He knows you're here and he's, like, jealous."

"Of what?" asked Donovan.

"Jealous that I have two men in my house."

"This is a business call. Nothing more."

"I tried explaining that to him. He's Chinese. I don't think you'd understand."

"So what happened," interjected Pron, "when she tried to blackmail him?"

Vcrinza Tong thought for a moment. "They argued after that," she continued. "The woman wanted the officer to leave his wife. I think he had children as well. But he wouldn't do it. She kept calling . . . and calling. Finally, he had enough."

"Yes. And then?"

"He told her to meet him. At West Lake. Do you know anything about West Lake?"

"Nothing," said Donovan.

"It's a man-made lake in Szechuan Province. It's a very famous place. A tourist attraction. Many Chinese people go there for their holiday. In Chinese it is called Sai Woo."

"And that's where they were to meet?"

"Yes. It was at night. She begged him to leave his wife. She pleaded with him. But he wouldn't do it. And then she threatened him again. Finally . . . he killed her. Right beside the waters of West Lake."

"We have to get hold of that story," said Donovan. "Do you have any copies?"

"No, and —"

"We know," said Donovan. "Everything was burned in the fire."

"Was that fire deliberately set?" asked Pron.

"I don't remember. I don't think so."

"Do you know anyone else who might have those back copies?" asked Donovan.

"I'm sure Li Ling has copies. Did you ask him?"

"He mentioned the book once, then refused to discuss it," answered Pron.

The telephone rang. Vcrinza Tong mouthed to them with her hand over the receiver that it was her boyfriend again.

"He's really quite jealous," she said, after hanging up the phone. "He wants to know if we're done yet. I can tell him we're not, if you have more questions. I really don't mind. This is more interesting than going out to some bar."

"We've bothered you enough for one night," Donovan said. "We better go. If you ever come across those stories could you call us at the paper, collect?"

Vcrinza Tong walked them to the door and got their coats. She seemed to want to say something, but wasn't sure if she should. Finally, she spoke.

"Ever since I read in the papers that Selina was dead and that she was Li Ling's girlfriend, I've had a lot of funny dreams. Even though I never met her, I feel I know what she was like. Probably really nice, sweet. For something like that to happen to someone, it's very terrible. I keep thinking that Selina's spirit is not at rest. You see, I am Buddhist. That is something we believe. Until her killer is punished, her spirit will never be at rest. Up until now I was scared because I thought her spirit might come to my door in the night but. . . ." Her voice trailed off. She looked very uncomfortable.

"There's something more you want to say," said Donovan. "What is it?"

"It's just that I'm not scared anymore. I think Selina's spirit has already come to my door. Tonight. Right now. Here. I think her spirit is in the two of you. I think it is behind what you are doing."

CHAPTER NINETEEN

An Innocent Man

Rui-Wen Pan could not understand it. None of the homicide detectives wanted to talk to him anymore. He'd been calling for days, leaving messages for Gus Riddell. But Riddell never called back. That was strange, Pan thought. He liked Riddell, trusted him, considered him a friend. They had talked many times. Pan found Riddell easygoing compared to other police officers, like the one who had ordered his brother to be fingerprinted the day his house was searched. Riddell had always returned his calls before. For some reason that had changed. Pan wondered why. Did it mean their investigation was over? Were they going to make an arrest? Were they coming for him? They couldn't do that. He had important information on the case. Information he had to give them. He had to get in touch with Riddell.

At the Asian Crime Squad offices in North York, Gus Riddell looked at the growing stack of messages on his desk, all from the same person, the chief suspect in the Shen murder case, Rui-Wen Pan. He had always returned Pan's calls before. In fact, the two had talked quite often, as many as twenty or thirty times, in person and on the telephone. But Riddell had been ordered to back off. Inspector Edgar had decided they were getting too close to Pan, and if they talked to him anymore, they would probably have to read him his rights. Everybody in the office knew about the gag order and helped by screening Riddell's calls. But there was a sense of urgency to the most recent message. It read: "Please call, important new evidence." Riddell couldn't ignore that. He picked up the phone and dialled. Pan answered on the first ring. After a bit of small talk, Riddell came to the point.

"What's this about new evidence?"

"I have important new information that shows I am innocent," Pan said.

Great, thought Riddell. He wasn't supposed to talk to Pan, but how could he ignore a comment like that from the chief suspect in a murder case? If it came to a trial, the police would be crucified for not following up on such a tip. Whether or not there was any substance to what Pan was offering, Riddell felt he had to check it out. Edgar was out in Lanark, investigating the Simpson murders, and he couldn't be reached. Riddell hoped he would understand.

"When do you want to meet?" he asked.

It took Riddell a few hours to make the preparations. A listening device called a Niagara was installed in his car; it would feed any conversation to headquarters, where it would be recorded. Because the surveillance of Pan had been cut back to spot duty, Riddell had to arrange for a team to follow him to his interview with Pan. Shortly before nine o'clock that night Riddell drove out to Pan's house.

"It's twenty-forty-seven on the fourteenth of September, and this is Constable Gus Riddell heading for Mr. Pan's house," Riddell said aloud, letting the technicians at headquarters know he was about to pick up Pan, who, he could see, was waiting at the front door, wearing a brown suit and a red tie and carrying a briefcase.

"Is this a new car?" Pan asked as he got in. "I wish I could have one."

"No, you don't. You don't want a Chrysler. What I need is some gas. Is there a gas station around here?" Riddell said, backing the car up then driving towards Queen Street.

"There's a gas station. Just make a left turn."

Riddell drove up Queen Street, then pulled alongside the pumps.

"Fill it up with super," Riddell said to the station attendant, then turned to Pan. "So, you've got something important to tell me?"

"Yeah. I will show you something. Then I will ask you to be spending one or two days on it."

"That's what I need. But I wish you'd told me earlier. What have you got to tell me?"

Pan, watching the attendant pump the gas, said: "Not here."

"No, go ahead. It's okay. Fire away."

"Should we talk here? In the car?"

"Sure."

"The problem is, whatever you already got, it is from somebody who is, in my personal opinion, lying."

"Well, there sure is a lot going on," Riddell said, handing his credit card to the attendant.

"According to my personal opinion you got some information I don't think is true," Pan said.

Riddell signed the credit-card chit and closed his window. "What have you got to tell me?"

"I do not know how much information you have got, but it is a case against me. I feel terrible and upset because people search my home. And my store. Because right now, like, every day, I do not have any more friends. Everybody won't even talk to me. The investigation has scared everybody. You treat me like a killer. That is why you did that search warrant at home and at my store."

"See, you keep saying *me*, but I didn't do that. That's not part of my investigation. My part of it was to deal with you, and I have dealt with you as fairly as I possibly can. If you think I've done something wrong, let me know."

"You're the only person I can talk to," Pan said. "I cannot talk to those reporters. You know, they try their best to frame me."

Riddell drove east along Queen Street towards downtown Toronto. When he got to University Avenue, he turned south, then got on the Gardiner Expressway going east towards the

Beaches. Pan wanted to talk and seemed comfortable doing it in a moving car.

"I am frustrated by what the press have said about you, as well," Riddell replied. "Because every time there's been something in the press about you, let's face it, that doesn't help the whole situation, does it? Where does all their information come from, anyway?"

Pan smiled, began talking more quickly. "Maybe we can find out where all these slanders come from. Maybe we will find out the people involved in doing that are the ones who killed her."

"You think they've been leaking things to the press?"

"Yeah. Maybe. Believe me, Gus Riddell, because I know Chinese people better than you do."

"I know you do."

"Some clue, maybe, that you did not pay any attention to. I got most important information. My girlfriend she disappeared after February twentieth. The information is that after that she still went to see somebody."

"Who?"

"I am just like this newspaper reporter. When people tell me something, I write it down. Like the Toronto *Star* newspaper. They had a story about an immigration scam the day of the press conference. So two days later Metro Toronto police say to the public, and Larry Edgar says, his force has not heard anything regarding to immigration scam. Police say that is smokescreen. Right? Somebody try to make things so complicated."

"Oh, yeah."

"I said I got some new information. I do not think the killer is that smart."

"Yeah," said Riddell. "I'll buy that."

"You know, we can find out some clue to resolve this case. Because my hope is the sooner the better."

"Right." Riddell slowed the car down as he reached the end of the expressway. He took the Leslie Street ramp.

"Everybody is going to be happy, you know. The newspaper, what they say is bullshit. Where does this slander come from?"

"Towards you?"

"Yeah. I have something — information or clues — but I have to be patient, until court," Pan said.

"You mean your slander case in court?"

"Yeah."

"But, you see, that's not helping me with this murder. Do you want to help me solve Selina's murder or not?"

"Yes," Pan replied, "of course I want to help you. That is my whole problem. I dare not tell you things without legal proof. If I told you some things I have to take legal responsibilities. I have to find out evidence to support, otherwise I make a mistake. You find out that it is not the truth, even if it is not my mistake, somebody will tell you that I tricked Gus Riddell. Because if I did that, you would say he is pretty shrewd, he tried to fool you, he tried to make things complicated, he tried to make the story international. I do not want to do that."

"What is the truth?" Riddell asked in exasperation, turning into the parking lot of a Loblaws store near Lakeshore Avenue. He stopped the car but kept the engine running.

"Okay," Pan said, "the truth is, like tonight, why I want to see you, I give you something regarding this case to prove I am innocent."

"That's the first thing you should have done. That's what I need. But I want to tell you something first," Riddell said, reaching into his pocket and taking out a card. "This is the usual little thing we read to people, okay?"

"I know this."

"You've probably seen something like this on TV. You may be charged with the murder of Selina Shen. It says, if you wish to say anything to that charge, you are not obliged to say anything. But whatever you say may be used in evidence or given in evidence against you."

"I know that," Pan said, looking straight ahead and nodding.

"Okay. This is a secondary caution. It says if you have spoken to any police officer or anyone in authority — do you understand what I am saying? — or if any such person has spoken to you in connection with this case, I want it clearly understood that I do not want it to influence you in making any statement. Okay, that's the usual stuff. I think you understand."

"I understand. First I will say to you I want a copy of search warrant. The one at my house."

"Mr. Pan, I will endeavour to get one for you. There's another thing you asked me on the phone today, about the rest of your stuff that was taken during the search. You got it all back, didn't you?"

"I got most of the things back. Some things still missing."

"I think it was just something that was overlooked. They had so much stuff from your house to go through. We're still having trouble getting it translated. You know, we all speak English, where do we get somebody who speaks Mandarin?"

"It is hopeless," Pan said, shaking his head.

"You've got to appreciate this whole thing — especially what happened to poor Selina—is so difficult for us to understand. We've investigated lots of murders, but when have we ever had a murder that was like this one? This is a very difficult investigation."

"Very difficult, indeed."

"Sure it is," Riddell agreed.

"I am so confused right now. When you told my friends, Peter and Andrew, 'We have enough evidence against Mr. Pan,' I said, 'Fine.' "

"What's that?"

"Once, some officer told them that there is enough evidence against me to take me to trial. Police told them, 'We have a lot of evidence against him.' "

"Listen, I've talked to them twice, I never said that."

"I do not know who said it. Fine. So why do police not arrest me? Charge me. Put me on trial. I say I am ready any time, anywhere."

"Where are those two fellows now?"

"In Vancouver. They are scared. They run away. They will be back. They do not want to be bothered anymore with the problem here. Because of the strongest pressure."

"Pressure, Mr. Pan? Pressure about what?"

"I think they will not do business with me anymore. You know, all my friends who you talked to, everybody keep long distance from me, do not talk to me."

"What can I say about that? I'm sorry about that."

"Could you pass message to Larry Edgar? If you think I did this, okay, why do you not arrest me? Now! And put me on trial. I am ready any time. Could you please pass message to Larry Edgar? I have strong evidence that can prove I am innocent."

"That's what we need."

"You put on the search warrant, on February twentieth, I did murder Selina Shen. I told you what I did on February twentieth. My brother told you."

Pan took several newspaper clippings from his briefcase and showed them to Riddell. "February twentieth was a Saturday. Okay, write this down."

Riddell pulled out his notebook and took out a pen.

"In *Sing Tao*, largest-circulation Chinese daily newspaper, there is advertisement."

"What for?"

"My house, 76 Puma Drive, advertisement that my house was for sale. I was only asking one hundred seventy-five thousand. See? My telephone number there, too. Let me explain to you. On February twentieth, in the morning, my brother and I drove to our store. Then, during the nighttime, we came back together. Then after that, at least more than fifteen people came to my place."

"So on the —"

"February twentieth."

"The twentieth."

"More than fifteen people saw this advertisement."

"And came to your house?"

"More than fifteen people who I do not know. Actually more than twenty. I put it at fifteen right now, because I do not want to make any mistake. More than fifteen —"

"People —"

"Who came to my place."

"To view it?"

"Yeah, I show them!"

"For the house sale?"

"Yeah, the house."

"How much was it again?"

"One hundred seventy-five."

"Thousand?"

"Yeah, there was no such price lower."

"Why were you selling so cheap?"

"More than fifty people called me, asked me information about the house. That means I was always busy from when I arrived home. Until after midnight the telephone was still ringing."

"Okay."

"I mean, like, at such a good price, I did this kind of business."

"Okay, let me get this straight in my mind. On that Saturday —"

"The twentieth."

"You told me before you dropped the letter off to Mrs. Chan about eleven or eleven-thirty in the morning."

"No more than eleven-thirty."

"What time did you get home on that evening?"

"I think seven or eight o'clock. I cannot remember exactly."

"And you had, from seven or eight o'clock to, say, midnight, you had a whole bunch of people coming through your house."

"After midnight, telephone still ringing."

"What time did these people come to your house until?"

"Between eight o'clock and eleven o'clock."

"Okay, help me understand this. Fifty people at least called."

"Fifty, at least that many."

"So that would mean these people could give you an alibi. Who are they? They must have given you their names. They could tell you that, yes, he was at his home from eight o'clock to eleven o'clock on the twentieth."

"Well, whatever they are going to tell you I do not know."

"Do you know any of their names?"

"I have some right now."

"You do?"

"I do."

"I would appreciate having these names. Why didn't you give me this before?"

"You would have wasted your time. You didn't believe me then."

"I would have. Why didn't you give me this before?"

"Okay, let me explain this. After you did search warrant, I realized I had to prove I am innocent here. Otherwise I am going to die."

"Wait a minute! You know that nobody dies in this country. For anything. We don't have a death penalty anymore."

"No, I do not mean this that way. All my life is finished."

"Can you give me some names?"

"I can give you whatever I have here." Pan opened his briefcase and took out a photocopied piece of paper with a list of names on it. There were no addresses, just a few telephone numbers. "I find out their names when they came to house and wrote them down on pad of paper."

"Okay," said Riddell, taking the paper.

"Maybe someone say, 'You did this on purpose. You put advertisement here just like a trick, to fool police.' Okay? Let me explain. If you plan to murder somebody, do you want to show somebody your house? And, the same day you killed this victim, do you still want to show the public you have connection to her by passing a letter? You understand what I mean?"

"I know what you're saying. And then on the twentieth you had a lot of people going through your house. Was it twenty you said?"

"Yeah."

"Excellent."

"I am innocent, because I do not know those people at all. I never see them and never call them. You go ask one if he called me. I remember it was busy that night, schedule was full up."

"So all these people, they came between the twentieth and the twenty-first?"

"Or the twenty-second. I cannot remember for certain which date."

"That's fine, Mr. Pan."

"You ask them. And another thing I would like to tell you, Gus Riddell. After you kill people and cut the dead body in pieces, would you show people your house? People who would spend one hundred seventy-five thousand dollars, these people would be very careful. They would check everything. The roofing, the basement, everywhere."

"Sure."

"The washroom, the kitchen, everywhere."

"Uh-huh."

"You understand what I mean? The back yard. After you kill people, I think you can find some blood. You ask these people. You check everything. I give all this to you to check."

"Mr. Pan, I'm going to get back to you when I finish with these people."

"You do investigation."

"This is excellent. This is just what I've needed."

"I don't have telephone numbers for all."

"That's all right."

"Most of the people come from Scarborough, and fifty people called me at least, like this Mr. Ho."

"Let me tell you something, Mr. Pan. I'm mad at you. You've explained this to me, but I still don't understand. Why didn't you take the bull by the horns when you knew she was missing and come to the police?"

"That is exactly what I want to tell you. My brother remind me, Mrs. Chan, she went to my store several times when I was not there. She find out something very strange about Selina, that she is missing, but without proof I dare not go to police. You understand what I mean, Gus Riddell?"

"No. I don't."

"Okay. If somebody told me, 'Do not look for her, maybe she is dead, maybe she is —' "

"Who told you that?"

"Maybe she is cut into eighty pieces. According to newspaper report she is cut into eighty pieces. So how does this person know that?"

"Who told that to you?"

"I dare not tell you that right now."

"Come on."

"Okay. This person's brother was killed by gun two years ago. Nobody find the killer."

"What's his name?"

"And this person —"

"What's the name?"

"Let me finish. This person, the member of his present family who, how do you say in English, uses the knife to cut chicken?"

"Butcher?"

"Butcher. Let me explain everything to you. This person Selina was always complaining about. Like he was dirty. Every time he saw her he always tried to . . . you know what I mean."

"A Chinese guy?"

"He always tries to touch her and —"

"No. Don't tell me."

"Yeah."

"You think you know him? Is he Chinese?"

"He is Chinese, but he is from America, not from China. Maybe he comes from Chicago. So that is why I say I do not know him, Gus Riddell. I am not sure what his original nationality is. He comes from another country, so if I say he is Chinese, maybe his passport is Indonesian, Singapore, or from Hong Kong. I do not know. And I dare not tell you who this person is. Give me time."

"But you are going to find out his name."

"When time is right, I let you know. Right now, time is not right."

"Do you know who it is?"

"Of course I know."

"Tell me."

"I know a lot of things, maybe I write a statement for you."

"When are you going to give me that?"

"Give me time."

"I don't have time. I want to get this settled now. How many months have we been doing this now?"

"Listen, if you find out this Chinese man did not do this, maybe you say I tried to make things complicated. I have to take legal responsibility, whatever I say, whatever I do. Sooner or later, I let you know, because I am doing some investigating."

"Listen, you know how difficult the Chinese community can be to work with. But I'll tell you something, eventually I'll find out, I will."

"Another thing I can prove. There is certain lady who told me after February twentieth Selina went somewhere to see somebody, a guy."

"You mean Selina was still alive after February twentieth?"

"Still alive, and went somewhere to see somebody. After I heard this, I try very hard to find out. Finally I got this information. I cannot tell you because this lady, she said she does not want to be a witness of this at court."

"But this lady saw Selina after the twentieth?"

"Definitely. And a guy who saw her absolutely knows this. But they do not want to say anything. And they do not want to be witnesses to that."

"I need a name."

"I try."

"Now."

"Okay, I was successful in one thing: I got a tape of what she said. They are so scared. I said, 'Do not worry, police can protect.' They said they do not want to see any police."

"Who are they? How can you know this and not tell me?"

"You should go right now and see this lady, she will tell you the story."

"Where does she live?"

"York University. I give you her address and telephone number, everything. But do me a favour, do not say I brought the police to her place."

"Okay, this is great, what's her name?"

"I give it to you, okay? But you just tell her you need some information. Just try to generalize, because she is so scared. If you are friendly, she will tell you all the story."

"I need a name."

"Just try, you know, to relax and take it easy with her. She will tell you something."

"She knows Selina was alive after the twentieth?"

"She said, 'Let me tell you something. After your girlfriend disappear, she went somewhere and see somebody, and, of course, caught somebody.' I paid attention right away, but she refuse to talk."

"What do you mean, she caught somebody?"

"She realized I paid attention and then she dared not tell me anything more. Whatever she told me, you ask, you find out."

"Okay, what's her name?"

"Zhang. Mrs. Zhang." Pan gave Riddell a telephone number and address.

"So what else?"

"I also know the other person Selina went to see after the twentieth. This person had a nightclub on Yonge Street. They have a nightclub, but this I do not want you to write down. They do business like prostitute, but do not write down because I have no proof."

"Did Selina work there?"

"I do not know. Sophie asked if I thought her sister would go to these nightclub people."

"Where's the nightclub?"

Pan told Riddell it was on Yonge Street near the Eaton Centre.

"Let's go see it," said Riddell, starting the car.

As they drove downtown, Pan continued to describe the nightclub. "They do immigration business. Maybe you find out it is the scam, maybe not?"

"What does Selina know about an immigration scam?"

"I do not know. That is why I asked the Toronto *Star* to do me a favour. Trace this information source. You ask this lady, you do your investigation, they do immigrating business, maybe legal, maybe illegal, I do not know. That is your job."

"No problem."

"They bring people from United States, Hong Kong, Mainland China, and Taiwan. Exactly like in Toronto *Star* story. And my girlfriend told me several times —"

"Selina?"

"Yeah, they are powerful and great and make money."

"This woman you mentioned, Zhang, she's going to tell me about these powerful people?"

"She actually does not know too much about them. But she knew something about them."

"Who are these powerful people?"

"I do not know."

"You told me before that Selina was afraid of something."

"Yeah."

"But you don't know who the people were?"

"Yeah. And let me tell you another thing. Sophie, whatever she told you, I think most of it was lies. And she hid something. I remember after her sister disappear, she call me. I hope you go back to ask her about that call. She told me Selina told her those guys are very powerful and very great. And very useful in immigration field. She will deny, but you ask her. I know she is lying to you. She hid a lot of things. Even I can say she is a suspect. But right now I do not want to say anything because it is so complicated."

"Uh-huh."

"What I mean is, after February twentieth, Selina saw or called certain persons. You ask Sophie, did she tell me, once by phone and once in person, these people were very powerful in immigration field? And also, after Selina disappear, Mrs. Zhang asked me if I thought Selina went to these persons in the nightclub."

They reached Yonge Street and headed north. "Are you going to show me where this nightclub is?"

"Go straight up Yonge Street."

"Is it a Chinese nightclub?"

"Sometimes it is Italian, sometimes Chinese. You have to check record. Also I want to take you to another place, where there are people who know about immigration."

"Do you think they're bringing them in here illegally?"

"I do not know. That is why you must not write down that I said that. It is your job to investigate. Right now I have no evidence."

"All right, where's this nightclub?" Riddell was driving slowly up Yonge Street, looking from side to side.

"That is it, right there! Make a right turn, but do not park here, you will get a ticket."

"I don't give a goddamn about tickets," said Riddell, stopping the car on Yonge Street. They got out and looked the club over. Riddell made a few notes, then told Pan he'd check the club out the next day. They got back in the car.

"Okay," said Riddell, "that's where these people who are in immigration stuff are from?"

Pan nodded.

"And she saw them after February twentieth?"

Pan nodded again.

"Let me look into it."

"You find out. Because I think there is no difficulty for you because a lot of people know this. We go to another place now, Spadina, go to Dennison and Spadina."

"Spadina? She used to go there?"

"I do not know for sure. That is your job."

Riddell looked for a break in traffic, then turned left on Elm Street, heading west.

"This place I will show you, they open it maybe a year ago, I do not know for sure. My girlfriend worked for them. You check the record. I cannot remember exactly."

"Whose record am I going to check?"

"You get name when we go there, check the registry."

Riddell drove.

"Make a right turn here," said Pan, when they reached Spadina Avenue. "Then a left."

"It says no left turn," Riddell pointed out.

"Yeah, I know, but you can."

"Oh, okay," Riddell said, turning into the laneway. They drove behind a building and parked near a truck that was backed up to a loading dock. A man was standing in the open back doors of the truck. They watched in silence for several moments, then Pan spoke.

"If I told you maybe Sophie involved in this case, would that surprise you?"

"I don't know if I'd be surprised."

"But do you remember you asked me something about her?"

"Yes, I did."

"So far I am collecting evidence," Pan said. "And information, that is what is so complicated, so I just give you basics. You figure out the truth and fact. Right now I can prove something."

"What's the point?"

"You write down the name," Pan said, pointing to the sign at the top of the building, which identified the place as some sort of training school. "I did not want my girlfriend to go to these people. I know these people. You check the record, they were raided by the police. One day before that these people invited her several times to work there. You ask, you see."

"Well, you've given me enough work for another week here. So when are you going to court against those Chinese newspapers?"

"The next step is to examine the documents. We both exchange documents. After that, we go to trial. But right now, so far, one hundred percent we will win this case. I show them my school certificate from China."

"You studied some type of medicine?"

"Yeah, I did."

"What did you call it?"

"You take X-ray pictures."

"Like a general practitioner?"

"No. I never general practitioner. I never give needles or prescription. I never had chance to do that. I never have chance to use operating knife. I never had a chance to go to operating table. I never was a doctor. I told you all that before."

"What about autopsies?"

"What?"

"Examining people after they are dead, finding out the cause of death. What about that kind of medicine?"

"No, no, no, no. I was never that." Pan paused for a moment. "Let us go back. Drive me to my residence."

Riddell took another look at the building, then backed out the laneway.

"Maybe you were afraid of the police?"

"No, no, no, no. I was not afraid to report it. The truth and fact was I do want to report."

"But you couldn't get Sophie to do it?"

"This is one big problem."

"Why didn't you just grab her and take her?"

"I did, yeah, I did. But she hid something from you and she is lying. It is terrible. She cheated you. She taped my conversation, she said something, but realized she made a mistake. She said some words in front of me. She said, 'Do not worry about Selina. Do not look for her. I think she is okay.' "

They pulled into Pan's driveway, and Riddell stopped the car. "What you've told me is going to change the whole aspect of the case."

"Right now the certain thing is my girlfriend, she run away, she move out suddenly without any reason."

"That's right."

"I do not know what kind of people she was dealing with or staying with. But I know one person, that is Sophie. She knows where my girlfriend lived. She was lying to me when she said she did not know anything about her. Once she laughed, like very shrewdly. I said, 'Could you please do me a favour. I just want to know where she lives. I will report this to the police.' She refused. 'I care, I worry about her,' I was crying. Ask her. Ask Sophie. I was crying." Pan started sobbing.

"Don't worry about it."

"I said, 'Do me a favour, no matter what trouble you have between you and her, if you do not want to bring me to her, just let me know where she lives.' She refused. Why? Why?"

"Well, that's a good question," Riddell said, patting Pan, who was sobbing uncontrollably, on the shoulder. "Listen, don't get so upset."

"Everybody stop me. They had enough out of me. 'You are not a man,' they said. 'She just threw you in the garbage. Threw you out.' So why should I care about her?"

"Don't worry about it," Riddell said, opening his door and walking around the front of the car to Pan's side. "Let me go to work on it.'' He opened the passenger door, but Pan sat there, still crying. ''What time do you go to work tomorrow?''

''Usually twelve o'clock.''

''I'll phone you before then,'' said Riddell, helping Pan out of the car. ''Go to bed. I'll talk to you tomorrow. I've had you out too late.''

''Until now, I did not eat anything. I do not have any feeling to eat anything. I am innocent,'' Pan said suddenly.

''Go in the house and get something to eat and go to bed.''

''I am innocent,'' Pan repeated, wiping a hand across his eyes. ''And you will find out.''

Riddell took Pan by the arm and escorted him to the front door. ''Go in and eat something. Get a good night's sleep. I'll talk to you tomorrow.''

Pan opened the door, stepped inside, then turned to Riddell. ''I just want to prove to you I am innocent.''

CHAPTER TWENTY

Final Confrontation

"Go away," Rui-Wen Pan shouted, as he peered out the small window in the front door of his house. But the two late-night visitors on his front step didn't move.

"We have some questions for you," Kevin Donovan shouted. "May we come in?"

"If you don't go away," Pan threatened, "I will call the police."

"Call them," replied Donovan.

"You are trespassing."

"Why won't you open the door, Mr. Pan? What are you afraid of?"

Pan turned and shouted something to Peter Wang, who was standing in the kitchen. Wang immediately picked up the telephone and started dialling. Pan watched him for a moment, said something else to Wang, then wheeled around and threw open the front door. His face was flushed, the veins in his neck bulging.

"You are going to be in big trouble now," he said. "Yes, you will see. I have called the police. They are coming here to arrest you."

"You killed her, didn't you, Pan?" Donovan said, moving threateningly towards him.

"Why are you saying such a thing?" replied Pan, stepping back. "You are trying to put me into jail."

"All part of the big frame-up, eh, Pan?" Donovan said, smirking. "They're all out to get you, everyone."

"You have no right going to my relatives. Who told you to go to Montreal? I have heard what you have been doing. No one gave you permission to do this."

"We have every right, Pan," said Donovan. "You gave us that right when you told us to find the real killer."

"I did not do this! This is wrong! This is all part of the police plan to have me destroyed."

"You know what I'm tired of?" said Donovan, pointing his finger at Pan. "I'm tired of all your lying. Right from the start, all you've been doing is lying to us. With your phony leads and your phony tips. Why don't you just admit it?" Donovan edged closer, close enough to bump Pan's shoulder with his own. "You killed Selina. There's no one else."

"How can you say such a thing?"

"She wasn't killed by a gang. Or a professor. There's no lawyer, there's no big shot who might have killed her. It was you! Admit it, Pan! You're the one who did it!"

"You are crazy!" replied Pan.

Nick Pron stepped between them. He put an arm on Donovan's shoulder and gently pushed him back.

"Let's take it easy here," said Pron. "Mr. Pan, there are a few questions we'd like to ask you. Then we'll go away. We won't bother you anymore."

"You will have to answer to the police," said Pan.

"Yeah," replied Donovan, "so will you, someday."

"Mr. Pan, we talked to people who said you wrote a murder mystery with a woman in it who was just like Selina. She wore the same kind of dress and she was killed in the end. Is this true?"

"If you write such a story, I will law suit you," replied Pan.

"Sure you will," Donovan interjected, "but is it true?"

"Write such a story and you will find out."

"This isn't getting anywhere," Donovan said, again moving towards Pan. "All you know how to do is lie."

"You are garbage," Pan said to Donovan. "You write trash. You interfere with people's lives. You have no morals. You have no scruples. You have no right talking to my relatives, talking to my uncle."

"He's not your uncle," challenged Donovan.

"Who told you this?"

"He's a friend of your dad's who sponsored you. And you want to know something? He didn't even want you in his house. You free-loaded off him."

"If he told you this, it is wrong."

"We know all about your murder book, Pan," continued Donovan. "So don't try to deny it."

"I beg your pardon?"

"You heard me. *Murder by West Lake*. That woman who was killed in your book, Pan. Was her name Selina as well? Is that where you killed Selina? By West Lake?"

"I will not answer any more of these questions!" Pan replied, his face reddening. "You don't know what you're talking about! You're talking nonsense! You are bothering people's lives! You are trash! I don't want to see either of you ever again!"

"You're wrong there, Pan," said Donovan. "We'll see you again—in court."

"Get away from my house!" Pan shouted. Saliva was bubbling from the corners of his mouth. "Don't ever come here again." And with that he slammed the door.

"Now what?" Pron asked Donovan as they walked back to the car.

"I guess we better wait for the cops."

A cruiser arrived within minutes. There were two police officers, a black man and a white woman. Pan strode out of his house as the two officers stepped out of the cruiser. Wang was close behind Pan, trying to put a jacket over his shoulders.

"What's the problem here?" the black officer asked, looking at the people crowded around the cruiser.

"These two men," said Pan, pointing to Pron and Donovan. "I want you to arrest them."

"Is that so?" the officer replied. "Can you tell me why?"

"They are trying to kill me," said Pan.

"We're reporters," said Pron. "We came here because we got an anonymous call that something was going to happen. We're not trying to kill anybody. We've talked to Mr. Pan before. Many times."

The officer turned to Pan. "Is that true?"

Pan shook his head. "I do not know these men," he said.

The officer looked at his partner. "I think we better split these people up," he said. He motioned for Pan to go to the rear of the cruiser, while his partner took Pron and Donovan to the front.

"Can I see some identification?" she asked. After they showed her their press identification, they repeated their story about getting the anonymous call. After a few minutes the black officer got everyone together again.

"Now look," he said to the reporters, "I don't think anything wrong has been done here, but it's pretty plain that this gentleman" — he pointed to Pan — "does not want you coming around his house again and bothering him. Is that clear?"

"Very clear," said Pron. He turned to Pan. "We're sorry if we bothered you, Mr. Pan."

"Now I've told him that if you do come here again, to his personal residence, he's to call us. In that event we might have to charge the two of you. Do both of you understand this?"

Pron and Donovan nodded.

"Okay. Fine. Now I think both of you better be on your way."

They went back to Donovan's apartment and sat out on the front stoop drinking beer, arguing late into the night about Pan's guilt. A baby was crying in one of the apartments in the building across the street. A pizza delivery car pulled up and the driver ran in carrying two large flat containers. Farther up the street, a motorist pulled over, parked behind a truck and watched the two reporters for several minutes. Then he drove away, turning into a side street near Donovan's building. A few minutes later a man walked quietly along the narrow laneway between Donovan's building and the one beside it. He stood in the shadows for a few moments, watching and listening. Finally, he stepped forward.

"You guys sure talk about stupid things," said Harvey Loxton. " 'Specially you, Pron. How could you still think he's innocent?"

Loxton had startled them, and for a moment they were speechless.

"You guys just keep pushing it and pushing it, don't you?" said Loxton. "Those coppers should've charged you. I would've."

"We didn't do anything wrong," said Pron.

"Both of you deserve to be in jail just for being general nuisances. Do your bosses know what you guys do?"

"Never mind all that threatening business," said Donovan. "You want a beer?"

Loxton nodded. He took out a cigarette but didn't light it. He stayed where he was, partially hidden in the shadows, waiting for Donovan to return with the beer.

"We've got a question for you," Donovan said, after he gave Loxton the beer. "Just what is this incident by the pier?"

"What incident by the pier?" asked Loxton.

"How many incidents by the pier can there be in this case?" replied Donovan.

"Sounds to me like you're just fishing, Donovan. Sounds to me like you don't know shit."

"Maybe I don't, right now. But I damned well intend to find out."

"Oh? And how would you go about doing that?"

"You know our methods," Donovan replied. "We'll find out. Someone will talk. They always do."

"That's what worries me about this case. Too many god-damn leaks. If you were to find out about this so-called incident — and I'm not saying it happened — would you tell Pan?"

"How can we tell him?" said Pron. "We don't know anything about it."

"That's not what I asked," said Loxton. He spoke slowly. "If you did find out would you tell him?"

"We knew he was under twenty-four-hour surveillance," said Donovan, "and we didn't tell him about that."

"That means nothing," Loxton said. "He probably guessed that all by himself."

"What's so secret about this incident?"

"Evidence. It's about evidence. Without it, the case against him is shit."

"Now for sure I want to find out," said Donovan.

"If I were to tell you about it," Loxton said, lighting his cigarette, "you could never tell Pan, or print it in the paper. Is that understood."

"I think we're both aware of what happens if you double-cross a cop," said Pron.

"It's way more than just that," said Loxton.

"How do you mean?"

"It's more than just having a bad rep with the force. You two already have that."

"What are you getting at?" asked Donovan.

"If I told you, and you were to tell Pan, or if I saw a story in the paper —"

"You won't."

"But if I did, you know what I would do?"

"What?"

"I'd shoot the pair of you. And I mean that."

"Sure you would," said Donovan. "Look, we're not going to write anything about this, so why don't you just tell us what happened at the pier."

"I'm taking a real chance being here. I could lose my hooks," Loxton said, tapping his left arm with three fingers.

"Your what?" asked Donovan.

"My hooks, my sergeant's bars."

"You're too paranoid," said Donovan. "You put us on to Mrs. Chan and we never burned you. How about a little trust?"

"I never told you about Mrs. Chan. I don't know what you're talking about."

Pron stood up, took out his car keys. "I'm getting tired of this. I'm going home."

"I don't like it around here," Loxton said, glancing down Vaughan Road, "Too bright. Too many people. Too much chance of being seen."

"We could go inside, have another beer," suggested Donovan.

"No," said Loxton. "Things get recorded inside of houses. I'd rather talk outside."

They went around to the back, going single file along the narrow walkway between the two buildings. Loxton sat on the fire-escape steps and waited for Donovan to bring him another beer before he began.

"It's funny the way things happen," Loxton said. "The surveillance team wanted to quit early that night. Fucking good thing they didn't." He paused to belch. "Pan started spinning right after he left the restaurant with his two pals, Wanger and Fanger. Up one street, down another, left, right. He was all over the map. Just like you drive, Donovan. When targets start doing that, you get real excited. You just know something is going to happen. He ended up down at the Beaches, left Wanger and Fanger in the car, grabbed something from the back, a box and a bag, and started walking towards the water. One of our boys got out and did the same.

"Pan was acting like he was out for an evening stroll. Sure, he looked around once in a while, but he didn't see our guy." Loxton took a swig from his beer. "Nobody sees our guys. He walks down to the boardwalk, then out on a pier. Which leaves our guy in a tough spot. He can't walk out there with him and hold his hand. But if something is going on out there, he can't be too far away. Fortunately, our guy was on the ball that night. You'll like this one. He takes off his jacket, kinda ruffles his shirt a little, musses up his hair and staggers, understand, staggers over to the nearest park bench and makes like he passes out. But, of course, he's eyeballing Pan, who thinks he's all by his lonesome.

"This is nighttime, don't forget. Maybe there's a full moon but our guy loses sight of Pan when he gets to the end of the pier. But he's got ears, and he hears something. Like something going into the water. Several times. Splashes. Just when our guy is wondering what to do, Pan comes back off the pier. Pan's still got the bag and the box but both are looking empty. He goes right by our man again and into the park. He loses the bag in one garbage can, rips up the box and dumps it in a second can. Then he goes back to his car, wakes up Wanger and Fanger, and he's off home." Loxton studied his beer can, which was empty.

"So what happened?" asked Donovan. "What did your guy do?"

"What do you think he did?" replied Loxton. "He went and grabbed those bags and called in some divers. And I gotta tell you, we get some dirty jobs. When our boys went through those bags later, they found shit from just about every dog in the Beaches."

Donovan handed him another beer. They waited for Loxton to continue. He took his time about it, lighting a cigarette, smoking it slowly.

"It was quite hilarious, all them cops at the end of the pier, waiting for them guys with the webbed feet to find something. Never thought much of the guys in the marine unit. Always thought of them as just riding around in a speedboat, working on their tans. But I gotta tell you, they earned their paystubs that night. One guy was nearly into his second air tank before he found something, other than pop cans, syringes, and used condoms, that is. You really had to see that scene. Swear to God, just like something out of a movie. Police boats all around the dock, big torchlights on the water, all these cops crowding around the dock, trying to get a better look, pushing each other out of the way, nearly falling in. The frogman was a fair bit out when his line stopped moving. He came up with something." He paused, then took another swig of beer, but didn't seem to be in any hurry to finish his story.

"Well, what did he come up with?" asked Pron.

"From what I hear, that searchlight added a nice touch."

"Harvey, what was it?"

"It was shiny, dripping water. And it was sharp."

"A knife?" Pron asked.

"No dickhead, it was a ball-point pen. What do you think it was? He threw away a whole set of knives, just like the ones in his store. A butcher knife, paring knife, meat cleaver, the works. All lying on the bottom in a semi-circle, like some fucking ritual or something. Far as I was concerned, Pan should've been bagged right then and there.''

"Why wasn't he?"

"Don't ask me. Ask Larry Edgar.''

CHAPTER TWENTY-ONE

A Detective's Dilemma

Larry Edgar had a tough decision to make. Rui-Wen Pan was asking for permission from the police to take a business trip to China, and he wanted to leave in a few days. The only way Edgar could stop Pan would be to arrest him. But was he ready? It was eight months into the case, and Edgar had put together a thick file on Pan. He knew a great deal about the man. Edgar and his detectives had compiled a profile from hundreds of interviews and several thousand pages of wiretaps. If one was to believe what Pan had been telling people, he was certainly an accomplished man. His list of self-proclaimed achievements was impressive: freedom fighter for democracy; world-famous writer and editor; successful businessman; community leader.

Here was a man who boasted that he had his pick of the most beautiful women in Chinatown, and that he chose the Shen sisters. What a terrible blow it must have been to Pan when first Sophie, and later Selina, walked out on him. The jealousy over Robert Fisher, the other man in Selina's life, must have been the final straw. Those two factors were the key to his investigation. Loss of face plus jealousy. It was a simple equation, and for Larry Edgar it added up to murder.

Pan had done his best to throw suspicion on Fisher, saying the professor had lured Selina away from him, then killed her. That's what Pan had been telling his investigators, and he had gone to the media with the same message. But the reporters had lost interest in the story, and were not buying his theory. After the initial flurry of excitement over the slaying, the reporters had gone on to other news. There hadn't been a story on the murder for weeks now. Pan's multi-million-dollar law suit against the *Sing Tao* and the *World Journal* seemed to have cooled the Chinese press as well.

Edgar was glad the media never took seriously Pan's accusation that the professor was the one who killed Selina. It just wasn't true. Pan would have been wiser to pick someone who at least looked like a killer, thought Edgar. The mild-mannered, soft-spoken academic hardly looked the part. Where was Fisher's motive? He had no reason to kill Selina. He had liked her and had wanted to get to know her better. On the Saturday and Sunday Selina disappeared, Fisher and his estranged wife, Anna Leung, had hosted two dinner parties. The guests had already vouched for that. There was nothing in Fisher's background to suggest he had ever taken any training in dissecting a body.

But the same could not be said for Pan. He told everybody he was a doctor but had given up his practice to devote his life to battling communism. There were a number of people who would testify to that. But Edgar needed more. He wanted proof of Pan's medical background, official documentation, something written down on paper that showed he had trained to become a doctor. If he had a doctor's certificate, Edgar wanted a copy of it. He recruited Jack McCombs to his team and sent him to Montreal to see what he could dig up.

McCombs was an experienced investigator with the OPP's Intelligence Unit who had worked with Edgar when he was on the biker squad. The burly detective knew Montreal well from other investigations. He was an excellent interviewer and his laid-back style put people at ease — an asset in a case full of jittery witnesses. Edgar gave him a list of people to talk to in Montreal. A few weeks later, McCombs was finished.

When McCombs, a meticulous note-taker, walked into Edgar's third-floor office at OPP headquarters, he sat down at the other desk in the office, put on his reading glasses, and opened his black book.

"I thought you were going to quit," McCombs remarked. Edgar, who was seated at his desk, was lighting up a Player's.

"I should, you know," replied Edgar. "I plan to. When you quit, Jack, was it hard to do?"

"You have to go cold turkey," said McCombs. "It's the only way."

"How long has it been since you had a smoke?"

McCombs looked down at his stomach and patted his belly, which was edging out over his belt. "Twenty-five pounds ago," he answered.

McCombs told Edgar he had talked to Jony Mark, Pan's uncle, who had sponsored Pan when he immigrated to Canada. As expected, Mark had been quite nervous, afraid to say anything. It took several interviews before he opened up. Mark finally admitted he really wasn't Pan's uncle. He was an acquaintance of Pan's father, who had asked Mark to sponsor his son. Pan's father said he needed a favour. The Pan family wanted to emigrate from China and wanted Rui-Wen to get established, then bring the rest of the family over. Besides his restaurant, Mark also ran a small business that imported cooking supplies from China using Pan's father as a business contact in China. He and his wife and their three children didn't need a boarder, but he was afraid that if he refused it might be bad for his importing business. So he agreed to do it.

Pan came to Canada with little more than the clothes he was wearing. But he did bring plenty of documentation, including his academic records. They were all in Chinese and had to be translated into English for the immigration officials. Mark knew a Roman Catholic priest, a native of China, who did translation work. He took the documents to him. McCombs got the name of the priest and arranged for an interview. Like Mark, the priest was reluctant to talk, but for a different reason.

"I think he was worried that he might be breaking some clerical vow," McCombs explained to Edgar.

"Only if he did the translation work in the confessional," said Edgar.

McCombs said that was the way he had put it to the priest, who agreed the detective was right. He confirmed that he had done the translation work for Pan and, luckily, had kept some records. Pan had brought over all his school records, from grade school on. The records confirmed Edgar's assessment of Pan as a very intelligent man. He had been a top student right from grade school, where his average had been in the high nineties. Pan's father worked at the Szechwan People's Hospital, and that's where Pan had gone for his training, but not to become a doctor.

"He took nursing," said McCombs.

According to his school records, Pan specialized in radiology. He was an accredited X-ray technician but he had taken training in other fields as well. And in those courses, as in the others, his marks had all been in the nineties. McCombs paused before continuing. Brian Kennedy and Garnet Rombough had joined Edgar in his office to hear the report. With Rombough and Edgar both smoking, a bluish haze was gathering around the ceiling in the small office. McCombs adjusted his reading glasses, then glanced up to ensure that his audience was attentive. Then he continued.

Pan had taken classes in pathology, anatomy, surgical techniques, and fundamental Chinese medicine, said McCombs. One of Pan's instructors had written some comments on his academic record. McCombs read them out.

"His performance during our school time was wonderful," the instructor wrote. "His deep and vast knowledge gave him an excellent result at final exams. Hard working in his studies . . . especially outstanding in medical and surgical techniques."

"That just about clinches it," said Edgar.

"So how about it, big guy?" Kennedy asked. "Do we arrest him, or let him go to China and hope we get more back than a postcard?"

"Come on, Larry, we got so much evidence," said Rombough, "we could save some for the next murder case."

Edgar knew they were right. He had enough evidence to make an arrest. He could show a jury that Pan had both the motive and the opportunity to kill Selina Shen. The motive was double-edged: the jealousy of another man's attentions to his girlfriend and the humiliating loss of face in the community when she left him for the third and last time.

As for opportunity, Pan had the time to carry out the crime. Kennedy and Rombough had checked out his alibi, interviewing the people who had supposedly visited his house on the weekend he put it up for sale, the same weekend Selina disappeared. But most of the people on Pan's list didn't know him, and were never at his house. A few of the people had called to set up appointments to see the place, but hadn't been there on that fateful weekend. Mrs. Zhang, the woman Pan said had seen Selina after the weekend in which she vanished, told the two detectives she had caught a quick glimpse of a woman who looked like Selina, but she didn't think it was the murdered violinist.

The school records were evidence of Pan's medical background. They had the knives Pan had thrown into the lake, with his thumbprint on one of the blades. They could show a jury he knew how to use them, his training in pathology and anatomy had given him the knowledge. And they had the testimony of four people that Pan had injured his hand on the weekend Selina disappeared. On Friday the hand was fine, but on Monday it was so bruised that when the landlord came around for the rent at one of his stores, Pan had trouble writing out the cheque.

Edgar was confident he had enough evidence to show premeditation and get a first-degree murder conviction. Any forethought, even if it was only a few minutes before the crime, was premeditation in the eyes of the law. Pan's letter to Selina showed premeditation. Pan, apparently so confident that the police weren't going to charge him, gave Edgar a copy of the letter, the one Selina had read on the day she disappeared. It was strongly worded, as if he meant to provoke her, draw her out of hiding. In it he had called her ''an unbearable bitch,'' someone who could have a venereal disease or AIDS because she slept with so many men. Then there was the statement from Anna Leung, Fisher's estranged wife. Pan had gone to her complaining that Fisher was paying too much attention to his Selina. During one conversation he told her that "something shocking" was going to happen, but had been vague as to details. The "something shocking" was obviously murder.

Means, motive, and opportunity: they were all there, along with premeditation, all of it backed up by plenty of evidence. But the problem was, most of it was in Chinese, literally thousands and thousands of pages of wiretap conversations that had to be painstakingly translated into English. Edgar already had quick translations that gave him the gist of the conversations, but to go to court the conversations had to be presented in their entirety. And that took time.

Stephen Tsai, the security guard at the forensic sciences building who was the lone translator on the case, had told Edgar he needed more time. At least another three months. If Edgar were to make an arrest right then, Pan would be entitled to a trial within a reasonable time under the Canadian Charter of Rights and Freedoms. If he were to arrest Pan, Edgar would probably have to delay the trial until the translations were completed, a delay that might give a defence lawyer grounds to apply for a dismissal. Edgar didn't want all the hard work his team had done on the investigation to get tossed out of court on a charter argument made by some shyster lawyer. Besides, he could use more time. There were still gaps in his case. Edgar didn't know where Selina worked after she left Pan. And parts of her body were still missing. If they found the head, for instance, they might be able to determine a cause of death.

Kennedy stood up, jabbed Rombough on the shoulder, and nodded at McCombs. "Come on, you guys. All this lack of decision is making me starved. Let's get some lunch." He looked at Edgar. "How about you, Sherlock Holmes? You coming with us?"

Edgar reached for one of the communications that Tsai had already translated. The blue binder contained what he considered to be the most damning of all the conversations that had been picked up by the room probe. He looked up at Kennedy and shook his head.

"Bring me back a sandwich," he said.

The transcript was a lengthy conversation between Pan, Wang, and Fang the night Pan threw the knives into Lake Ontario. While the trio were talking at Pan's Pridham Place home, the divers were busy scouring the lake bottom. Like all Pan's discussions, this one was a rambling conversation that went on for nearly five hours. But there were some pertinent points that Edgar figured a jury might like to hear.

"Why do I talk to you about this on this evening?" Pan had asked Wang and Fang, after telling them how much he had been suffering since Selina's death. "Because maybe there is not too much more time. I have a lot of things to arrange and take care of. This girlfriend of mine, she was a very good person, very kind, but she was also an extremely unfortunate, ill-fated. I am not a person who cries easily, but often I wake up in the middle of the night and cry on account of her suffering. She looked like a typical Chinese girl. Gentle and kind, with a kind of inner beauty that was dignified and good."

"A classical Chinese?" Fang had asked.

"Not classical. To look at her—well, beauty is in the eye of the beholder. To love a person is happiness and to be loved is also a happiness. You know what was my unusual encounter? At the same time, the two sisters both fell in love with me. The older sister loved me and the younger sister loved me. Was that strange or not? Finally I chose the older one because I felt she was suffering so much, so pitiable. It aroused a kind of sense of responsibility in me, a kind of sense of mission. I said, rather than just talking empty words about saving the country and saving the Chinese people, I might as well first save her."

Edgar paused a moment, thinking to himself that Pan had not done a very good job "saving" Selina. He flipped ahead a few pages, to a spot in the transcript where Pan had blamed Selina's mother for his girlfriend's troubles.

"Her mother doted on her younger sister, didn't like the elder sister since she was small. The immature spirit of a child is extremely sensitive. If it receives even a slight injury, it will influence the child in both mind and body. I will give you an example. Her mother shipped a piano to her younger sister from Hong Kong because her younger sister was carrying on her mother's life work of studying piano. The elder sister, Selina, played the violin. She bought it with her own savings, her own spare cash. I felt she had no love. No one to love her. That was very pitiful."

"Of course, Selina was psychologically unbalanced," Wang had replied.

"Her mother came here and secretly gave her younger sister money to buy a house. If you were her, how would you think of this? At that time I had just started in business. I had nothing at all. Completely destitute. Her mother said, 'In the future, you will have nothing.' After her mother came for a visit, she was forcing her to break up with me. From that point on, from the time her mother left, everything changed. Every time she got a letter from her parents she told me, 'My mother and my father insist I leave you.' When I was together with her, so much trouble and pain. Happy moments were few."

Edgar skipped ahead a few more pages.

"I told Selina," Pan had said, "that only in adversity and suffering is a great person formed. Later, I said, we'll invite guests over to our house. And by coincidence that professor from the University of Toronto came. He entrapped her with honey words as soon as he came in here. After she was entrapped she moved out within two weeks. I didn't even know where. Finally, the fourth day after she moved out, it was a Tuesday I think, she gave me a call and gave me a great tongue-lashing. She wanted to find excuses for leaving me. I said, 'What is the matter with you? What are you up to? We should have a good talk about it.'

"She hung up the phone. At that point I became even more anxious. Every minute I was worrying about her. I waited, waited, waited, waited, right through to Saturday, but there was still no word from her so I wrote her a letter and gave it to the parent of one of her students. I expressed to her that she should turn around and come back."

Edgar stopped for a cigarette. It was as if Pan was on the witness stand, recounting the case. His version, that is.

"After that," Pan had continued, "another week went by and there was still no news. She had already broken away from her original agreement with me. Where did she go to? What does this mean? How do I know whether she has had relationships with eight or ten men? Damn! Maybe with someone with syphilis or AIDS. I cannot be a cuckold. I cannot myself lose face. So I wrote her another letter. I declared to her from this point on I no longer loved her. 'In the past I was unable to part with you but now I no longer love you because you are not worthy of my love. So beginning from today, because you are so cheap, I look down on you in my heart. I will not assume any responsibility or duty toward you.' Perhaps I should not have written this letter. Now I hear when she read this letter she was stupefied, dumbfounded."

"Her sister called me," Pan had continued, "it was two or three weeks after she moved out. Later, I told her sister, 'Let's go and report to the police right away.' The younger sister didn't report. She said, 'What if I reported to the police but later she reappeared?' "

Edgar found that remark by Pan interesting. According to Sophie Shen, Pan was the one who said it was a waste of time reporting Selina's disappearance.

"When she left," Pan had gone on, "I was truly pained. It was a great shock to see that empty house. And now she is dead."

"What do you plan to do?" Wang had asked.

"What can I do?"

"You could provide some information."

"What information could I provide?"

"The murderer has still not been arrested," said Wang.

"Right, but what information could I provide? This is where the difficulty arises. I wanted to talk of her past. The newspapers all say how gentle and refined she was. How intelligent. But they don't know what a mess she was in. Those who knew her character looked down on this person. When I was with her, my friends all knew. My own reputation was completely destroyed. But I have been truly unwilling to say anything that would damage her reputation. To damage her reputation is equivalent to injuring myself. It is like the Chinese saying, if there is a rat on the jade vase, you do not strike the rat for fear of breaking the vase."

"That is right," agreed Wang.

"The police, they have investigated me, and there wasn't anything. This is a country ruled by law. Even if I shoot and kill a person in public you do not say I am a murderer. You can only say I am a suspect, right? There must be evidence. There must be proof. As to this obstacle, I have a one hundred percent absolute confidence. It is the largest murder case in the world. I will tell all the people in China and abroad, to be Chinese is very sorrowful and woeful."

"The way she ended up could be foreseen," said Fang.

"I anticipated it long ago," said Pan. "So many times she wanted to commit suicide. The knife was lying right in front of her for her to kill herself but she didn't dare. Seeing her like this, I cried and she cried. She very much wanted to die. She had no mother's love. But she felt that to die here, it would be like an abandoned spirit that couldn't go back home. She felt that to die she had to return to her own native land. I encountered her in a dream. She was crying. 'You still won't come to save me. You still won't come to save me,' she said. When I woke up, there was nothing.

"There is a saying, 'If a person has done nothing shameful, if you knock on my door in the middle of the night, I will not be startled.' As for the police, I should say, if you want to charge me as a suspect, that's okay. If you want to detain me, that's okay. If you want to ask me in for questioning, that is your affair. It doesn't matter to me. They have not dared to do anything. They know that I am not one very easy to pick on. God is still protecting me. I've wanted to leave Toronto. Even if it's one day for rest. If police want to watch me, then watch. Their twenty-four-hour surveillance is not something I didn't experience during the Cultural Revolution in China. I have been through it all. As a result, the one who won is me. No matter how great my suffering I will just go about my work in order to revive and recover."

Edgar mashed out his cigarette and lit another. This part of the transcript was particularly helpful. Pan apparently planned to continue living and working in Toronto. He skimmed over a few more pages.

"And now the police are doing investigation of new leads. Go ahead and investigate. Don't you think that in such a big affair there would be some clues. As to selling my house, the ad I put in the paper was before she disappeared. If it was after she disappeared, I would not be able to wash clean even by throwing myself in the Yellow River. In addition, that letter I wrote is in hands of police. I told her I was willing to give up everything, business career or whatever, for her. We will settle down, together forever. Fortunately, thanks to God, this is a country of law. They don't dare act recklessly. If I was in mainland China, I would have long since been arrested. Arrested and jailed."

"Right," Fang had said. "Dismemberment of a corpse is a deep enmity and great hate in the world."

"There was no deep enmity between me and her," noted Pan.

"No, the question is," continued Fang, "if they really want to find out this thing, I feel that as far as you are concerned, you are the most suspected."

"The most what?" asked Pan.

"The most suspected for the police investigation," repeated Fang.

"How could they pin it on me?"

"Why I think this? You have more understanding about this affair than anyone else."

"I don't know anything," said Pan. "If you think I did it, go ahead and charge me. And that's the end of it. I am not speaking mixed-up words to you. I don't know anything. I never knew anything, right?"

"Right," agreed Wang.

"It is all too late," continued Pan. "There is nothing to do but depend on the police. I was intent on helping and healing her psychological wounds for two or three years. Damn it. She was so confused. This is a possibility. She went to work. She needed money. If someone gave her a glass of something to drink, and made her intoxicated or something and so on and so on. Or coerced her to become a prostitute or take drugs or whatever. She resisted. But why would someone want to dismember her?''

"The person wanted to silence her?" asked Wang.

"Silencing her has no connection. If you kill her, you have silenced her."

"Someone killed her. He would have to find a place to put it," said Wang. "Easier to dispose of —"

"Even if disposal is more convenient, would it not be, that is to say . . . like maybe . . . that is, that is to say . . . there is . . . is easier to get rid of the corpse, and eliminating the traces, you know, than a complete corpse?" wondered Pan.

"It would be very easy to be located," said Wang.

"He would not be freely able to throw in any place," said Pan. "If it happened this way. As you say, I had no deep enmity or hatred for her. I swore at her for leaving and then had nothing to do with her. When she left, I had no idea where she went. Really, this is what they mean by saying a beautiful woman can bring calamity. Once she's dead, for her, it's finished. Really, the one who is suffering most is me."

"Naturally," agreed Wang.

"You have no need to worry," continued Pan. "I will get through this, no question."

"We both believe you," Wang added.

"We should keep doing our business and developing our careers, as before," said Pan.

"But you must be on your guard," cautioned Fang. "They could arrest you."

"How could they arrest me?"

"Very simply. Just say you intentionally provoked her."

"How could I provoke her?"

"For example, the letter you wrote."

"Yeah . . .?"

"It was written before she disappeared. You already had intention."

"How could I have an intention?"

"It's premeditation. Now, I am just speaking hypothetically."

''You cannot speak this way! How can writing a letter be premeditation? The content of this letter, there is no premeditation. If I had any intention in advance, I would not write one word. If I want to kill her I would not let her move out, right? What advantage would there be to me in killing her? What mouth would I be silencing? Just what need was there for me to silence her? This is a country ruled by law and it gives great weight to evidence. Even if there is premeditation, they don't have direct evidence against me. The Crown attorney will not be able to prosecute. If he prosecutes, the judge will say bullshit, and you will be released and declared innocent on the spot. In the last analysis, it's what murder weapon did you use? In what kind of a way did you kill her? Where are witnesses, material evidence, corroboratory evidence? Are there, or are there not, your fingerprints on this knife? Yeah. Blood traces were found on your floor. Her blood stains appear on your wall. Afterward, we had someone who saw it clearly. She screamed, and after that, saw you kill her, and hit her. Yeah. Only in such a case can you be convicted. Right? It's very simple.''

Edgar looked up from the transcript. That's right, Pan, he thought, it was all very simple. He had refreshed his mind on two points by rereading the conversation. One, he was more convinced than ever that Pan was guilty of first-degree murder. Maybe they didn't have a crime scene, but they had the next best thing. The killer's description of what must have happened. Although Pan was speaking in the third person, he had described, in graphic details, a murder, the slaying of Selina Shen. The second point Edgar picked up from the transcripts was that Pan didn't think the police had a case against him. The very fact that he had given police the second letter, the one Selina read the day she disappeared, showed that. Over and over again, Pan said he had no motive to kill Selina. At one point in the transcripts, Pan commented that even if he did have a motive, there was no still no case against him because police had no ''direct evidence.'' Apparently Mr. Pan had never heard of circumstantial evidence. Maybe that's all the police had, Edgar thought, but it was great circumstantial evidence.

But he was still faced with a tough call.

If Edgar let Pan go to China, what guarantee did he have that Pan would return? His investigators were pressuring him to arrest Pan. They feared that Pan was planning to make a run for it. If Pan decided not to come back from China, there wasn't much Edgar could do to get him, short of kidnapping. Canada had no extradition treaty with that country. They had more than enough to convict him, his detectives argued. Why take the chance that he won't come back?

Edgar thought about what to do for a long time. The decision was his alone to make. If he went to court before he was ready, he risked having the case tossed out on a legal technicality. But if Pan never came back, Edgar might finish his career pounding a beat at Wasaga Beach. Was this why the investigators with the CID were given so much freedom? If they screwed up, there was no one to blame but themselves. If he let Pan go, it would be a calculated risk. But he was sure that Pan would come back. Toronto was his home now. He had his magazine, his businesses and, of course, his law suits. Pan seemed sure that the two Chinese newspapers had libelled him, and he was about to become a quick millionaire from the damages. Yes, he would let Pan take his little trip because it would be a long, long time before he ever got home to China again.

Kennedy poked his head in the door, then walked over and dropped a sandwich on Edgar's desk. Edgar looked at it.

"Egg salad?" he asked, with a sour look on his face.

"It's good for you, big guy," Kennedy said, smirking. "So, Sherlock, when do we arrest Pan?"

"When he comes back from his little trip."

CHAPTER TWENTY-TWO

Late Arrival

Amtrak train Number 98 from New York City was late getting into Toronto that night. Larry Edgar and Garnet Rombough were waiting by the arrivals area on the main floor of Union Station when the announcement of the delay came over the public-address system. They went for a coffee. There was nothing much they could do but wait.

Edgar and his team of investigators had met that morning in Rombough's suite at the Holiday Inn to discuss the evening's operation. The hotel in the heart of Chinatown had been like a second home for Rombough and Brian Kennedy. The two men had stayed there for most of the fourteen months since the discovery of Selina Shen's legs on the Parkway.

Edgar's pager went off. He left the coffee shop and called Kennedy from a pay phone. Kennedy wanted to know what was going on. Edgar told him everything was on hold. The train was about an hour late. It was scheduled to arrive at 9:11 P.M.

Edgar rejoined Rombough at the coffee shop. They drank their coffees in silence, each smoking, staring absently at the travellers scurrying about the station. The strain of the investigation was starting to show on Edgar's face. There were dark lines under his eyes. He was smoking more than usual. Although neither detective would admit it out loud, both were a bit nervous. The other teams of investigators were in place, all set to move.

It had taken months, but Sophie Shen had finally given Edgar the missing information he needed. She told him where Selina had worked during those several weeks after she walked out on Pan. It was at Fred's Coffee Shop on University Avenue in downtown Toronto, a small mom-and-pop business run by a Korean couple.

There was a reason for Sophie's silence, but it had nothing to do with the murder. Since Selina was on a student visa and not allowed to work, she had assumed her sister's identity, telling the Korean couple her name was Sophie. Her paycheques were made out in Sophie's name. Sophie had cashed the cheques, then given the money to Selina. Since what the sisters had done was illegal, Sophie had been afraid to tell Edgar. She didn't want to get into trouble. Edgar had assured her he didn't care about any of that. He just wanted to fill in a gap in his case. Pan suggested that Selina might have worked at a bar as a prostitute after leaving him, and perhaps met her killer during that time. Edgar knew that was nonsense, but until Sophie finally admitted the truth, he had no evidence with which to dispute Pan's lies. He sent his investigators to interview the Korean couple. They said that Selina had been a model employee, punctual, always cheerful with customers. Selina said she had left her boyfriend and didn't want him to know where she worked. The man she really loved, a person she had met in Hong Kong before coming to Canada, was living in Australia. She wrote to him often and one day they planned to marry.

By 9:20, the passengers from the Amtrak train from New York started to file out through the arrivals area. Edgar and Rombough were standing off to one side, silently scanning the faces. The man they had come for was one of the last off the train. He was carrying a single suitcase, staring ahead as he walked, as if looking for someone. He went right past the two detectives but didn't see them. They followed him into the lobby. A woman was waiting for him there. Edgar and Rombough approached the couple from the rear, unnoticed. Edgar reached out and put a hand on the man's shoulder. The man swung around to see who it was.

"Rui-Wen Pan," said Edgar, "I have a warrant here for your arrest. You're charged with murder, the first-degree murder of Selina Lian Shen."

He turned to Rombough and nodded. Rombough took a small card from his wallet and began reading Pan his constitutional rights.

"I am arresting you for first-degree murder," he began. "It is my duty to inform you that you have the right to retain and instruct counsel without delay. You have the right to telephone any lawyer you wish. You have the right to free advice from a legal aid lawyer. Do you understand? Do you wish to call a lawyer now?"

Pan said nothing. There was no indication that he was surprised to be arrested now, at the end of a trip to New York that he had taken shortly after returning from his business trip to China.

"I will now give you a caution," said Rombough. "You are charged with first-degree murder. Do you wish to say anything in answer to the charge? You are not obliged to say anything unless you wish to do so, but whatever you say may be given in evidence. Do you understand this?"

Pan remained expressionless.

"Do you understand what I have just said?" Rombough asked again. Pan nodded.

"I will now give you a supplementary caution," said Rombough. "If you have spoken to any police officer or to anyone with authority or if any such person has spoken to you in connection with the case, I want it clearly understood that I do not want it to influence you in making any statement."

"I only think it is so ridiculous," said Pan, shaking his head.

Edgar took Pan firmly by the arm. "Mr. Pan, you'll have to come with us," he said, leading him towards the exit.

The woman who had been waiting for Pan followed the two detectives through the station lobby.

"What right have you got to do this?" she demanded.

Edgar took out the warrant and held it up for her to read.

"I want to see your badge," the woman said.

Edgar took it from his pocket and showed it to her. Other travellers had stopped and were milling about. Edgar, glancing at the crowd around him, took Pan by the arm once again and continued towards the door.

"Call my brother," Pan shouted to the woman. "Tell him to arrange my bail."

Much later that evening, after Pan had been fingerprinted, photographed, and formally charged with the first-degree murder of his former girlfriend, he was taken from the OPP's waterfront headquarters to the force's Downsview detachment, where he would spend the night in a prison cell. There were three people waiting outside the main office as Edgar and Rombough led Pan out the front door. One of them was a photographer.

Jim Wilkes shoved his camera in front of Pan's face and snapped off several frames before Pan was put in the back seat of Edgar's Chevrolet. As he got in beside Pan, Edgar glanced at the other two men, who were standing just to the rear of the car.

"Those two fellows," Edgar said to Pan, nodding in their direction, "do you know them?"

Pan swung around and looked at Nick Pron and Kevin Donovan for a long time. He was still staring at them as the car drove off.

"No," he said to Edgar. "I never saw them before."

CHAPTER TWENTY-THREE

Prison Blues

The guard behind the bullet-proof window punched the name into the computer.

"Oh," he said, giving Nick Pron a quick glance. "Him. He's in super-protective custody. He's not in with the general population. You have to come back later, after six."

The waiting room for the Don Jail was packed that evening when Pron returned. Most of the visitors were women, several with babies. Off in one corner, a florid-faced woman with a tattoo of a rose on one arm was bottle-feeding her baby while keeping up a steady stream of chatter with the woman beside her, who was older and heavier, and was missing two front teeth. When she laughed, her whole body jiggled and her massive breasts, barely concealed by a thin T-shirt, flopped in either direction. She yelled at two children who were both wearing stained T-shirts. They stopped fighting for a moment, then when the woman with the raspy voice looked away, they went back to wrestling. One of the children bumped against a tall man, elegant in a dark blue business suit, polished Florsheims and camel-hair coat. He brushed the child away, as if trying to shoo off a pesty fly, then backed up a step, trying not to touch anything or anyone in the cramped room. A sign over a door at one end of the room read: WAIT UNTIL YOUR NAME IS CALLED.

After a half hour's wait, Pron heard his name on the loudspeaker. He walked through the door under the sign and into the next room.

It was larger, brightly lit, and divided in half with a thick, plexiglass window heavily stained with fingerprints. There were chairs on either side of the glass, with black telephone receivers in front of each one. Standing alone in a cubicle, clad in a blue V-necked T-shirt and blue pants, his shoulders stooped, was Rui-Wen Pan. When he saw Pron, the passive expression on his face changed to confusion, then anger.

"What-what-what are you doing here!" he demanded, yelling into the phone. "I did not ask you to come here. I do not want you here. Who told you to come? The police?"

"No. I —" Pron started to say.

"You have no right coming here. I-I am defenceless."

Pan put the phone down, turned away from Pron, and bowed his head. A moment later, the corners of his eyes started to redden. Then they glistened and welled up with tears. Tiny droplets rolled down his cheeks through the stubble on his unshaven face. The tears flowed slowly at first. But then the tiny droplets falling from his eyes turned into a torrent of tears. The tiny rivers on his cheeks widened, and when they came to his chin the droplets tumbled through the air, landing on the collar of his prison blues, his new business suit.

For nearly five minutes, he cried unashamedly, ignoring the other prisoners who glanced over from their side of the plexiglass. His body slumped even more, as if all the air had been let out of him. Finally, he took some tissue from his pocket and brushed weakly at the tears. He picked up the phone and turned to Pron.

"I did not want you to come, to see me here, like this," he said. "Do you enjoy this, seeing me here" — he looked around the visiting room—"like an animal in a cage?"

"I came to see if you were being treated well," replied Pron.

"I am allowed visitors only twice a week. You have stolen a visit from my family."

"They didn't tell me that. I can leave, if you want."

"Everything I have fought for, everything I have achieved, all that is finished now. My life's work . . . over."

Pan put the phone down. He looked around the room for a few minutes, then reached for the phone.

Crime Story*

"I do not want you to write that I cried like this," he ordered. His eyes were still red and puffy. "If you do, I will law suit you."

"I'm just here to visit. I can't write any stories now because of the trial."

Pan looked away again, deep in thought. After a few moments he turned back to Pron. The tears were gone. He straightened his shoulders a bit.

"It's very clear now what is left in life for me," he said. He took a deep breath, let it out gradually. When he spoke, his words were measured and slow. "I have three choices. One is that I could kill myself. I could commit suicide. This I have thought about very, very hard." There was another long pause. "Second, I can accept what they have done to me, the police and the media. I can stay here, in jail and just rot. I have been framed. You have helped to do this to me. I can accept this and do nothing." He paused again. "There is one more choice. I can fight, fight against this horrible wrong that has been done to me."

A guard walked past and tapped on the glass, a signal that the visit was over. Pan watched the guard as he walked over to the other prisoners with the same message. Then he turned back to Pron, started to get up. He still had the phone in his hand.

"I have made my decision," he announced, nodding to himself. "I have decided, Mr. Nick Pron, that I will fight. I will fight this injustice. You will see. I will get justice."

He put the phone down and started to leave, but stopped and picked it up again.

"Will you be at the trial, Mr. Nick Pron?" he asked.

"Yes. Of course."

"Good," he replied. "When the trial is over, then you will finally learn the truth."

282

CHAPTER TWENTY-FOUR

A Reasonable Jury

Fred Rowell shoved back his chair and stood up, grabbing the transcript off the defence table. For a long moment he stared at the two typewritten pages. Then he turned slowly towards the prisoner's box, where his client, Rui-Wen Pan, sat making notes. Pan stopped and looked at his lawyer, a bear-like man with a thick, black beard and bushy eyebrows. Rowell gave Pan the briefest of smiles, then wheeled around and strode towards the lectern, his black robe billowing behind him.

Rowell purposefully shifted the wooden stand closer to the jury, six men and six women who had already listened to more than a month of testimony in the Ontario Supreme Court murder trial. The prosecution had called seventy witnesses and introduced thousands of pages of intercepted communications. With a quick motion, Rowell flicked the robe off his arms, tugged down his vest, and grasped the lectern with both hands. He leaned towards the man on the witness stand, Metro police constable Ken Yates, a Crown witness whom Rowell was cross-examining. To Rowell's left, the trio of Crown prosecutors, Glen Orr, Gary Clewley, and Mike Innes, sat silently. Rowell glowered at them as he began.

"Your Honour, we seem to have a serious problem," Rowell said, addressing Mr. Justice David Doherty. "Earlier in the trial the defence was told through disclosure that no tapes existed of Mr. Yates's interview with Anna Leung Fisher. But late yesterday it was brought to our attention," he said, looking at co-defence lawyers Ed Hung and Anne Tierney, "that the interview was, in fact, tape-recorded by Mr. Yates."

Rowell paused, stepped to one side of the lectern, hooked his thumbs in his vest pockets, and turned towards the jury. He continued.

"To the great credit of Mr. Yates, he has come forward with this tape. It seemed after the interview the tape was misplaced. Is that not right, Mr. Yates?"

Yates, wearing blue jeans and a sweatshirt, had been pulled from an undercover assignment and rushed to the courtroom to give his testimony. He had apologized to the judge for his appearance, saying he didn't have time to change.

"After I did the interview, I put the tape in a drawer at my office, and it has remained there ever since," Yates said, adding that the tape had been mislaid when the Selina Shen investigation was still a missing person case.

"Your Honour," Rowell said, holding up the two typewritten pages, "I've taken the liberty of making a transcript of the relevant portions of this tape. I would like to enter this as evidence and, with Your Honour's permission, play the tape to the court. I also have copies of the transcript for each juror, and for my learned friends here," he said, motioning to the three prosecutors.

An audio system had been set up in the wood-panelled courtroom so the jurors could hear the wiretapped evidence against Pan. Each juror had a headset, as did the judge, the defence lawyers, and the prosecutors. For days on end, the courtroom had been virtually silent as the tapes were played. Rowell handed around the transcripts as the headsets were put on.

Constable Yates had interviewed Anna Leung Fisher in April, 1988, nearly two months after Selina Shen vanished. Anna Leung Fisher was the estranged wife of Robert Fisher, the university instructor who Pan claimed was trying to steal his girlfriend. Anna Leung had met with Pan twice in the days before Selina's disappearance. At her testimony in the first week of the trial, Leung had described those meetings. Pan had said her husband was seeing a Chinese woman, whom she assumed was Selina. She told the court that he then went on to say: " 'Something very shocking is going to happen. . . . You'll be very surprised. . . . It will be beyond your wildest imagination. . . . It will happen very soon, within a week or two.' " Pan had then tried to kiss her, something she testified she found "very distasteful."

Rowell walked to his seat at the defence table. Picking up the cassette tape of the interview, he turned back to the jury.

"Ladies and gentleman, I want you to cast your mind back to Anna Leung's testimony and listen very carefully to this recording of her earlier interview with Mr. Yates." He then put the cassette into the tape recorder and hit the play button. Yates was asking Anna Leung Fisher about her meeting with Pan at his shop on Broadview.

"So you saw him on Wednesday?" Yates asked.

"Right," she replied. "I met him at his shop on Broadview. We went to a restaurant just opposite his shop. I kept asking him, 'Tell me what this is about. I have things to do in the afternoon. I have to work. I have to go to school.' He kept beating about the bushes. He said, 'You will be so surprised, you'll be so shocked about this thing, you know.' He said, 'I haven't got enough information yet, but maybe in a few days or a couple of weeks I will have more information.'

"I said, 'What are you talking about?' He kept talking in terms like that, and then he made some oblique reference that Bob is seeing another woman. And very soon this woman is going to move in with Bob. I said, 'Bob is seeing Selina. Is it Selina?' And he said, 'I couldn't tell you.' So I said, 'Look, you know you just have to be straight with me. I don't believe in wasting my time like this. I don't even know you and you're asking all these personal questions. I have to go to work.' So he dropped me off at the hospital."

After the tape was finished, Rowell went back to the lectern and leaned towards Yates.

"Was that Anna Leung's voice on the tape?"

Yates said it was.

"Earlier in the trial," Rowell said, "the defence was told the tape of Anna Leung Fisher's interview with police did not exist. And now we have the tape and the two pages of transcript taken from an interview soon after she had the conversation with Mr. Pan.'' Rowell held the two pages aloft, slapped his hand on the lectern, and faced the jury. ''And this transcript, taken from a tape made when her memory would have been the freshest, contradicts what Anna Leung Fisher said earlier in this trial. Not that something shocking was going to happen in two weeks, but rather it would take two weeks to get information on something surprising.'' With that, Rowell walked back to his chair, glancing over at his client, who was smiling. A recess was called.

A red-faced Larry Edgar was one of the first out of the courtroom. He was furious. The missing tape was going to hurt their case. Rowell made it sound as if the investigators had tried to mislead the court. Nothing was further from the truth. As far as he was concerned, he had a solid case against Pan. He and his team of investigators had gathered a huge amount of evidence showing that Pan had killed and cut up Selina. They had showed how Pan had lured Selina to her death with a letter, how Pan had ditched the knives in Lake Ontario, and how Pan had incriminated himself on the wiretaps. Doctors Ming Lee and Ian Taylor, anatomy specialists from the University of Toronto, along with Dr. Hans Sepp, had testified that those knives were capable of making the precise cuts that had dissected Shen's body. By sheer luck, Shen's skull had been found in the Cataraqui River by two fishermen just before the trial began. The precision of the cut at the vertebra showed it was done by someone with medical knowledge. During the seven-week trial, various witnesses had told the jury that Pan had received medical training in China, that he was a top student in courses such as pathology and anatomy. Then there was his injured hand, his lack of an alibi, and the bitter argument he had had with Selina just before her death.

There could be only one verdict, thought Edgar, as he stormed into the small room beside the court that served as his makeshift office during the trial. Pan was guilty of first-degree murder. That's the way Edgar saw it. But the trial was not going well. Even he had to admit that Rowell had scored a direct hit with the missing tape. And they had looked bad, no doubt about it. The question was, how much damage had it done to the case?

Garnet Rombough and Brian Kennedy joined Edgar in the office. Rombough immediately pulled out a pack of cigarettes and lit one.

"I should start smoking again," Edgar said to Rombough, eyeing the cigarettes.

He had quit cold turkey after the preliminary hearing. That had been a good day. Judge John Kerr had committed Pan to trial, saying: "I think that a reasonable jury, properly charged, would find this man guilty of first-degree murder." But just how reasonable was this jury?

"Pass me a cigarette, Garnet," Edgar said to Rombough.

"Are you sure, Larry?" Rombough replied, flicking his package of cigarettes across the table. "Bad enough that I'm smoking."

Rombough was still recuperating after spending several months in the hospital. Just before Pan's preliminary hearing, he had suddenly taken ill and nearly died. Doctors found a blocked artery and repaired it with open heart surgery. But the stay in hospital had been hard on the wiry Rombough, who had lost about forty pounds from his illness.

Edgar stared at the cigarette package for a long moment, before picking it up and reading the surgeon general's warning on the side. He took out a cigarette, held it between his fingers, and started to put it in his mouth. Just then the door opened.

"Is the case going that badly, Larry?" asked Glen Orr, the chief prosecutor, staring at the cigarette package. Edgar looked at the cigarette again, then put it back in the package.

The smile on Orr's face quickly faded as he walked into the room. He took off his black robe, the special silk one given to Queen's Counsels, and threw it on the table. Then he dropped his lanky frame in a chair across from Edgar. He sat carelessly, his arms dangling limply over the sides, his legs stretched out under the table. He did not look like one of the country's top prosecutors; his trousers were wrinkled, a shirt-tail was hanging out, and one side of his collar was sticking up. This was not the same Glen Orr who had lost only one case in his twenty-year career. Orr was still mourning the death of his son, who'd been killed in a car accident just two months before Pan's arrest. Orr had been planning to leave the Crown's office and go into private practice with his son, who was about to enter law school. The accident happened on a remote highway in eastern Ontario, ironically not far from where Shen's body parts were found. With Kennedy's sister dying, Orr's son getting killed, and Rombough's brush with death, Edgar was beginning to believe the Shen case was jinxed.

While some Crown prosecutors had told Edgar he didn't have a case, not even enough evidence to lay a charge, Orr disagreed. He took the case, telling Edgar there was more than enough proof to convince a jury of Pan's guilt. Orr had seen this as his last trial, a fitting end to an illustrious career. He would win, retire, then go into private practice. But those plans were finished. When Orr slipped into a depression after his son's death, Edgar had been advised to find a new prosecutor if he wanted to win. But Edgar, known for his loyalty to friends, stuck with the man who had backed him. He believed Orr was the best man for the job, and that the trial was just what Orr needed to get his mind off his son.

There had been times when Orr demonstrated the courtroom theatrics that had earned him a reputation as a winning prosecutor. One of his best moments came when he infuriated Pan's defence team by repeatedly brandishing one of the knives in the air, holding it up long enough to show the jury it could be a murder weapon and not a kitchen utensil. An angry Rowell had jumped to his feet, protesting: "Perhaps Mr. Orr can emphasize his point even better if he throws the knife so it would stick into the wall, Your Honour." Orr didn't reply. He sat down, point made. But there were times when Orr, overcome with grief, had left the courtroom and wandered the halls. The judge had finally remarked that no one should leave the courtroom without a good reason. It was said as a general comment, but everyone knew it was directed at Orr.

"It's all my fault, Larry," Orr said, slumping even deeper into his chair.

"Forget it, Glen," Edgar said. "The missing tape's not your fault."

"No," Orr said sullenly, shaking his head, "I mean the way the whole trial's going. I just can't shake my depression. I haven't been sharp enough. I let you down."

"Don't worry. No matter what Rowell says, he's not going to come up with an explanation for the knives. What possible reason can he give for Pan going down to the lake at midnight and throwing four knives and a cleaver into the water? We've got nothing to worry about. Pan is going down for first-degree murder."

Fred Rowell looked straight into the eyes of the men and women in the jury box and began his defence.

"Rui-Wen Pan did not kill Selina Lian Shen," he said, his deep voice booming throughout the silent courtroom, crowded that day with high-school students on a field trip.

Rowell had moved the lectern so it was directly in front of the jurors. Although he had prepared some notes, he barely glanced at the page as he spoke.

"Then why did he throw the knives into the lake?" he continued. "Isn't that the Crown's case? You have heard much expert testimony, from pathologists to weathermen to cottage owners who found the body parts. You have heard all of that evidence. But if Mr. Pan is innocent, why would he throw knives into the lake? That's the bottom line. Why would he make comments about our legal system, under which you can't be hauled off to jail as in China? There is a term in law called consciousness of guilt. You look at what this person did and you say, 'Wasn't he feeling guilty and that's why he did it?'

"We have heard much about the throwing of knives into Lake Ontario after Shen's name had been released to the media. That's not the issue. The issue is whether there is anything else in Mr. Pan's background that is consistent with this action. We will be delving into consciousness of guilt, trying to find out what was inside a person's mind when he did something. A mind is not like a goldfish bowl. You can't just look at some balance sheets to find out what a person was thinking about.

"We have a problem here. The mind that we want to look inside belongs to a culture we know very little about. This makes your task," Rowell said, his eyes sweeping over the jury, "ten times more difficult. We're going to go to China for a couple of days. Well," he said, pausing to tug his black vest over his ample belly, "to be more accurate, we're going to bring China here. You'll be hearing a lot of testimony. I want you to listen to it critically and carefully. Maybe there is an explanation, other than consciousness of guilt, for Mr. Pan throwing the knives into the lake. You'll be hearing about authority and the police in China."

Rowell leaned forward, shifting the lectern even closer to the jury box. "Rui-Wen Pan said and did a lot of things you might not expect. His background will explain this. Your Honour, the defence calls Peter Mitchell to the stand."

The back doors of the courtroom opened and a thin man walked in. Mitchell, an associate professor of humanities at York University in Metro Toronto, was born in China and immigrated with his parents to Canada when he was five years old.

"Mr. Mitchell," Rowell began, "how does the legal system in China differ from our system here in Canada?"

"In China, the law is always viewed as a method in which the state orders society, not one in which you get protection from the state," Mitchell replied, speaking slowly, as if he were lecturing at the university. "The authority in China is the collective over the individual. Chinese authorities wanted to purify society, and in 1966 Chairman Mao Tse-tung declared a new revolution, the Cultural Revolution. He said the revolution of 1949 should happen again. The country should go through a process of chaos to build a new purified form. Chairman Mao started the revolution because he found himself out of power with his party. He turned first to the army, then to society to oppose his enemies. The universities were essentially shut down from 1966 to 1969 and never really opened to 1971. All academics were targeted to see if their thoughts followed the thoughts of Chairman Mao and the

Marxist-Leninists. Anything associated with Western values, such as curled hair and Western clothing, disappeared."

Edgar swivelled his chair around and frowned at Rombough and Kennedy in the first row of the gallery. He then glanced at Pan, who had stopped taking notes.

"In traditional China," Mitchell continued, "the value of the group is placed above the individual. The individual finds identity only in the group. You are identified by your group. That's why Chinese people always give their family name, rather than their first name, if you ask them. When you ask them where they live, they will give their family's residence as their address, even if they don't live at home anymore. Someone is a renegade, an outsider, if they don't conform to the dictates of the group.

"Criminal law and process are regarded as an arm of the state to assure conformity to group goals. When you are arrested, the system is geared to finding you guilty. The person is aware that once the arrest is made it is inevitable that he will be found guilty. There is no protection to the individual after the arrest. Until 1989, it was a society without lawyers. Once the arrest was made, then, to society, that is a guarantee the person is guilty. There are no institutions, no legal process by which individual rights are looked after. There are no laws, no institutions, to register a complaint about how you are treated after your arrest. There is no bail-hearing process. The person just disappears. The family is unaware what has happened until the authorities contact them. It could be hours, days, months. There is no procedure the authorities have to follow. The steps are arrest, trial, conviction, appeal, and then execution. It goes quickly. It can take only forty-eight hours. The execution process is held to impress the public of the need to conform. The condemned man is paraded through town, often wearing a tall hat and carrying a banner on the way to the execution grounds."

"What about the rights of an accused man?" Rowell asked.

"There are no rights in China," Mitchell replied. "Concepts we take for granted, such as the presumption of innocence, are non-existent. The concept of proof beyond a reasonable doubt? There is no such thing. The authorities in

China are viewed with caution. The right to remain silence? There is no such right.''

Rowell's next witness was Enching Long, a fifty-nine-year-old doctor who once practised medicine with Pan's father in China. He had flown in from Atlanta, Georgia, where he now lived. Long said he had suffered through the Cultural Revolution and was jailed in 1967 for being an anti-revolutionist.

"You can't use your own name when you're in jail," he testified. "They give you a number and they call you by that number. You're not allowed to speak to your cell mates or to read."

"Can you explain to the court why you were jailed?" asked Rowell.

"They said I said something against the Communist party. I couldn't speak to a lawyer. My sister-in-law ran away from China, and because of that I was classed as an enemy of the nation. I was sentenced to a year in a labour camp where I cleaned toilets, dug holes, made bricks, and repaired houses. One man who was in jail was a hero of the Korean War. They just took him off the street and beat him up."

At this point Judge Doherty interrupted the testimony and called for a recess. While the jury was out, he asked Rowell what point he was trying to make with Dr. Long. "We're hundreds of millions of miles from anything of relevance," Doherty said, an exasperated look on his face.

Rowell said he didn't have many more questions and promised there was a point to the testimony, which would become clear with his next witness.

"Dr. Long," Rowell began, when the jury returned, "could you describe for us the type of persecution you faced in the labour camp?"

"They would not let you alone. I had to write my thoughts down on paper. There were meetings and I was shouted at. Day in and day out they held meetings and shouted against you. My wife was in another camp. My eldest daughter was not allowed to finish junior high school. We were watched continuously."

"What is your attitude towards the authorities and the police?" asked Rowell.

"After our experiences, we were all very frightened of the police. The police never reason with you. If you resist, they just beat you up. After they beat you up, they can just put you in jail. They can put anyone in jail, even ones who are innocent. The people of China all hate policemen. I have been in the United States two years and I'm still fearful of police."

"Thank you, Mr. Long. Your witness, Mr. Orr."

The prosecutor rose slowly to his feet and straightened his robe, which had fallen from one shoulder. He had a day's growth of beard and his hair looked as if he'd started combing it and given up. Orr leaned an elbow on the jury box and began.

"So, Mr. Long," he said, rubbing a hand across his stubble, "you were quite afraid of the police in China?"

"Yes. Very afraid."

"And down in Georgia — that's where you live now, Georgia?"

"Yes. Two years."

"And I gather you've been there for two years and you're still afraid of the police? Now these would be the Georgia police, would they not?"

"Yes. I am as scared of the police in Georgia as I am of the police in China."

Orr put both arms behind him on the railing of the jury box and leaned back. He looked around the courtroom, his gaze stopping on Pan for a moment, before he looked back at Dr. Long. Orr sauntered over to the witness box, with the relaxed manner of a man walking around his own living room.

"Now, Dr. Long, you came up here specifically to testify?"

"Yes."

"And I gather you flew up here?"

"Yes."

"And you've been up here for a few days?"

"Right."

"And I gather you've seen our police driving around in their cruisers?" Orr said, resting his forearms on the witness box and leaning close to Dr. Long.

"Yes, I think maybe, yes."

"Well, doctor, tell the court . . . the police here in Toronto, are you afraid of them?" Orr's face was just a few inches from the witness.

Doctor Long paused for a moment, shifting back in his seat, away from Orr. "Here? Toronto? No. I have no fear at all."

In a stern voice, Judge Doherty said: "Would you please step back, Mr. Orr. It's not necessary to be so close to the witness."

Orr mumbled an apology and sauntered back to the lectern.

"Mr. Long, you know Mr. Pan's family. Correct?"

"Yes, very well."

"And your evidence was that there's a lot of persecution in China? A lot of people being jailed by the police?"

"Yes, all the time."

"And I gather that's what makes people afraid of the police?"

"Yes."

"Being put in jail, I mean."

"Yes."

"Now Mr. Pan's family, you say you knew them quite well?"

"Yes."

"And were any of his family, that is Mr. Pan's, were any of them ever put in jail during the Cultural Revolution?"

"No."

"Thank you, Dr. Long. No more questions."

Rowell called Dr. Hung-Tat Lo to the stand. Lo was a psychiatrist with the Clarke Institute of Psychiatry and the Queen Street Mental Health Centre in Toronto. He was describing his expertise in transcultural psychology—the problems that arise when people move from one culture to another—when Orr asked for the jury to be excused so he could discuss the relevance of the witness.

Speaking in a tone defence lawyers referred to as Orr's "angry voice," the prosecutor asked why Rowell was bringing to the stand a psychiatrist who had never even examined Pan. "M'lord, it's quite clear Mr. Rowell is trying to get in the back door what he won't put through the front door. I'm referring to, of course, Mr. Pan's state of mind. If he wants to describe Mr. Pan's state of mind, well, let him put Mr. Pan on the stand. If I can use an example, just because one Chevrolet might have bad brakes, that doesn't mean all Chevrolets have bad brakes.''

Rowell got to his feet and, in an equally loud voice, replied: ''M'lord, the defence is trying to show the problems faced by immigrants who come to this country from authoritarian regimes. We're trying to get at the 'head space' these people bring with them. Are Pan's actions consistent with guilt, or of immigrants from authoritarian communities. In China there is a common saying: In life, do not enter the door of any government office. And in death, do not enter the gates of hell. In China, government authorities are equated with hell.''

Judge Doherty said he would allow the witness and ordered the jury brought back in. They filed in slowly, looking tired. During the long trial, there had been numerous delays to discuss legal matters. On some days, the jury heard only a few hours of testimony while the rest of the time was taken up with heated legal arguments between Orr and Rowell.

''Dr. Lo,'' Rowell asked, ''we've heard there is a widespread fear of the authorities in China in general, and of the police in particular. We've also heard of the absence in China of presumption of innocence and the right to a fair trial. When people come from that country to ours, do they bring that with them?''

''Yes,'' Lo replied, ''they bring those attitudes with them. For some, it takes quite a while to shed those skins. For others, they never shed them at all. Some may have a paranoia tendency regarding the police. For instance, if they pass by a police car they might become unsettled. It might affect the way they behave. That is, they see the police car and they turn and take another route. It's called an 'adaptive response behaviour.' ''

Rowell walked over to Lo and handed him a thick blue folder labelled 'Communication Number One,' 328 pages of a conversation between Pan, Peter Wang, and Andrew Fang, secretly recorded by police shortly after Pan threw the knives into the lake.

Lo said there were at least three instances in which Pan's comments showed he was afraid of being falsely accused of Selina Shen's murder. He read aloud one passage on page 311, in which Pan was talking to Wang and Fang: " 'It is that damned sister of hers. The bitch. I am just afraid she might do something and push it onto me.' " Lo looked up from the transcript and addressed the court. "That could be described as a fear of false accusation. Or it could show guilt. Whether it is guilt or fear of false accusation, that is open to debate."

"Are there other such passages in the transcripts?" Rowell asked.

"Yes. On page two forty-nine, Mr. Pan says, 'Even if they cannot find a single piece of evidence, I would not be able to wash clean, even by jumping into the Yellow River.' This could further be interpreted to show that Mr. Pan has fears of false accusation. On page three twenty-one, he says that 'Canada is a country ruled by law.' What he is doing is reassuring himself that he is in Canada and not in China. People who are under threat act in various ways to reduce their anxieties through defence mechanisms."

"Like people who whistle when they walk through a cemetery late at night?" Rowell asked.

"You could say that," Dr. Lo replied. He flipped through the blue book to another page. "There is another comment. Mr. Pan says, 'If I was in Mainland China, I would have long since been arrested.' This could show fear of arrest. I see a lot of fear behaviour consistent with both hypotheses. Either that he is afraid of false accusations or that he is guilty."

"Dr. Lo, we've heard testimony that Mr. Pan threw knives into Lake Ontario soon after Selina Shen was identified as the murder victim. Could he have been acting out of fear when he did that?"

"Based on what I have read, I'm quite mindful of the possibility Mr. Pan was aware he might be suspected or arrested. But whether this was fear of false accusation or a show of his guilt, I don't know."

Fred Rowell began his summation the next day. He stood in front of the jury, his hands folded across his belly, his reading glasses dangling part-way down his nose.

"Ladies and gentlemen of the jury, you must be satisfied beyond any reasonable doubt before convicting Rui-Wen Pan of first-degree murder. There's no direct evidence, no eye witnesses to this murder. It's a circumstantial case and you have to go through a Sherlock Holmes–type analysis of the facts. Ladies and gentlemen, you are the final arbiters in this function. Your responsibility is overwhelming. There is an unusual component to this case which you must consider, that is the Chinese culture and the attitudes brought into the courtroom by these people. I was struck by the eloquence of the language, the depth of the emotion in the love letters, almost Victorian in manner, that Mr. Pan wrote to Selina Shen.

"There are a lot of unanswered questions: how, where, and when she died. If you don't believe a witness, don't accept their evidence. The Crown's case is based on innuendo, half-truths, and outright lies. A circumstantial case is like a jigsaw puzzle. Each witness carries part of the puzzle. You can fill in the gaps with your own imagination. But the trouble with this case is there are just too many missing pieces and too many that don't fit.

"Take Anna Leung Fisher. She lied to you. She testified that two weeks before Shen's disappearance, Pan went to her and said that 'something shocking, something beyond your wildest imagination' would happen in two weeks. Ladies and gentlemen, that is clear evidence of first-degree murder. It's stunning, important evidence. But something very interesting happened. A mini cassette tape appeared that we didn't even know existed at the start of the trial. It's a tape of a police officer's interview with Anna Leung Fisher. It was put in a drawer and forgotten about. The history of this trial turns on that tape. On that tape, she said in a slow, calm voice that Mr. Pan would have more information in two weeks about her husband's love affair. She didn't say anything about 'wildest imagination.' "

Rowell paused, glanced at his notes, then leaned forward on the lectern. Slowly and carefully he looked at each juror over the top of his reading glasses.

"Mr. Pan never said," he continued, "that something would happen in two weeks. What he said was it would take two weeks to get information about this affair. This casts enormous doubts on the veracity of Anna Leung Fisher's testimony. If Mr. Pan was going to kill Shen, why would he tell Anna Leung Fisher? It's an awful thing to say you're going to kill someone. To say those words to Anna Leung Fisher is to put his head in the noose, not the type of thing you'd say if you truly were planning a murder. If Mr. Pan really said that, then she would have called the police. Anna Leung Fisher belongs in the penalty box. So does Sophie Shen, Selina's sister.

"Sophie Shen is an important Crown witness. She said she went to Mr. Pan's house shortly after her sister's disappearance and wanted to look in the basement; only he wouldn't let her. There may be some suggestion from that that the homicide took place there. But there's evidence to suggest that's not so. We have heard from one policeman who said Sophie Shen told him she did look in the basement that day and remembered enough to recall there was a freezer and a stove in one corner. That is an extremely important point in this case. She lied to you. Why? Perhaps she had an axe to grind with the man who left her for her older sister. That, ladies and gentlemen, ought to instill in you a pretty healthy scepticism about her evidence.

"You've heard a lot of evidence that whoever killed and cut up Selina Shen had a lot of medical training and could have been a doctor. You have to ask yourselves, do you think Mr. Pan is a doctor. He told everyone he was a doctor. But did he do this just to enhance his reputation, perhaps even to impress the ladies? The evidence is clear he is not a doctor; he is an X-ray technician. He did not have the qualifications to get into medical school."

Rowell stopped and looked at his client, who stared right back. Rowell tugged at his vest, absently toyed with his gold watch fob, then continued.

"Ladies and gentlemen, we all do dumb things in an emergency situation, especially when we panic. When Mr. Pan found out the body parts were his girlfriend's, can you imagine his horror? In the face of this panic, his fear of what the police might do to him, it was typical of those with his background to do something to throw suspicion away from himself. He threw the knives into the water, not because he was guilty, not as a sign of consciousness of guilt, but as a self-defence mechanism, a sign of the cultural paranoia felt by Mr. Pan and his countrymates towards authority. Had he not thrown the knives off the pier he never would have been arrested. It is a suspicious bit of evidence. Suspicious as it is, though, you can't convict him of first degree murder because he threw away some knives. There's no evidence the knives were the murder weapons.

"Selina Shen deserves to have the man accused of her murder tried as objectively and as fairly as possible. We don't want the tragedy of her death compounded by a miscarriage of justice."

Glen Orr began his closing summation after the lunch break. He spoke from memory.

"Has this case been proved to you beyond a reasonable doubt, ladies and gentlemen of the jury? I submit it has. It's a case based on circumstantial evidence. One might say, where are the eye witnesses? A circumstantial case is much more reliable than one with eye witnesses. Eye witnesses may lie. People lie. The facts don't. Let's start at the beginning."

Orr held up a picture of Selina Shen for the jury to see. He held it up a long time.

"Who had a motive to kill Selina Shen?" he asked. "There's no doubt Mr. Pan had the only real motive or reason to kill Selina Shen. A lot has been said about Mr. Fisher. Was he the real killer? Do you think for one instant that Fisher killed Selina? Where's the evidence of Fisher having any motive? He's a milquetoast. If he didn't kill Selina, well then, who did? Obviously Mr. Pan didn't have much respect for her. He always remembered her illegitimate child with that 'damned black' from El Salvador. Take a close look at the last letter he gave to Selina. If ever a letter showed contempt for a lady, this was it. He called her 'an unbearable bitch,' you might recall. To use the language of the street, he hated her guts. He did her in. He had a tremendous degree of jealousy towards her. Selina Shen was flying the coop. She wanted to be gone. In Mr. Pan's demented way he thought Selina was taking up with Mr. Fisher. Who had the motive to kill her? The only man was Mr. Pan. And what was the catalyst, you may ask? The dinner party, the day Fisher appeared on the scene. It was clear Mr. Pan did not want Mr. Fisher calling her and paying her any attention. It's clear Mr. Pan was intensely jealous of Mr. Fisher.

"Do you really believe Anna Leung Fisher came up here to lie? Just what was Mr. Pan referring to when he met her? That Selina was going to take off or that Selina was going to be done by him? He was referring to the fact that Selina was going to be done. . . . Mr. Pan is not a stupid man. He had to know the relationship was over. He tried to entice her back with a sweet love letter. It was a ruse, a nice letter, but it didn't work. He was like the fox, trying to entice the rabbit. If you don't succeed, you try again. When letter number one didn't work, he tried letter number two. He got nasty. He was using the letter as bait, to get her into his clutches. And did it work? I suggest it did, because she never showed up for her music lesson the next day.

"And there's another matter to consider. Mr. Pan had a bad hand at a very bad time. He told some people he injured his hand moving something. He told others he hurt it in a fall. It's very strange he had this bad hand at this bad time. Why would Mr. Pan not want his hand looked after? Because he was well aware that if he did, medical records would have been kept, medical records which could have embarrassed him. Mr. Pan had a bad hand because he used it on Selina." Orr stopped pacing a moment to look at the jury. "But of course that's for you to decide," he said.

"Why didn't Mr. Pan go to the police and say his dearly beloved had gone missing? Wouldn't an innocent man have done that? He had two reasons for not reporting her disappearance to the police. Number one, he couldn't go to the police station with a bad hand, someone would have noticed it. And number two, he needed time to dispose of the body.

"Where was Selina Shen killed? There are no witnesses to this awful murder. I suggest to you that the best description of the murder scene came from a conversation Mr. Pan had with Andrew Fang and Peter Wang the night he threw the knives into the lake. Let me read briefly from it."

Orr picked up a blue book from the lectern and faced the jury again. "Mr. Pan says, 'In the last analysis, it's what year, what month, what day you were at the place. What murder weapon did you use? In what kind of a way did you kill her? Are there, or are there not, your fingerprints on this knife? Blood traces were found on your floor. Her blood traces appear on your wall. Afterward, we have someone who saw it clearly. She screamed, and after that, saw you kill her. And hit her. Only in such a case, can you be convicted. Right?' " Orr put the book down and walked back to the jury.

"She was killed in a room and killed by Mr. Pan. You heard his interview with Kennedy and Riddell. That's a man who can get out of control. It's clear that Selina was dismembered by someone with more than a layman's skill. Who had that skill? Mr. Pan did. He got ninety-five percent in anatomy class. In my opinion that gave him all the expertise he needed. Fisher didn't have that kind of expertise. Forget poor old Robert Fisher. Let him go back to the University of Toronto.

"You've heard a lot about cultural paranoia. But not all Chinese people are on trial. Just Mr. Pan. If you're going to give any credence to this hopeless, hopeless defence, why weren't the other knives thrown into the water? Is there any evidence of Mr. Pan panicking? There is nothing! He was operating very coolly and very calmly on that day he threw the knives into the water. He went out to dinner earlier in the evening. Is that a man in a great state of panic? If you see any evidence of panic that supports this hocus-pocus defence, then by all means, acquit him. But there is no evidence of panic. It's nonsense.

"Then why did he throw the knives into the lake? He did it because he didn't want them ever to be found. That's the only rational conclusion. He never, ever wanted them to be found because he was concerned there was something about the knives that would cook his goose.

"What happened here is very simple. There is a man who was living with a lady who left him. And he killed her in a very, very methodical and able manner so she wouldn't take up with another man. He's guilty of first-degree murder. That's the position of the Crown. I ask of you that you return with a verdict of first-degree murder."

Fred Rowell was in the check-out line in the basement cafeteria of the court-house when Nick Pron and Kevin Donovan stopped to chat.

"This cultural paranoia stuff, Fred," Pron asked, "do you think the jury's really going to buy it?"

"Let me put it this way, Nick," Rowell said, pocketing his change, "how many days has the jury been out?"

"Five," replied Pron.

"I think you've just answered your question," Rowell said, taking his coffee and walking away.

A familiar figure was waiting for Pron and Donovan when they went outside the court-house to drink their coffees.

"You sure you want to be seen talking to us?" Donovan asked, looking around.

"Someone's got to talk to you fuckheads," Harvey Loxton said. "You've pissed everyone else off."

"It's been five days, Harvey," Donovan said. "Pan's walking. I told you to get someone with a university degree on this case."

"I've got a degree. A degree of tolerance for assholes like you. Look, it's not us who screwed up this case. It's the justice system. I know how the case went. I dropped in a couple of times. Never did trust juries. The big guy on the end? Looked like he was sleeping. Never trusted the jury system, never will. That cultural paranoia? All bullshit. But you watch, somebody will fall for it."

The defence and prosecution teams were drinking at Foster's, a bar near the court-house, when the word came that the jury was on its way back with a verdict. It was about suppertime and the bar was crowded with regulars from the court-house. Bills were hurriedly paid and everyone ran back in one group. Gary Clewley, one of the two assistant Crown prosecutors, was still putting on his black robe as he walked into the courtroom, which was rapidly filling with spectators and reporters.

"Pan's going to be convicted. I know it. I can feel it. What's that expression?" he asked, turning to one of the Chinese reporters. "*Yu chuet. It chie mo sa.* Guilty. Of first-degree murder." He joined Orr and Innes at the prosecuting table, while Rowell, Tierney, and Hung sat down at the table beside them, all waiting for the judge. Edgar, Kennedy, and Rombough took their seats behind the prosecution table. Edgar leaned forward and got Orr's attention.

"You did a good job, Glen," he said. "No matter what happens, thanks."

Everyone rose as Judge Doherty came in. He asked the court matron to summon the jury. A moment later they filed in. One of them, a woman, was crying. Another was shaking his head. Some looked angry. Most kept their eyes down as they took their seats.

Judge Doherty looked down at the jury.

"Ladies and gentlemen," he asked, "have you reached a verdict?"

CHAPTER TWENTY-FIVE

Unfinished Business

Nick Pron and Kevin Donovan were at a bar in the east end of Toronto when a man walked up to their table.

"Mind if I join you fellas for a drink?" he asked.

"Uh," said Donovan, glancing at Pron, "I guess you know you're not supposed to talk to us?"

"I don't care," the man said, pulling up a chair. "I'm still upset. What happened in there really bothers me. I have to talk to someone about it."

"What did happen in there?" Donovan asked.

"I should have known we were in trouble. Put twelve people in a room who don't know each other and what else could you expect? We couldn't agree on anything. We couldn't even get a foreman at first. The judge told us to go to a show one night, but we couldn't even agree on which movie to see."

"Sorry you got picked?" Pron asked. "Most people would love to get in on a first-degree murder trial."

"Being on that jury was probably the most interesting thing I'll ever do in my life. But I'd never want to do it again."

"Was there ever a chance of reaching a unanimous decision?" asked Pron.

"Actually, I thought we'd be done that night. I didn't think we were even going to get a free supper out of it. The way everybody was talking, I thought we'd find him guilty right off the bat. Let's face it, he was guilty as sin. If we caught him looking at us, he always turned away. Wouldn't look us in the eyes. For most of us, it was the knives that did the convincing. I was sure we were going to be in and out of there in a day—until we took the first vote. It was ten jurors to two for conviction."

"Was it a secret vote?" Donovan asked.

"Yeah, it took us a couple of days to figure out who thought he was innocent."

"So why did they think he was innocent?" Pron asked. "They must have been the only ones in Toronto who did."

"Cultural paranoia. Both of them bought it hook, line, and sinker. They believed everything that psychiatrist said, about how he was so scared of the cops and that's why he chucked the knives. Rowell did a good job. The rest of us thought it was complete bullshit. But not those two."

"So what happened next?" Donovan asked.

"We rolled up our sleeves and went through the case step by step, page by page, line by line. And believe me, it was a detailed case. The cops did their homework. We taped the walls with foolscap outlining all the main points in the case. By the time we finished, the walls were covered. Even the windows. We worked really hard. There was never a let-up over the five days. At night, when we went to the hotel, we just kept going. They set up a special room for us. It's not as much fun as a lot of us thought it was going to be. We couldn't read the paper. They let us watch some television, but as soon as anything even remotely resembling news came on, the matron came over and flicked off the set. As far as television in our own rooms, forget it. The first night at the hotel, I saw one of the court clerks go running down the hall with all the cable hook-ups in his hand. Oh, yeah, we had room bars, but they wouldn't give us the keys."

Pron shook his head sympathetically.

"Eventually, one of the two hold-outs came around," the man went on, "but there was no way the other would budge. It's not that she thought he was innocent, it's just that she couldn't find him guilty. She kept referring to the judge's charge. 'There's a reasonable doubt,' she kept saying. Maybe she believed that, but nobody else did. The judge kept calling us back in. We kept telling him we were making progress. But after five days we realized there was just no way she was ever going to change her mind. Most of us felt sick. All that court time and money and all the work on the investigation. And our only job was to make a decision and we couldn't do it. We didn't do our job."

"Is that why some of you were crying when you came back into the courtroom?" Pron asked.

"Of course. We felt we had let everybody down. The worst part was at the end when we had to walk out of the courtroom after the judge dismissed us. We could feel everybody's eyes staring at us. None of us wanted a mistrial. Not after what we went through. We wanted a verdict. But there was no way eleven of us were going to swing over and let Pan go free. So what choice did we have? It still bothers me, probably always will. We just weren't able to finish the job."

"I wouldn't worry about it," said Donovan.

"Why not?"

"Somebody else will."

CHAPTER TWENTY-SIX

A Man of Detail

The waitress smiled as she plunked down the big, frosty mugs of draught beer onto the table.

"Guess you fellas will be running up a tab tonight," she said to the four men at the table in Foster's bar.

"That'll be on Inspector Edgar's tab," Brian Kennedy said with a droll expression. "Garnie and I are tired of always catching the bill for the chief detective. And this gentleman," he said, pointing to prosecutor Gary Clewley, "he'll get the next one."

"I can't believe he's taking the stand," Clewley said. "I tell you, he's going to be up there for a long time. He's got a lot to answer for."

Clewley, who had assisted Glen Orr at Pan's first trial, had remained on for the second trial, while Orr moved on to other cases. Bob Ash replaced Orr in the second trial, which was into its seventh week. Although Ash was the senior Crown, he had decided to stay in the background, to oversee the case, and let Clewley handle the prosecution since he had done the first trial. 'Pan I' and 'Pan II' were pretty much the same, with one exception. Tomorrow, a very special witness was going to take the stand: Rui-Wen Pan.

"All I ever asked for was a fair fight," said Clewley, hoisting his mug of beer. "We put forward our best case and then he gets on the stand and tries to beat it. If he does, he walks. If he doesn't, he goes down for the big twenty-five."

Around the court-house, John Rosen was known as Mr. Murder. The pleasant, cherubic-faced lawyer had defended well over a hundred people charged with murder during his career. He had replaced Fred Rowell and Ed Hung after the mistrial, and was assisted by Anne Tierney, who had remained on the case. After the Crown had wrapped up its evidence, Rosen decided that his client should take the stand to face his accusers. It was not an easy decision.

"This case is not some sort of a mystery novel being written by the Crown or the defence. You are here," he said to the nine women and three men on the jury, "to decide the fate of a real person. If you or I were charged with murder and faced with all the innuendo and questions of credibility raised by the Crown in this case, how would you defend that charge? What can you do? The only thing you can do is get in that box," he said, pointing to the witness stand to the right of Mr. Justice Hugh O'Connell, "take the oath, tell the truth, tell what you know. You must understand that there is no onus on Mr. Pan to prove his innocence to you. In our country, the accused has the right to remain silent. But by taking the stand, he leaves himself open to scrutiny by the Crown. We have elected to undergo that scrutiny. In order to assist you in the difficult task of reaching a verdict, I would like to call to the stand Rui-Wen Pan."

Pan scooped up a pile of notes he had taken throughout the second trial and walked eagerly to the witness box. He took the Bible in his right hand and swore to tell the truth.

"Mr. Pan," Rosen asked his client, "did you kill Selina Lian Shen?"

"No, sir," replied Pan without hesitation.

"Did you have anything to do with her disappearance or dismemberment?"

"No, sir."

Pan wore a dark blue suit and grey tie. His appearance had changed in the two years he had spent in jail since his arrest. The diet of Western food had put pounds on the slightly built frame, and his suit looked one size too small. His face had gotten puffy and harder-looking. Hair that had always been well coiffed was greasier, cut in simple bangs. Rosen led him through a series of questions about his background and his education in China. At first he spoke so softly, the judge told him to talk louder. Pan blamed the Cultural Revolution for his inability to get into university. Instead, he said, he had had to enrol in the Szechwan Provincial Hospital Nursing School.

"What did you study to be?" Rosen asked him.

"An X-ray technician," he answered.

"What kind of anatomy courses did you take?"

"Anatomy of physiology. How people get energy from digesting food. There was another course on the muscles and bones, but that was called gross anatomy and I did not take that."

"Mr. Pan, did you have any hands-on experience in the dissection of bodies?"

"No, sir," he replied earnestly, without hesitation, his eyes riveted on Rosen. "All I did was take X-ray pictures and develop them."

"You've heard the doctors testify about the knowledge needed to cut up a body. Do you think you have the necessary knowledge?"

"Do I have it? I cannot answer this question because I have never done it."

"You graduated in 1976," Rosen continued. "Where did you go to work?"

"I was assigned to the Chinese Academy of Blood Transfusion. Before any donor gave blood I took X-rays."

"Did you have a title?"

"Everybody called me Dr. Pan."

"Did that mean you were a doctor?"

"No," Pan replied firmly. "In China, everybody who works in the medical field is called doctor."

"How did you meet Sophie Shen?" Rosen asked, after Pan had described how he first settled in Montreal, where he started the Chinese democratic movement before moving to Toronto.

"A friend of mine introduced me to her when I was still in Montreal," he answered. "I arranged for her to live in a flat in Toronto and then I moved in with her."

309

"Why did you and Sophie break up?"

"We found that we had different interests. But she really loved me and called me almost every day after we broke up."

"How did you meet Selina?"

"Sophie told me her sister needed a job and I had just opened my first store and needed help. Sophie did not like to work."

"When you and Selina developed a romantic relationship, how did that affect Sophie?"

"She was jealous. She said, 'You have to choose. If you want my older sister to work in your store then I must leave you.' "

"Sophie has testified that you followed her from place to place and harassed her. Is that true?"

"That is not true. It was her first husband who harassed her. Sophie would always come to me crying and trembling for help."

"What happened when Selina's mother came for a visit?"

"It is very sad story. Selina's mother came all the way from Hong Kong but stayed with Sophie. Everything was turned upside down. Selina said her mother made her feel meaningless. She gave money to Sophie for a house but none to Selina. Selina and I had discussed marriage but her mother said to me, 'You can only marry my daughter if you give me money, maybe fifty to one hundred thousand dollars.' " He paused to take a sip of water, then brushed a tear from the corner of an eye. "I told her mother, 'Forget about it. Selina is not merchandise to buy.' "

"Did you and Selina ever have temporary breakups?"

"Yes, two or three times. One time she left me and I got a call from my bank manager who said Selina was there trying to take eight thousand dollars from our joint account. I went there and saw Selina with a man but she left without speaking to me. I signed so she could have money and later found she had taken money from two more accounts."

"At this time, did you know about Selina's baby?"

"Yes, but I was still happy to live with her. I felt very sorry for Selina and told her not to abandon herself," he said, pausing again to wipe tears from his eyes, "or give up hope for our future."

He went on to describe how he learned that part of the money, three thousand dollars, had gone to a boyfriend in Australia and thousands more had gone to other boyfriends.

"Did that bother you?" Rosen asked.

"Yes, I was upset. My brother was living with us now and he was upset. He said, 'What kind of man are you? She is living with you and she is sending all her money to her old boyfriends.' So I told her to move out and she went to live with her sister. But then she came back."

"Did you have a party in January of 1988 and meet a woman named Anna Leung and a man named Robert Fisher?"

"Yes, I had a big party. Selina was complaining she had no social life and so I invited many people. Selina prepared all the food. My brother greeted the guests and I chit chatted. I saw Selina talking to Robert Fisher in the kitchen."

"Did you ever talk to Robert Fisher after the party?"

"Yes. He started calling late at night for Selina. I would answer the phone and then he would make me wake her up. They spoke a long time. Then Selina started coming home late at night, sometimes one in the morning. One time she didn't come back at all. Then this Robert Fisher would call me at the store. I was getting a little pissed off."

"Did you ever say anything to Fisher about being upset?"

"Yes. I told him, 'You are influencing my business and my life.' I said, 'Selina is my girlfriend. Please don't bother her. Leave her alone.' "

"Why didn't you and Selina ever get married?"

"Both sides have to agree. It is not right to force her. There were times when she left me but every time she came back. She was always crying, saying, 'Rui-Wen, give me work.' I think Selina was a victim of society and her family."

"Did you love her?"

He bowed his head and buried his face in the palm of his hand. When he looked up again, his eyes were glassy, moist.

"Yes, I did," he replied softly.

"Were you jealous of Fisher?" Rosen asked.

"Not any reason to be jealous. I knew that if she ran off we would have a talk and there would be no problem."

"In January, when Fisher was around, was she talking?"

"No. We were not talking like we used to. I had a feeling it was because of Fisher."

"Did you speak with Anna Leung Fisher about this?"

"Yes. I told her I had something important to discuss. She asked if it was about her husband and another woman. I didn't come right out and say it, but then she just collapsed and started crying. She said her husband was having troubles. She was so upset, she said it was very embarrassing for her. She wanted to know who was the girl. I did not tell her it was Selina but I said probably in a few weeks I will give you some more information."

"We have heard," said Rosen, "that something surprising, something shocking was going to happen. Did you say that?"

"How could I tell her that?" Pan replied. "I really didn't know what was going to happen."

"After Selina moved out on February 6, did you know she was working at Fred Carter's Coffee Shop?"

"No, not at all."

"Did you ever talk to Selina again?"

"Yes, she called me at eleven at night on a Tuesday. She gave me a tongue-lashing. She said she wasn't important in my heart and my mind and I didn't love her. I didn't spend enough time with her. She blamed me. I said, 'That's not true. I do love you. I do care about you.' I asked her what was the problem? She just hung up on me. After she hung up, I was very upset. I realized I should take part of the blame. Maybe I did not spend enough time with her. So I decided to write a letter. The next day was Valentine's Day. She had been away for a week so I bought her some chocolates. I gave the chocolates and the letter to Mrs. Chan, my next-door neighbour, to give to Selina. In my letter, I took part of the responsibility."

"Mr. Pan, did you have any sinister motive with this or any other letter to lure her back or cause her harm?"

"No. I had thought maybe she doesn't want to come back. Maybe she has found somebody else."

"When you got no response from that letter, you wrote a second letter that was in a totally different tone. In fact, you said some not very nice things, didn't you?" Rosen asked.

"Yes, because I was thinking she had gone back to her old past and given up on herself. Before I met Selina she had many, many affairs with other men. She had been a bad girl."

"Were you angry when you wrote that letter?"

"Yes, I was angry. I told her she was acting in an irresponsible way. I said I was not going to take any more responsibility. She had ended the relationship."

"Did you ever see Selina again?"

"No."

"When you knew she was missing, why didn't you go to the police?"

"I couldn't do that. I didn't know where Selina was living. If I went to the police station and they asked where she lived, what her telephone number was, I could only say, 'I don't know.' So they would say, 'How do you know she is missing?' Then police would think I am an idiot."

"When many weeks went by and you didn't hear from Selina, what did you think?"

"I felt something was wrong for sure. It had been such a long time. Then I hear on the radio that police find Selina and that she was dismembered. Early the next morning, I went to the bus station to pick up my friends Andrew Fang and Peter Wang. I bought a copy of Toronto *Star* and became extremely paranoid. The story said she was cut up clean and neat, like by a professional. I felt very scared, paranoid, panicked. I had a feeling I was in a trap already because I was the boyfriend and they would always suspect the boyfriend. I was so concerned that somebody related to my political work would frame me. I also heard from Sophie that when Selina got my letter her face had a big change, like going to a death party. I was afraid of false accusation because I was boyfriend. Then, at about five in the morning, I read the story again and thought that the only thing that would give me trouble was the knife, so I went to my kitchen, opened the drawer, and took out all the knives. I found a box by the kitchen counter and I put all the knives into the box. When it was daylight, I put the box in a plastic bag and put it in the car. At that time I felt that I didn't want any knives in my residence."

"Are those the knives you later threw into Lake Ontario?"

"Yes."

"Where did you get them from?"

"They came from my store. When Selina and I lived on Puma, Selina started bringing the knives home to use in the kitchen. They were from all different sets because sometimes in the store a few people would steal knives and we would just sell other knives separately."

"Did you take anything else down to the lake that night?"

"Yes. I also took some manuscript material that had names of Chinese democracy supporters. I didn't want any of us to be framed. My feelings were very complicated. I had a headache. I was dizzy. Crying."

"Did the knives have anything to do with killing or cutting up Selina Shen?" said Rosen, asking his last question.

"No, because all those knives were direct from my kitchen. If, let's put it this way, if those knives had anything to do with the case, why should I keep them in my kitchen for so long, to use them for food and for cooking? Also, I come from Communist China, and although Canada is a country ruled by law, I always think police are police. There is no difference in the world. If I was a guilty man, I would not have kept the knives, I would have thrown them away immediately."

The gallery was packed for Clewley's cross-examination. Reporters, other Crown attorneys, lawyers along with several groups of high-school students filled the courtroom. Those who couldn't get a seat were turned away, told they couldn't get in until someone left. But nobody was leaving. Jia-Wen, Pan's brother, sat several seats back with a Chinese woman. He looked angry.

It was only Clewley's third year as a Crown prosecutor. Called to the bar in 1979, he had worked in Toronto for a large law firm for several years before moving to New York, where he worked on Wall Street. Most of his clients had been businessmen accused of white-collar crime, such as defrauding their companies. The native of east-end Hamilton came back to Canada in 1989 and took a job with the provincial Crown's office. Clewley liked the idea of being a prosecutor. He had never felt comfortable on the other side.

"Mr. Pan," he began, picking up a document from the lectern, "this indictment alleges Rui-Wen Pan committed the murder of Selina Shen on or about February twentieth, 1988. Are you Rui-Wen Pan?"

Pan, his eyes following the prosecutor, replied, "Yes."

"Have you always been Rui-Wen Pan?"

"No."

"Used a lot of aliases in your day, haven't you, Mr. Pan?"

"Yes."

"Li Ling, Wen Hue, and, of course, Dr. Li. Ever call yourself Wang Tao Po?"

"No. Maybe. I don't remember. I could have because I was involved in democracy movement and I used many, many pen names for security reasons."

"So, is it fair to say that one purpose of a pen name is to conceal your true identity?"

Pan hesitated. "Yes," he replied.

"You've told us that in China you were called Dr. Pan," Clewley continued. "And over here you told people you were a doctor. Why?"

"Because when people think you are a doctor you get more respect."

"You like titles, don't you, Mr. Pan?"

"Yes."

"You were editor in chief of a couple of magazines. What does an editor-in-chief do?"

Pan brightened. "Very important job," he said. "He decides what articles to use, where to make correction, or where to make translation."

"Is it fair to say you are someone who cares about details?"

"Yes."

"But when you applied to live permanently in Canada you didn't care too much about details, did you?" He picked up a document from the exhibit table, dropped it in front of Pan, pointed to a section of the paper, tapped the spot several times, then turned to the jury. "Says here you're a doctor.

And that you went to medical school. Funny, I don't see the words nursing school or X-ray technician anywhere."

"Well. . . ."

"You decided you'd get preferential treatment if people thought you were a physician, right?"

"Uh . . ."

"You lied, didn't you?"

"Well —"

"You wouldn't be misrepresenting your medical background in front of the ladies and gentlemen of the jury, would you?"

"That is not true, Mr. Clewley. I would never tell anyone I was an X-ray technician unless someone asked if I was an X-ray technician."

"We've seen evidence that you got ninety-five percent in anatomy. But you told Mr. Rosen you don't know how a body is put together?"

"Yes," he corrected, "I do know."

Clewley walked back to the lectern, reached down, and took out a medical exhibit, the spinal cord of a human being. Holding it aloft, he walked slowly the length of the jury box so the jury could get a good look at it. Then he went over to Pan.

"And what about this?" he asked Pan in a loud tone, holding the spinal column by a vertebra near the neck. Then his voice dropped, almost to a whisper, just loud enough for the jury to hear. "What about this, Mr. Pan?" He pointed to the neck area. "If you look really closely, you can see how small the spaces are between the vertebrae. See the way the bones fit together like a saddle? Selina was missing one of these vertebrae, but you know what, Mr. Pan? It was done so neatly, the knife marks didn't show. You know about this, Mr. Pan. You studied anatomy."

Pan stared at the spinal column Clewley was holding. "I don't know about this in particular," he replied. "This would be learned in gross anatomy. I studied anatomy of physiology in China. And that has nothing to do with necks."

"You know something, Mr. Pan? We had a lot of doctors testify here. English, Chinese. Even one fellow who was German. And I'm going to suggest to you that the study of anatomy is a universal science. It doesn't matter if you're Chinese. A neck is still a neck."

"Yes, I agree."

"Thank you, Mr. Pan."

The court guard poured Pan a glass of water, and he took a long drink before facing the prosecutor.

"You used to date Sophie Shen, didn't you, Mr. Pan?" asked Clewley, taking off his oval-shaped glasses and rubbing the bridge of his nose.

"Yes."

"Why'd you break up?"

"We had different ideals. I dedicated myself to the student democracy movement. She just wanted business and money. And also I find out her personal life was so complicated."

"Sophie, was she a prostitute?"

Pan paused and looked at his lawyer, who was making notes.

"This is very hard to talk about," he said, still looking at Rosen, as if for direction. "I don't want to destroy her reputation."

"Just answer the question," ordered Mr. Justice Hugh O'Connell.

"Uh, yes. Could be."

Clewley picked up a transcript of a room probe from the exhibit table. "You say here that Sophie is just like a prostitute. But we know she left you, Mr. Pan. And that bothered you, right?"

"Uh, no. Not true. I, I told her to leave."

"Is that the case? Or is it more true to say that you care a lot about losing face? And that's exactly what happened to you when Sophie Shen left you."

"Not really."

"There's another woman in this case that left you, a woman named Selina Shen," said Clewley. "She left you a few times. And we've also heard that Selina gave a lot of your money to a boyfriend who she called her 'precious love.' "

"Yes. I told Selina, if you need more money, I will give you as much as I can. If you need help, let me know."

317

"Come on, Mr. Pan. That upset you, didn't it?" Clewley asked, in a sarcastic tone.

"Yes, I felt upset. I told her I didn't like that. And that's why she moved out one time."

"So you've got this girlfriend," Clewley said, his voice rising, a big smile on his face, his arms held out towards Pan, "and she's giving away all your money to all her boyfriends. So, how did you think you were going to finance this girl's sexual appetites? According to you, she meets a guy, goes with him, then she's back at the bank."

"I always felt that she deserved a chance. That is why I took her back. I hoped she would change. I had great sympathy for her."

Clewley, still standing in front of Pan, rocked back on his heels. He touched his forehead, scrunched up his face in a quizzical manner. "Wait a second," he said. "Didn't you call her a dirty garbage girl?"

"I tried my best to help her."

"Well, you helped her, Mr. Pan. You made her famous. She had a miserable life until good old Dr. Pan came along. We all heard how she'd meet a guy on a streetcar, a 'damned black' according to you, and the next thing you know she's six months pregnant and she didn't even know the guy's name."

"This is very hard," Pan said, his voice dropping. "We were boyfriend and girlfriend. But she was totally free to do what she wanted."

"What did you think of her?"

"She had a sickness."

"Now we've heard you refer to yourself as a legend. I've got a question for you. What is a legend doing with a dirty garbage girl? That's what your friends thought, didn't they?"

"Yes."

"Were you mad when she fooled around?"

"No."

"Did you punish her, beat her?"

"How could there be punishment? I loved her."

"Let me ask you the question again. What's a legend doing with a dirty garbage girl?"

"When living with her, I did not treat her like garbage. If I truly felt she was a piece of garbage, I would not live with her."

Clewley walked back to the jury box and put an elbow on the railing near one of the female jurors, a woman whose hair was done in a ponytail with a big pink bow that matched the colour of her skirt.

"Back in January of 1988," Clewley continued, "when you met the Fishers, you got it in your head that there was something going on between Selina and Robert Fisher."

"Yes."

"And you'd had it with Selina seeing other men. You weren't going to put up with it anymore?"

"Yes, that's right."

"Let me put it to you that in your mind it was finished between you and Selina. In your own words, Mr. Pan, she'd been 'honeyed up' by Bob Fisher."

"Uh . . ."

"And by February twentieth, the day Selina disappeared, you thought she had gone off with Robert Fisher."

"Could be."

"Is that why you decided to end the relationship? Because of Fisher?"

"She was very irresponsible."

"Why didn't you lock her in the basement? Keep her in the house so she couldn't run off with Mr. Fisher?"

"It was useless."

"You and Selina had a lot of separations," Clewley said, advancing on Pan. "But am I correct in saying that on February sixth, when she moved out, you knew it was final? And you had been left for good?"

"No, Mr. Clewley. I didn't have any idea if it was permanent or temporary."

"Mr. Pan, how'd you feel when she left you?"

"I was extremely worried for her. She didn't let me know where she was."

"You were so worried about Selina and Mr. Fisher you went to see Fisher's wife, Anna Leung, didn't you?"

"Yes."

"And one of the times you talked to her, you took her down to the Beaches, didn't you?"

"Yes."

"You like water, don't you, Mr. Pan? That's where you told Anna Leung something shocking was going to happen."

"No, no," Pan said emphatically. "I said surprise, something surprising."

"You didn't tell her what was going to happen, did you?"

"I didn't want to embarrass her. I didn't have enough information about Selina and her husband."

"Hmm, let's see, shocking. What could be shocking? How about, Selina's going to be hacked to death? Would you regard this as shocking?"

"No, impossible."

"We also have Anna Leung's testimony that you told her you liked driving down to the Thousand Islands area to clear your mind. You know, the area where certain limbs belonging to Selina Shen turned up." He walked over to the map set up on an easel beside the witness stand and thumped the map so hard it jerked backwards on the stand. "Your favourite area, right, Mr. Pan?"

Pan looked as if he didn't understand the question.

"You wrote a couple of letters to Selina, didn't you, Mr. Pan? The one on February thirteenth, for example. Why'd you write that letter?"

"The main reason was to leave the door open to Selina even though she had left me. I had told her in the letter, 'If you blame me for not spending enough time with you, I do hope you can forgive me because I worked very hard for us.' "

"Well, you may not have hated her by the thirteenth, but I put it to you that when you wrote the letter of the twentieth, you hated her."

"Actually," Pan replied, "I was very upset and pissed off. I felt she was very irresponsible."

Clewley read from the letter. He finished off by saying, "Here, Mr. Pan, you write to Selina, 'In my mind you are the most dirty, cheap, and shameful woman in the world.' Funny, Mr. Pan, when Mr. Rosen was asking questions the other day you just described this letter as fine, goodbye.'' Clewley slapped the letter down in front of Pan, on the wooden railing of the witness stand. ''This is fine? Goodbye? I suggest this is not just a nasty letter, it's a vicious letter.''

''I just thought she had a new boyfriend or something like that,'' Pan replied, staring at the letter. ''And I was not going to take any more responsibility.''

''You also say in the letter that Selina is going to be the dog that eats the shit?''

''That is just a Chinese proverb, Mr. Clewley. I don't know if you have ever had such an experience in your life, but it was painful. A big disappointment. She went back to her old past, her old sickness. In my mind, since I had such a feeling, there is no more love between us. And I should end the relationship. That's why I said, 'You are so cheap and dirty and shameful.' ''

''After you dropped that letter off to Mrs. Chan, did you go anywhere?''

''No.''

''Make it down to Rockport that weekend, by any chance?''

''No.''

''You told the investigators you showed your house to a lot of people that weekend. They investigated but none of the names you gave them checked out.''

''Yes, but problem was the names I had were people who said they would come in the future. The people who did come just came.''

''It would probably help you out if you had the names of the people who did show up.''

''Yes, there were people.''

''Who?''

''I don't know.''

''Give me a name. If you've got one,'' he said, holding out a hand, ''I'll take it right now.''

''I would have written the names down had I known I would be here.''

''That's right,'' said Clewley, ''because you're a man of detail. Remember you told us that you drove to Ottawa and back in a day and it really tired you out?''

"Yes."

"Would it surprise you that Ottawa is not too much farther away than Rockport? And you could easily drive to Rockport and back in a day."

"I don't have any idea where Rockport is."

Clewley walked over to the map, banged it again with a fist. "It's right here," he said, "right where those legs of Selina's were found. Sophie Shen saw you the Monday morning. She said you were exhausted. And later that night, she said you had a bad hand."

"Yes, I remember her saying that."

"Under the circumstances," Clewley said, turning to the jury, "wouldn't you say you had a bad hand at a bad time?"

"Yes. But if my hand had anything to do with wrong-doing, I would hide it. Right?"

"I'm asking the questions here, Mr. Pan," he said, walking back to the lectern, his back to Pan. Suddenly he wheeled around and pointed right at Pan. "But you did try to hide it. Sophie told you to see a doctor and you didn't go."

"Yes."

"That's because a man of detail like you knows doctors keep records, right?"

"I just thought, what could a doctor do? I could still move my hand."

"And you hid it from the police, didn't you? Isn't that why you didn't report Selina missing, because you didn't want to show up at some police station, fill out a report and have some police officer lean over the desk and say, 'Excuse me, Mr. Pan. You've got a bad hand at a bad time.' "

"No, I . . . I didn't go to police because I didn't know where Selina was living and police would just think I was an idiot."

"You told Mr. Rosen you hurt that hand moving some boxes. You didn't by any chance hurt your hand moving something other than boxes, did you?"

"That's impossible."

"You didn't hurt it by hitting someone, did you?"

Pan took a long time to answer. "No," he said finally, "that's impossible."

"You've told us you did your best to help police when they came to interview you."

"Yes, I did."

"I don't think so. You know why, Mr. Pan? Because you know all the answers. You didn't tell them everything, did you?"

"I did everything to help."

"You left out a few things, like the location of her head, or her arm. Did you think her torso would wash up on May fifth? You wrapped it up pretty well, didn't you? In a garbage bag. Who'd have thought it would wash up by Mr. Borisenko's cottage? You said you were sad. Were you?"

"Yes."

"But you were sad for yourself, weren't you?"

"No."

"And when was the last time you saw Selina Shen?"

"When she moved out."

"No," Clewley said, shaking his head. "The last time you saw her she was going into the Bay of Quinte. Right?"

"No."

Clewley picked up the four knives and the cleaver from the evidence table, then carried them slowly past the jury box and over to Pan.

"Are these the knives you threw into the lake?" he asked.

"Yes."

"Why didn't you just throw them into a dumpster?"

"I didn't want any trouble. I just wanted to get rid of all the knives in the house."

"Because you were panic-stricken?"

"That's right."

"And after your midnight stroll to give the knives the old heave-ho, you and Wang and Fang went back to the house. How'd you feel?"

"Very sad that Selina was dead."

"I've heard the tapes of the conversation." Clewley smiled at the man in the witness box. "You didn't sound too sad. You were laughing, joking."

"Yes, I was. Sometimes."

"You must have been relieved with the knives sitting forty to sixty feet out in the water. What I can't figure out is, if you were so worried about having knives around, why didn't you get rid of all the knives in your stores? There's not a whole bunch of knives out there in the lake, are there, Mr. Pan? Knives we should be out looking for?"

"No," replied Pan. "Knives in the store, they were all in sets. There's not any problem."

"With all those knives of yours gone, how'd you cook?"

"We used the microwave. We made a lot of noodles."

"Isn't it true you were getting rid of everything by putting it into or near big bodies of water?" asked Clewley. "Let's see, the torso, the head, the arm, and finally the knives."

"I heard this happened at this trial. But I did not do that."

Clewley picked up a blue binder from the lectern, a transcript of Pan's conversation with Wang and Fang on the night of the knives. He looked up briefly at the shield on the wall behind the judge. It was a symbol of justice in the Ontario courts, a lion on one side of the shield, a unicorn on the other. There was a Latin inscription ringing it, *"Honi soit qui mal y pense."* In English, "Shamed be he who thinks evil of it." Clewley looked at Pan.

"Just so it's clear," he began, "you had quite a conversation with Mr. Wang and Mr. Fang after you tossed the knives into the lake. Right?"

"Yes."

"I want to read a few of the statements you made. 'In the last analysis, it's what year, what month, what day you were at the place. What murder weapon did you use? In what kind of way did you kill her? Are there, or are there not, your fingerprints on the knife? Blood traces were found on your floor. Her blood traces appear on your wall. Afterward, we have someone who saw it clearly. She screamed, and after that, saw you kill her. And hit her.' Mr. Pan, what were you talking about?"

"I was just speaking hypothetically to Peter Wang. I cannot even remember who I was using as an example in this case."

"You talk about fingerprints on a knife. I'll just remind you that we have a fingerprint on a knife." He picked up one of the knives from the table and held it aloft. The blade glinted in the bright courtroom light. "The knife you threw into the lake. Your knife. Your fingerprint."

"No, the things you are saying are wrong. The translation from Chinese was wrong."

"Well, if you're speaking hypothetically, why did you say blood traces on a floor or on a wall? Why not say blood traces found on the Thousand Islands Parkway? Or on bushes or a rock near Rockport? You knew from all the stories in the paper that's where her body parts were found. And police never said anything about her being killed with a knife. Why didn't you say fingerprints on a saw? How did you know she was done with a knife?"

"Just common sense. Newspapers say she was cut up cleanly and neatly. So I figured she was cut up with a knife."

"How did you know she'd been hit?"

"I didn't know."

"You say here, in your hypothetical conversation, that she screamed. How'd you know? Lucky guess?"

"Not a guess," Pan replied. "What I mean is, I was just talking hypothetically. I was talking to my friends. I was scared of false accusations. That's why I was saying that no one can convict me without evidence."

"When you were speaking hypothetically, Mr. Pan, why didn't you add that her nipples were removed from her torso?"

There was a stir in the gallery, gasps. Pan took a few moments to answer. His response was slow and measured.

"I did not know that at all," he said.

"You sat through the trial, Mr. Pan. Did you hear Dr. Hans Sepp, the pathologist, say removal of the nipples had a sexual connotation?"

"Yes."

"And Selina Shen, she was your former live-in girlfriend, your lover. Right?"

"Yes."

"But when you say here that she was hit, there was blood on the walls and the floor, and she screamed," Clewley said, turning to the jury, ''I guess you were just speaking hypothetically?''

''Yes.''

''And the fact you were saying these words within hours of throwing those knives into the lake,'' Clewley said, pointing to the knives, ''is just a coincidence?''

''Yes.''

''So you had nothing to do with Selina Shen's disappearance, her death, or her dismemberment.''

''That's correct.''

Clewley nodded at Pan. ''Thank you,'' he said, and sat down.

On a cheery, sunny spring afternoon three years after Selina Shen's murder, Mr. Justice Hugh O'Connell sent the nine women and three men of the jury out to deliberate on the fate of Rui-Wen Pan.

CHAPTER TWENTY-SEVEN

Judge's Call

It was long past closing time at Foster's and the bar was empty, except for six men at a corner table. The cleaner had just finished putting up the chairs around them and was hovering nearby. But nobody was moving. The cleaner reached over Larry Edgar's shoulder and picked up four empty beer bottles, staring at each man in turn, trying to catch somebody's eye. But none of his looks was returned. He shrugged and wandered off. Crown prosecutor Gary Clewley finished his beer and stood up to go.

"You're wrong, Larry, it's not Juror Number One we have to worry about, it's Number Six. Didn't you see his face during my cross? He's definitely on Pan's side," Clewley said.

Detective Brian Kennedy pushed the bar tab towards Clewley, "Gary, you've got it all wrong, as usual. Number Six is definitely on our side. He kept nodding while I was giving my evidence."

"Sure, Kennedy," Clewley said, picking up the bill. He glanced at the total, then dropped it down in front of Detective Garnet Rombough. "He was nodding, all right. You were putting him to sleep."

"Gary," Kennedy began, looking at the bill that Rombough had passed back to him. He eased it towards Edgar. "That jury was asleep long before I took the stand. Someone wasn't doing a good job putting our case in."

"Well, if our case had found the crime scene we wouldn't be in this mess," replied Clewley. "What's tomorrow, day six of jury deliberations? Number One, there's our problem. They would have been back within half an hour if it weren't for her. It's 'Pan I' all over again. You've got eleven people who want to fry him and one who's probably fallen in love with him."

"Actually, I think we're going to be okay," said Edgar. "It was a long trial, they want to make sure before they convict him. They don't want to have second thoughts down the road." Edgar put his credit card down on the bill. "Didn't I pay last time?"

The eighth-floor hallway at the Holiday Inn across the street from Foster's was off-limits to the public. It had been that way ever since the jury began deliberations. Long after jurors had retired for the night, a woman in a crisp blue suit with an Ontario government crest on the breast pocket knocked on one of the doors. She was carrying a tray with a pot of tea. The door was answered by a woman with long brown hair bunched up at the back and tied with a red bow. Her eyes were red and puffy, brimming with tears.

"Here's the tea you asked for," the woman in the blue suit said. "Are you all right?"

"Can you come in? I've got to talk to someone. Something terrible has happened. I have to stop them."

For the first time in six days all twelve were smiling as they sat around the two tables in the hotel restaurant. Breakfast had just been served up; plates were heaped with pancakes, bacon, buttered toast, and mounds of freshly scrambled eggs. Sunshine was streaming in through the windows. There was laughter and joking among the twelve. One of them turned to the woman with the red bow in her hair.

"You haven't changed your mind, have you?"

"Just remember what I said last night," the woman with the red bow replied, and as she spoke all eyes turned to her. "I still feel exactly the same as I felt then."

A woman beside her reached over and hugged her shoulders. Another one started to clap. Soon, all eleven were clapping loudly.

"Don't start applauding," the woman with the bow said. "We're not in court yet."

Mr. Justice Hugh O'Connell pulled out two small pieces of paper from the inside pocket of his robes, slowly unfolded them, and lay the papers flat, smoothing out the rumpled edges. He read the note to himself, then looked up at the silent, packed courtroom.

"We have a problem," he said. "At nine forty-five A.M. I received this note from a member of the court staff. The note is two pages long, rather difficult to read in places, contains a number of misspellings, and appears to have been written on hotel stationery. According to a court officer, this note was written by one of our twelve jurors. This juror, who identifies herself as Juror Number One, has written to me complaining of being forced to make a decision by the other jurors. As I said, ladies and gentlemen, we have a problem."

In the second row behind the prisoner's box, Nick Pron scribbled a note to Kevin Donovan. "Another hung jury," it read. Donovan flipped to a fresh page of his own pad and wrote back, "This case is jinxed."

O'Connell passed the note to the registrar, who in turn handed it to a court clerk who then gave it to John Rosen and Anne Tierney at the defence table. After they read it, they passed it to Crown attorneys Gary Clewley and Bob Ash. Ash and Clewley huddled for a moment as they read the note, then passed it back to the registrar, who returned it to O'Connell.

Rosen stood and spoke briefly to Rui-Wen Pan, then walked back to his chair.

"Your Honour, I've never been in this position before," he said.

"That makes two of us," O'Connell replied. "Before I saw that note this morning I was preparing to bring the jurors in for a gentle exhortation to see if they could be urged to make a decision. It has been almost five days since they began deliberating. They've worked the equivalent of two and a half court days every day and I can imagine they are exhausted. If I do not exhort them, then my only other alternative is to declare a hung jury and order a third trial."

Ash and Clewley had been talking quietly with Larry Edgar. Now Ash stood up and moved to the front of the courtroom, where he stood beside Rosen.

"Your Honour," Ash began, "it's not clear from the note what are the intentions of this lone juror. But one thing is clear from the note. This jury has a verdict. One juror may have suddenly become uncomfortable with that verdict, but they do have a verdict. My position is that you should bring the entire jury in and give them a gentle exhortation. Hopefully, that will break the impasse."

O'Connell thought for a moment as he reread the note.

"There is also the possibility," the judge said, "that this lone juror, I believe it is one of the female members of the jury, could be brought in on her own to be spoken to."

Rosen shook his head. "Your Honour, I would oppose that. This jury must be dealt with as a group, or they must be discharged."

"I agree with my colleague," Ash said. "I urge Your Honour not to bring this juror in on her own."

"Very well," said O'Connell, "then we are faced with two choices. Bring the jury in and exhort them to deliver their verdict, or declare a mistrial. We have no indication from the note what the verdict is, whether they want to acquit or convict Mr. Pan. All we know is that the juror who wrote the note feels she was coerced by the others. Her request is that, after the verdict is read, all jurors be polled to show that the verdict is not unanimous. I don't have to remind all counsel present that the verdict must be unanimous or it is not a verdict."

O'Connell sat back in his chair and was silent again. Finally, he leaned forward.

"I have to think about this," he said. "When I return I will give you my decision, but I will still entertain comments from either side. Fifteen minutes' recess, please."

The defence and prosecution tables were swarmed the moment after the judge left the courtroom. Lawyers, other Crown attorneys and reporters who had followed the case gathered around each of the opposing camps. They all wanted to know one thing: What was in the note?

A tall man with wispy brown hair who had been sitting in the back row of the gallery walked slowly up to the front. Paul Culver, chief Crown attorney for Toronto, was frowning as he signalled Clewley and Ash over to one side. They talked in private in front of the jury box.

When John Rosen arrived at court that morning and heard the jury was coming back, he had been convinced they were bringing in a verdict of guilty. Like everyone else associated with the protracted case, he had heard how the jury from Pan's first trial had come within a vote of sending his client away for life. His gut feeling told him the jury in this case was coming back to convict. But his mood had changed after he read the note. He was beaming. Rosen leaned over the railing of the prisoner's box.

"Well, Mr. Pan," he said softly. "We've got a very important decision to make here. Do we want to hear this jury's verdict or do we press for a mistrial?" Rosen straightened and adjusted his robes. "Mr. Pan," he asked, "are you a gambling man?"

Pan leaned back in his chair and thought for a moment. He glanced over at the empty jury box, then looked back into the gallery, staring briefly at Pron sitting in one of the front rows. Pron stared back at him. Finally, Pan turned to Rosen.

"No," he said, with a shake of his head. "I am not a gambling man."

Donovan had gone to the pay phone outside the courtroom to tell the city desk of the latest development. The court was still in recess when he returned and took a seat beside Pron.

"The desk wants something for final edition. They want to know if we could somehow speed things up."

"Yeah, sure," replied Pron. "Why don't I just go into O'Connell's chambers and tell him to get a move on?"

"They want something else too," continued Donovan.

"Oh, yeah? What's that?"

"They want to know what's going on in that jury room," Donovan said.

"How are we supposed to find that out?" Pron asked.

"There's only one way I know. Talk to the jury."

"The last time I read the Criminal Code it said you can do jail time for that. Will the *Star* pay my mortgage and look after my family if I go behind the pipes?"

"Well," said Donovan, "I'm going to do it. Are you going to help me or not?"

"You keep wanting to cross the line on this story, don't you, Donovan?" Pron reached into his jacket pocket and handed over a piece of paper. "Maybe this will help you get across the line faster."

Donovan looked at the piece of paper. On it were the names of twelve people.

Spectators had lined the wall at the back of the courtroom by the time O'Connell returned.

"I've given this a great deal of thought," said the sombre-faced judge, turning first to the Crown attorneys, then to the defence team. "I'd like to hear your thoughts first."

Bob Ash rose. "Your Honour," he said, "I would like to ask you to bring the jury back and deliver an exhortation. We may find we are very close to reaching a verdict. Juror Number One's note said they have a verdict. We have no indication what that verdict is. I say, let's hear it."

O'Connell turned to the defence, "Mr. Rosen?"

John Rosen looked back at Pan. Then he turned to the judge. "Your Honour, my position is that you should declare a mistrial."

O'Connell picked up the juror's note and read aloud one of the lines. "She writes, 'I feel I have made the right choice.' That is what this juror says in her letter to me and that is significant. I have thought about this and thought about this, and I believe this juror has been coerced into making a decision she does not agree with."

O'Connell motioned to the court matron. "Bring them in, please."

The nine women and three men walked in smartly, led by Juror Number One, a woman with long brown hair tied back with a red bow. The foreman, Juror Number Six, clutched a piece of paper in her hand. It was the verdict. She sat forward on her chair, as if preparing to stand and read it to the courtroom.

But instead of addressing just the foreman, O'Connell spoke to the jury as a whole.

"Ladies and gentlemen, I have a letter from one of you that was sent to me this morning," he began.

The comment drew a sharp reaction from most of the jury. They turned to the woman with the red bow. She ignored their stares, looking out into the courtroom, then back at O'Connell.

"I cannot reveal the contents to you," he continued, "but I can say that the information contained in it has forced me to come to a difficult decision.

CHAPTER TWENTY-EIGHT

End Run

One end of the couch was gently writhing. Donovan, sitting at the other end, eyed it warily.

"You want some juice or something?" the woman with the red bow asked him.

"I'll pass," said Donovan, shifting uneasily, still staring at the other end of the couch. The stained, flower-patterned sheet that covered it was hiding something. Something alive.

"You caused quite a stir with your note," Donovan said, pushing himself even tighter into the corner. He glanced around the room at the jumble of cardboard boxes, animal cages, and mismatched pieces of vinyl-covered furniture. The air was stale, likely with animal feces and urine, Donovan thought as he glanced at the wire-mesh cages.

"I never dreamed it would end up like this," said Juror Number One. "Oh, don't mind them," she said, pointing at the moving mass under the sheet.

"What is it?" asked Donovan, leaning closer to the moving sheet.

He jerked back as a wedge-shaped, fur-covered, snarling head suddenly poked up. The head was followed by a long, tubular body that crawled across the couch and right into Donovan's lap. The animal's short, clawed legs pawed furiously at his suit jacket until they got a foothold, then it shinnied up his arm to his shoulder, where it curled into a ball.

"What the hell is this thing?" Donovan shouted, jumping up and trying to untangle the animal's claws from his hair.

"That's Joe," the juror replied. "One of my ferrets."

"*One* of your ferrets?"

"They're such adorable creatures," she said, smiling as she watched Donovan trying to get it off his shoulder. "I've got seven more." The juror whipped back the sheet. "Here! See?"

In a writhing, sticky, oily tangle were seven other ferrets, all different colours and sizes, some sleeping, some crawling lazily around. Donovan finally freed the one from his shoulder and tossed it onto the moving pile.

"Ma'am, I wonder if we could talk a little bit about the case?" Donovan asked, cautiously sitting back down on the couch. A black ferret with a half-white face crawled onto his lap. He picked it up when it got too close to his crotch and threw it back onto the pile.

"I guess you know the other eleven jurors wrote to the attorney general of Ontario," Donovan continued. "They're complaining that a terrible injustice has been done to Mr. Pan. They say he would have been a free man if you hadn't sent that note to the judge. This mistrial they say you caused means Pan will face a third trial. Who knows what will happen in that one.

"I'm not saying I agree with this, but the other eleven jurors say you were incompetent, on drugs, and couldn't see or hear properly. They also say you were seeing a psychiatrist during the trial. According to them, you were unfit to sit on a jury."

Donovan reached into his pocket and pulled out a copy of the letter from the jurors. He held it in his teeth while he peeled another ferret off his shoulder.

"They say it was your — and I'm quoting here — 'misconduct and clandestine behaviour' in sending the note to the judge that screwed things up."

Donovan handed her the letter and pulled away another ferret that had been burrowing under his jacket. A large brown dog followed by a black-and-white cat wandered in from the next room and started sniffing around his shoes. He ignored them for a moment, then gently pushed them away.

"To be perfectly straight with you, ma'am, I've interviewed some of the jurors who wrote this letter and, well, they're not your biggest fans."

The juror leaned her head forward, grabbed a handful of her waist-length hair with one hand and swept it back. She fussed with her red bow for a moment before shaking her head and chuckling.

"You know what I think?" she said. "I think they're having these sandbox tantrums because a person they pinned as an airhead got one over them."

"Why would they think you were an airhead?" Donovan asked.

A grey ferret with yellow teeth was gnawing on his watch strap. He picked the animal up and dumped it behind the couch. He wiped his greasy hands on a corner of the sheet.

"All those other jurors had college degrees, nice makeup, great clothes," she said. "Me? I look like someone who stepped right out of the sixties."

"Were you on drugs, like they suggested?"

The juror laughed lustily. She picked up one of the ferrets and cuddled it. "Can I tell you a little bit about myself? A little human-interest stuff that might make you understand where I'm coming from? I live in Metro Housing, as you can tell. It's not the best place to live in the world, but it's home for my husband, my daughter, and our pets. I guess you could say I'm kind of a concerned person. I'm a spokesperson for the tenants in this building. They come to me with problems and I help them with their complaints. I also try to help the police if I can. I even sing sometimes with the Coppertones, you know, that police band that plays at community events.

"So I'm not stupid. I know what's going on. They don't like what happened, so they're attacking me. They had their verdict of innocent and I wouldn't go along with it. It's kind of funny, though. . . ."

"What's funny?"

"Well, when they were picking the jury, Gary Clewley stood me aside because he didn't want me. They had to bring me back because so many jurors were dismissed for other reasons. So Mr. Pan would be free if I hadn't been on that jury. As far as drugs go, I was not drugged-out or in any way incapable of rendering a decision. The only drugs I was on were anti-depressants and tranquillizers prescribed by my own psychiatrist. And I guess I was taking Tylenol for migraine headaches. But I wasn't zonked-out."

Donovan asked about the psychiatrist.

"Geez, I'm starting to feel like I'm the one on trial! Like I told you before, I'm kind of a concerned person. I have this tendency to take on other people's problems. Last year, there were two people I knew who had really severe problems, and I got too involved. So I went to a psychiatrist to get help. I wanted to learn to say no to people when they were asking too much of me. I told the other jurors about the psychiatrist because we were friends. At least I thought we were. Now they're using it against me."

"What about your hearing and eyesight?" Donovan asked.

"Well, I'm blind in one eye and I don't see too well in the other one, but I hear as good as the next person. I always feel that a handicap is only a handicap if you give in to it. Judge O'Connell knew perfectly well that I can't see out of one eye. Since I could read the transcripts fine, he said it was okay. So why are the jurors making a big deal out of these things now? I'll tell you why. They didn't get their way. But let me tell you, if I was such a drug-crazed, disabled person, how come I was able to sit quietly through the trial and then stand up to the abuse they put me through afterwards?"

"What's this about abuse?" Donovan asked, turning sharply as one ferret, climbing onto a shelf to get away from the cat, knocked over a plate, which shattered on the floor. The juror didn't seem to notice.

"It was more like hell on earth in that jury room!" she replied. "I just think that anything that would be considered a crime outside the jury room should be considered a crime inside the jury room."

Donovan got off the couch and moved to a chair, shooing away a ferret that was trying to crawl up his leg as he walked.

"Just what did happen in that room?"

"I was assaulted. That's what happened," the juror said. "Everything was going along fine during the first few days of deliberations. Other jurors were nice to me, always saying how intelligent they thought I was. At the start, it was just like I expected a jury to be. We all had different opinions. At first, it was maybe half to convict and half to acquit. And then what happened was people that I thought were backing me started to shift over to the other side, the innocent side. Well, I wasn't buying that. In my mind, he was guilty.

"That last day of deliberations was when it got really tough. They were all against me. But there was no way I was going to give in. I knew what I was doing. But . . . but . . . they kept on to me. I was so tired I started crying hysterically. The cops could take a lesson from these guys on interrogations. One would be yelling something at me, another would be saying, 'No-no-no-no-no, you've got it all wrong. This is what we should be telling her.' Then another one would be hanging over top of me, saying, 'No wonder we're not getting anywhere. You've got her all confused.' They were browbeating me to a point where I was just crying all the time.

"One of the men told me I would be locked in that jury room until I reached the decision they wanted, which was innocent, and I didn't feel Pan was innocent. So I freaked out. I ran for the bell to call for the sheriff, or whoever was guarding us. One of the other men grabbed me and I was physically manhandled, pulled back, and they made sure the door was locked. I was terrified. So you see, there is a reason why I did what I ended up doing. I knew I had to do an end run on them. I had to pretend to go along with them if I was ever going to get out of that room. I said to them, 'Let's go over the case one more time.'

"I'm amazed that they didn't know what I was doing because I sounded so sarcastic-like. They would say to me, 'What about so-and-so's testimony that made Pan seem guilty? I would say, 'Oh, so-and-so must be lying.' That made them happy. They loved to hear that. By the end of the night the only person telling the truth in this whole case was Rui-Wen Pan. The cops, the Crown, her sister, the pathologists, his uncle, the lecturer, the real estate people—all liars! That's what they thought I believed when they went to bed that night.

"That was the only way to get them off my back. And it worked. Some of them hugged me, others thanked me, and we all went back to our rooms for the night. But then I started getting scared. I kept thinking about that poor girl getting cut up like that. It was up to me. I had to stop them from bringing in a verdict I didn't believe in. The court matron came in to check on me because she knew I was upset. I said to her that I had to find a way to get to the judge. The matron brought me a pad of paper the next morning. That's when I wrote my note to the judge. The matron put it in an envelope. She never looked at it. She said she would try and get it to the judge.

"One of the women on the jury came into my room just before breakfast and gave me a hug and said it was a pleasure working together on the jury. She even carried my suitcase down to breakfast. They were all so happy. I was still worried because I didn't know if the judge would get my note in time. The foreman already had the verdict typed out. I was afraid they were on to my little scheme when they asked me at breakfast if I changed my mind. I thought I was quite clever when I said that my mind hadn't changed."

"Did you ever have any doubts about his guilt?" asked Donovan. "One of the jurors told me the reason they were acquitting him was because they believed Communist agents had framed him."

"But that never came up in the trial," she replied. "They were playing detective, and Judge O'Connell warned us not to do that. We were just supposed to look at the evidence that was presented to us."

Donovan put away his notebook and got up to go. He petted one of the ferrets before walking to the door.

"When I was talking with one of the jurors," he said, "I told her that the jury in Pan's first trial had the same split, but it was eleven-to-one to convict him. You know what she said to me? She said she wasn't surprised, that she could see the case going either way. What about you? Think you'd ever change your mind?''

Her reply was quick. ''I'll think that man is guilty until the day I die.''

CHAPTER TWENTY-NINE

A Taste of Freedom

Rui-Wen Pan gave a friendly nod to the commissionaire as he walked out of the court-house and into the bright sunshine of a crisp winter day. It was his ninth month out on bail after two years behind bars. He spotted someone he recognized and hurried to catch up.

Donovan had been walking towards a hot-dog vendor when a strong hand locked onto his shoulder. He turned.

"Oh, Mr. Pan. How are you?"

"Better," said Pan. "Much better after this morning."

"Looks like your side scored a few points," Donovan said. The hearings to decide whether the murder case should be tossed out of court because of the problems with the last jury had just adjourned for lunch. "If Rosen keeps on like he did today, maybe there won't be a third trial."

"I cannot talk about the case with you," Pan said, putting down his briefcase and buttoning up his overcoat. "You were in Kuwait and Iraq, weren't you?"

Donovan nodded. He had covered the Gulf War for the *Star*.

"I will go to those countries one day," said Pan. "I am very interested in the Middle East. And also, I will go to Saudi Arabia. I have important business opportunities awaiting me there when this is over. You know, Mr. Donovan, I clipped all of your articles from the Gulf War. I clip all stories that you and Mr. Nick Pron write. I keep them in folders. Both of you are very important to me."

"You're the important one, Mr. Pan. I know a lot of cops and Crowns who think you're just about the most important person in the world."

"What are you doing right now?" Pan asked. "Will you have lunch with me?"

They walked to a Chinese restaurant around the corner from the court-house. Pan was first to the buffet, filling his plate with mounds of lemon-fried chicken, egg rolls, rice, sweet-and-sour meatballs, spare ribs, and vegetables, along with a bowl of won ton soup that slopped over the sides of the bowl as he carried the tray back to the table. He dug into the meal using a knife and fork, the sleeves of his tight-fitting jacket sliding up his arms.

"I think you've put on a few pounds, Mr. Pan," Donovan said.

"Yes, I eat many doughnuts these days."

"Doughnuts? Four years ago you said you never ate anything but authentic Chinese food."

"When I was in jail I was very upset, very worried. I ate a lot. Doughnuts, Chinese food, it does not matter what, that is why I am a bigger man now. Put yourself in my shoes and you will see what it is like. I was in jail for two years. Now I am a free man since Mr. Justice Richard Trainor gave me bail. But I still like to eat."

Pan laughed. He picked up an egg roll, dipped it in a bowl of sweet sauce, coating it thickly, and lifted the dripping roll to his mouth. Some of the sauce dribbled onto his jacket. Pan stopped a passing waiter and grabbed a handful of fortune cookies from his tray. He cracked them open until he found one he liked. He handed it to Donovan. It read: "This is your lucky year."

Pan chuckled. "I need all of the luck I can get."

"Mr. Pan, you've changed," Donovan said. "You've developed a sense of humour."

"I learned many things while I was in jail. They treated me very well in that place. The black man and white man would always fight with each other, but me they would treat me with great respect. They all thought I was innocent. Even the guards. One time, forty people signed a petition. They told me to use it if I was convicted. I am confident I will not need it." Pan leaned forward across the table in a conspiratorial way. "The guards even told me that when my friend Andrew Fang came to visit me in jail, the Ontario Provincial Police had put a bug on him so that they could hear what I said. You see, Mr. Donovan, I am well respected."

Pan asked the waiter to bring Chinese tea. "I must tell you now," he continued, "that I think I will be acquitted at this trial. I feel the tide turned for me at the last trial when eleven normal people decided I was innocent and one person with mental problems thought I was guilty. How could they put someone on the jury who takes drugs and cannot see and must go to a psychiatrist? Very unfair. But if there is a third trial this jury will be different. It will not be like the first trial. Then maybe you and Mr. Pron will report that I was framed. Both of you have been very fair to me in your reporting."

"Why do you keep taking chances with these trials? Wouldn't it have been easier just to have stayed in China when you must have known you would probably be arrested if you came back?"

"Because I am so dangerous to the Communist government I have always known that they would arrest me if I stayed too long in China. I have always thought it is better to be in prison in Canada than to be in prison in China. But I am going to win this year. I hear this is also a big year for you, Mr. Donovan. You are getting married."

"Who told you that?"

"My lawyers told me. I congratulate you. I always used to say to you that you should get married. Mr. Nick Pron is married. If you love someone, then you should marry them. That is the way I felt about the deceased."

"The deceased? What do you mean, the deceased?"

Pan looked puzzled. "Selina Shen, of course."

"Isn't that a little strange, calling your poor girlfriend, the woman you almost married, 'the deceased'?"

Pan shrugged. "She is dead, is she not?"

"Mr. Pan, there's something we've always wanted to know about. This book that you wrote, what was it about?"

"Yes," Pan replied, pouring Donovan another cup of tea. "I can confirm that I wrote a book and that I am writing two more books right now. The book that I wrote in Montreal is a very famous book. I cannot tell you the name except. . . . Okay, maybe I can tell you the name now. It is called *Death by West Lake*. It is mainly a book about the Cultural Revolution in China. It is about the great struggle for democracy which —"

"Hold on a sec, Mr. Pan. Doesn't somebody get killed in your book?"

"Yes, I can tell you now that is also in the book. There is a young army officer who wants to better himself. He wants to have a higher rank and he works very hard to become more important. He is married, but he begins to see a very beautiful woman. He is very much in love with her and he buys her a white dress. They often go away together to Sai Woo."

"Which means West Lake, right?"

"That is right. It is a beautiful lake where lovers often go. But China is not like Canada. In Canada, you are allowed to have one mistress. It is against the law to have a mistress in China. The beautiful woman wants him to leave his wife but he cannot because his marriage is very important to his standing as an army officer. She threatens to blackmail him. They meet one last time at West Lake."

"And that's where he kills her?"

Pan took a moment to answer. "Yes."

"How? Did he cut her up?"

Pan laughed. "No, Mr. Donovan. Do not be ridiculous."

"Well, how did he do it? Did he strangle her? Drown her? Shoot her? What?"

"He makes her go to sleep."

"What do you mean?"

"He gave her pills."

"Sleeping pills?"

"Yes."

"An overdose?"

"Yes."

"So that way there's no pain, right?"

Pan stared straight ahead. He said nothing.

CHAPTER THIRTY

Closing Argument

. . . The headline stretched across the top of the front page of the Toronto Star: SCATTERED BODY PARTS IDENTIFIED AS SCARBOROUGH WOMAN. Rui-Wen Pan stared at the words as he fumbled through his pockets for some change. He felt dizzy, put a hand out on the newspaper box to steady himself. He hurriedly dropped the change in the slot and yanked out a paper. He walked over to one corner of the deserted bus terminal and read the story. It said that police had identified the body parts found in eastern Ontario. The victim's name: Selina Lian Shen. The story quoted a source saying the body had been cut up cleanly, as though professionally dissected. But police had not found the instruments that had been used to do it. Pan felt sick to his stomach. They knew it was her. They knew the killer had some sort of medical training. That could mean only one thing. Soon they would be knocking on his door. He read the paragraph again. It was time to act. He had to do something. And quick. When his friends arrived on the late bus from Vancouver he drove them home. After they went to bed he got the knives. All five of them. The meat cleaver. The paring knife. Three long-bladed knives. There were others. But they didn't matter. Just those five. He had to get rid of them. But where? Water? Why not water? He liked water. Water washed things clean. When? It had to be tonight. At the lake. At midnight. When nobody was around. He would do it, and then it would be over. . . .

Crown Attorney Sarah Welch paused for a moment and looked up at the jury, trying to gauge their reaction to the picture she was painting of Rui-Wen Pan, a killer with no conscience. The six women and six men at Pan's third trial stared back impassively. Welch turned to face Pan in the prisoner's box. His arms hung limply by his sides. He was staring down at the floor. Welch, the chief prosecutor, was the sixth Crown Attorney to work on the case. She was known around the court-house for her dogged persistence; there was a resolute toughness behind her soft smile. Welch continued with her closing summation.

"Ladies and gentlemen of the jury, I say to you that until the body parts of Selina were identified there was no reason for Pan to get rid of the knives. Without a link between the dismembered body parts and Selina, the knives had no significance. They were, on the surface, just ordinary kitchen knives. It is only when the press reported that Selina Shen had been dismembered and that the instruments used had yet to be found or identified that it was necessary for Pan to dump the murder weapons. I would also remind you the knives thrown into the lake weren't just any assortment of knives. They were knives suitable for the dismemberment done here.

"The man who cut up the body knew exactly what he was doing when he began the dissection. There was no 'learning curve.' The killer didn't gain in experience as he made the cuts. He didn't have to. He had medical training. Only one man had both the opportunity and the necessary knowledge and skill to dismember Selina Shen in the manner seen here. That man is the accused before the court, Dr. R. W. Pan. Don't be fooled by Pan's attempts to distance himself from his medical background. The study of anatomy was crucial to his training. As a young child, he watched his father perform surgery. On his own admission, he saw a dissection performed back in China. In short, the accused had more than enough training, knowledge, and experience to do the job.

"But Selina Shen's murderer not only wanted her dead, he hated her so much and with such intensity that he sliced her nipples from her breasts. We do not know if she was alive or dead when her nipples were removed. We do know, however, that this was done by a man determined not only to murder her but to mutilate her as well. There is one, and only one, person whose feelings for Selina were such that he felt compelled to sever her nipples from her breasts. That man," she said, turning to the prisoner's box, "is Dr. Rui-Wen Pan.

"When they started dating, Pan was bothered by the fact that Selina had had an illegitimate child by a black man from El Salvador. He was tormented by the fear that Selina would leave him for another man in the future. That is why, as you heard in this trial, this man "— she pointed at Pan — "made Selina write out what he called 'An Overall Statement of Loose Morals.' In that statement, Pan made Selina write that if she wasn't honest with him she might as well die. And when Pan wrote his last letter to Selina the day she disappeared he included that same passage. I suggest it is no accident that those words appear in that letter. Having concluded that Selina had betrayed him he decided she might as well die. In Pan's mind, Selina had broken the agreement by her actions with another man, a casual acquaintance, University of Toronto lecturer Robert Fisher. Selina had been dishonest to him. Therefore she must die.

"The accused before you put a great deal of planning into the murder of Selina Shen. Upon deciding to kill his ex-lover, I suggest to you that Pan selected each one of these knives," she said, pointing to the evidence table, "with a particular aspect of the dismemberment in mind. For example, this small paring knife was precisely the instrument necessary to perform the intricate and delicate task of dismembering Selina's neck. And after she was dead his actions were marked by a total absence of grief.

"So I put to you, ladies and gentlemen of the jury, that the murder of Selina Shen was carefully planned right up to the steps Rui-Wen Pan took to scatter her body parts across eastern Ontario. You'll hear a lot from His Lordship about reasonable doubt and how you cannot convict if you have reasonable doubt in your minds. But I put it to you that on the evidence before you there is no reasonable doubt as to the murderer of Selina Lian Shen. That person is Rui-Wen Pan. Rui-Wen Pan is guilty of first-degree murder."

The five key people in the prosecution's case against Rui-Wen Pan sat glumly in Room 212 of the University Avenue courthouse as the jury deliberations dragged into a fourth day.

"If I lose this case, that's it, I quit," said Larry Edgar.

"But not before me," said an equally sombre-faced Brian Kennedy.

No one spoke for several moments. Garnet Rombough got on the phone and arranged for headquarters to send a truck to remove the last of the boxes of evidence they had kept in the tiny office.

"What's with this case, anyway?" asked assistant Crown attorney Pat Bryant, who had worked with Sarah Welch during the three-month trial.

"It's a typical Pan jury," said Kennedy. "You send them out and they just never come back."

"Look, Edgar said, "it was a long trial. They want to do a good job. They don't want to have second thoughts years from now. They're just taking their time."

"Didn't you say that at the last trial, Larry?" Rombough asked.

"It was such a clean case," Welch said. "Everything went so well. Does anybody have any Rolaids? I'm starting to get worried."

The phone rang. Edgar picked it up, nodded, and hung up. "The jury's coming back and they've got a verdict."

Although it was late Friday afternoon, the sixth-floor courtroom was quickly filling up as word spread that the Pan jury was coming back.

"If it's another hung jury," Crown attorney Gary Clewley said to chief Toronto Crown attorney Paul Culver as the jury filed in, "the tie goes to Pan."

Mr. Justice David Watt asked Rui-Wen Pan to stand. Pan's eyes were puffy. His hands trembled. He stared straight ahead, not even looking at his defence team of John Rosen and Ann Tierney.

Watt turned to the foreman, Juror Number Six, a man in his thirties with neatly trimmed short hair. "Have you reached a verdict?" he asked.

"Yes, we have."

"How do you find the accused?"

"We find Rui-Wen Pan guilty of first-degree murder."

Edgar and Kennedy, seated behind the Crown attorneys, swung around in their chairs and stared at Pan. He showed no emotion, just stared straight ahead. Tierney, who had steadfastly protested Pan's innocence from the time of his arrest, was almost crying.

Watt thanked the jury and dismissed them. Then he turned to Pan. "Do you have anything to say before sentencing?"

Pan leaned forward on the railing of the prisoner's box. "It was exactly one year ago that I was in this building and there was a verdict that was not guilty. One year later, based on the same evidence, I am convicted of first-degree murder. As a matter of fact, I have been tried three times. The first trial I wasn't convicted. I insist I am innocent . . . I will for the rest of my life. I never did it."

Watt waited a moment after Pan had finished. "I am fully satisfied the jury came to the correct conclusion," he said. "It is not generally my practice to comment on the verdict of a jury. So far as this case is concerned, let me put it this way. If there were thirteen jurors the verdict would be precisely as delivered. It was a despicable crime, followed by dismemberment. Mr. Pan, I sentence you to life in prison with no chance of parole for twenty-five years."

EPILOGUE

Sophie Shen got to the city morgue early that morning. She identified herself to the clerk behind the desk and was told someone would be with her shortly.

A brand-new Ford Taurus was parked down the street from the morgue. Harvey Loxton turned to the two men in the back seat. He offered Pron a cigarette.

"No, thanks," said Pron. "I quit when the case ended."

"It's not over," growled Loxton. "The lawyers will drag this out in the appeal courts for years."

"Thirty-six jurors," said Donovan, "and only two-thirds voted guilty. Maybe Pan didn't do it."

The door to the morgue opened and Sophie Shen walked out, carrying a small box under her arm.

'Bout time Selina was cremated," said Loxton, watching as Sophie Shen walked down the street and out of sight around a corner with her sister's remains.

ABOUT THE AUTHORS

KEVIN DONOVAN has been a reporter at *The Toronto Star* since 1985. He graduated from the University of Western Ontario where he served as editor of the campus paper, *The Gazette*. He has won several journalism honours including a National Newspaper Award in 1989 for his coverage of the police shooting of a black youth in Mississauga, and Ryerson's Udo Award in 1991 for his coverage of the Persian Gulf War. Mr. Donovan currently works for *The Star's* investigative team. He lives in Toronto with his wife Kelly.

NICK PRON is a veteran reporter with *The Toronto Star* who has covered the crime beat for the past decade. The native of Winnipeg graduated with a Bachelor of Arts degree from the University of Manitoba and studied journalism at Ryerson Polytechnical Institute before joining *The Star*. He is currently working on a book about the Colombian drug cartel in Canada.

TRUE CRIME BOOKS FROM SEAL ALWAYS ON TARGET

HUNTING HUMANS
Modern pressures have created a new kind of murderer—the mass killer. *By Dr. Elliott Leyton*

LIFE WITH BILLY
How Jane Stafford's abusive marriage drove her to murder.
With Brian Vallee

HIGH SOCIETY
Who are the real pushers are in our society?
By Neil Boyd

A CANADIAN TRAGEDY
An account of the death of JoAnn Thatcher.
By Maggie Siggins

FINAL PAYOFF: THE TRUE PRICE OF CONVICTING CLIFFORD ROBERT OLSON
What is the true price of buying-off of a murderer.
By Ian Mulgrew

SLEEPWALKER
Ken Parks killed while he slept. Murder?
By June Callwood

RITUAL ABUSE: CANADA'S MOST INFAMOUS TRIAL ON RITUAL ABUSE
The precedent-setting custody trial.
By Kevin Marron

CRIMINAL NEGLECT: WHY SEX OFFENDERS GO FREE
A searing indictment of Canada's justice system
By Marshall & Barrett

SOLE SURVIVOR
What makes a child murder his family ?
By Dr. Elliott Leyton

The Mark of Canadian Bestsellers

SL/TC-4/93